PUBLISH A MEMOIR

A Step-by-Step Guide to Saving Your Memories for Future Generations

by DINA C. CARSON

IRON GATE PUBLISHING
Niwot, CO

Publish a Memoir:

A Step-by-Step Guide to Saving
Your Memories for Future Generations

by Dina C. Carson

Published by:

Iron Gate Publishing
P.O. Box 999
Niwot, CO 80544

Copyright © 2015 by Dina C. Carson, Iron Gate Publishing
Printed in the United States of America
      ISBN   1-879579-65-0   ISBN 13 978-1-879579-65-1
      LCCN   2014914856

Publisher's Cataloging-in-Publication Data

Carson, Dina C, 1961 -

    Publish a Memoir: A Step-by-Step Guide to Saving Your Memories for Future Generations
by Dina C Carson.

        p.   cm.
    Includes index.
    ISBN 978-1-879579-65-1 (softbound) $24.95

    1. Reference—Writing.
2. Language Arts & Disciplines—Publishing.
3. Self-Publishing—United States   I. Title.

CT5. C239 2014   [Z285.5 C239 2014—Self-Publishing]
070.593

To Aunt Gladys and Uncle Ben,

You told me the best stories.

I love and miss you both.

Acknowledgments

My kindest, most deeply held thanks to:

Dad—who supported my efforts in genealogy and who loved hearing about every delicious find I have made.

Mom—who had enough patience to read every word in this series of books and made each book better.

Charly Miller—whose Harry Potter Places travel guides have charmed me through and through, and who has supported every last thing I have done to make these books possible.

Buzzy Jackson—who wrote the stories of her ancestors in an enviable way, and was kind enough to lend her expertise to launch this project.

Silvia Pettem—whose remarkable local histories encourage me and so many others to poke about Boulder and write about our discoveries.

Dr. Thomas W. Jones—whose kind words and brilliant edits inspired me to share what I know about publishing.

Pat Roberts and Mona Lambrecht—who inspired an entire workshop on writing, research and publishing that lead directly to this series of books.

Sandi Pearce—my grammar goddess, who keeps me from tumbling headlong over my own words.

Gena Philibert-Ortega—for the most amazing week of social history studies. I have never had so much fun in a class.

Dr. John Philip Colletta—for providing the inspiration to take the next step to finish these books.

My friends at the Boulder Genealogical Society, the Jewish Genealogical Society of Colorado, the Boulder Heritage Roundtable, and the Colorado Council of Genealogical Societies—who have encouraged me to write, to lecture, and through steadfast community spirit have kept me going.

It is hard to be old, but there's something liberating
about old age, too, because finally you realize
that you can claim your history in all its fullness,
that you can give voice to your memory
and speak its truth, and that it is not a betrayal
or an indiscretion to do so.

—Millie Werber and Eve Keller
Two Rings: A Story of Love and War

Memories are simply moments
that refuse to be ordinary.

—Diane Keaton
Then Again

Updates

Websites come and go or change their structures. If you find a broken link or a website that has moved or changed its name, please help me update the book for the next generation of readers. Send an email to: alert@irongate.com.

Contents

Preface

The question I get most often when I lecture on the topic of writing and publishing family or personal histories, is "How did you go about it when you wrote your first book?"

In the preparation for writing my own family history, one thing I found frustrating was that there were so many authors or instructors who told me *what* should be done, but very few who told me *how* it should be done, and done well. A lot of that, I had to figure out on my own.

I had to determine whether I could borrow from fiction or creative non-fiction. If so, just how much? Or, must I stay within the rules of non-fiction and write like an historian, although historical fiction could hold some lessons? If there is a line we cannot cross as memoirists or family historians, where is it? And how close can we come to it?

To answer my own questions, I started with a well-researched register-style genealogy. I am confident *that* book will be of use to the next generation of researchers, but I also wanted to leave behind a family history my non-genealogical relatives would read. So, I wrote a narrative family history. Then I re-wrote it. And I re-wrote it again. Each time experimenting with how to entice the best stories to come out. As an exercise to begin writing a narrative, I wrote about myself a little bit every day. Although I have not put my own story together as a memoir, I will ... some day.

I sought out professional writing assistance, and I have had the pleasure of learning from the best. I studied genealogical writing with Tom Jones during his "Writing and Publishing for Genealogists" course at the Institute for Genealogical and Historical Research (IGHR) held at Samford University, and John Colletta's "Producing a Quality Family Narrative" course at the Salt Lake Institute of Genealogy (SLIG). I am not going to give away their secrets here. It is well worth attending these Institutes yourself.

I am willing to try anything and everything that promises to make my work better, and I am not afraid to make mistakes. If, like me, you have ever been called out for using a malapropism, grouched at for run-on sentences (or other grammatical horrors), or even for missing the point of the writing assignment entirely—at those tender moments in a class full of fellow writers, you know *exactly* what you do not know, and then some. I have spent enough time in writers workshops, genealogical institutes, local history seminars, and national conventions featuring the best writers and speakers, to put the pieces together.

At the point at which years of ruminating over classes and seminars and books about writing became "A-ha!," that I wrote this book and the others in this series.

Take heart.

You do not have to get a degree in English Literature to write your memoir. You can learn to tell your own story in a captivating way.

You do not have to know much about research to glean enough historically accurate details to enliven your prose.

And, you do not have to have any experience with publishing to take your manuscript and mold it into a beautiful book.

Just keep reading.

Introduction

This book is a guide for anyone interested in writing a memoir—to record your memories and to pass on your experiences to the next generation.

This book is a conversation between you and me—one writer to another. I have been where you are. I have sat in my office wondering how to put the words down on paper. I have slogged through far-away repositories and courthouses to gather information to aid my memory. I have accumulated a pile of research and notes, and scratched my head over how to put it together. I have made sense of it, and so can you.

So, what if:

You have a lifetime of memories but nothing written down?

You have a box of old photographs but nothing written about the people in them?

You have notes but no stories?

You have legend or lore but no images?

For the beginner, this book contains the elements needed to start with a box of inherited photographs, or notes scribbled in a journal and end with a finished book. For the intermediate, there are ideas for organizing your research, adding social and historical context, and writing in a vivid, believable way. For the advanced, it is a polishing cloth for your writing and your research, to make your book the best it can be.

This book has technical explanations. If you are technologically challenged, there are suggestions for hiring help in critical areas that you may not wish to tackle yourself.

This book contains some drudgery. Writing is hard work and some of the rules for publishing are no fun to implement, but are endured by publishers everywhere for the sake of the reader.

This book is not death by grammar. There are suggestions for catching and correcting the little bugaboos we all use because our first inclination is to write as we speak. Even the most prolific professionals do not write perfect books on the first try. They, however, have the benefit of professional editing. Most of us do not. Trust me when I say that I can turn my editor, my grammar goddess, into a grammar grouch in one short phrase. The painful process of editing is not a punishment, it is performed so that the words on the page for posterity convey your meaning.

PUBLISH A MEMOIR

This book is lengthy. If you would rather jump right in and start with what interests you most, go right ahead. For the rest of you, I have organized the book in the steps that publishing projects follow.

Section One is full of ideas for additional publishing projects, describes how to pick a doable project, explains how traditional and self-publishing works, and examines the tools to facilitate the jobs of organizing, researching, writing, typesetting and layout.

Section Two describes the preparation for writing—identifying who you are writing for, conducting a research review of what you already have, adding research and images to make the stories come to life, what happens when you stare at a blank page one and have no idea what to do next, and how to draft an outline to jump start the storytelling.

Section Three is all about the writing—becoming a better storyteller, saving time by creating a style sheet, writing the first draft, and editing.

Section Four tackles the ins and outs of print publishing. The books that look the best are also the easiest on the eyes to read. This section will give you the instructions you need to make your book look its best.

Section Five will show you how to spread the word far and wide that your book is finished and available.

By the end of this book, you can expect to choose a doable project, to perform the kind of research that will give you a sound footing on which to tell your stories, to write in a way that is compelling to readers, to successfully publish a book, and to let the world know it is available.

Throughout the book you will find references to:

Baby Steps. Baby Steps are essential. My objective, always, is to encourage you to do what you feel comfortable doing and to enjoy the process. It is not to make your book project a burden. If the only steps you take are the Baby Steps, no problem. Baby Steps also may identify more complicated tasks that you can skip if you are feeling overwhelmed, and still create an enjoyable book.

Next Steps. Next Steps build upon the Baby Steps and require more effort but will make the book look and read better. Many of these steps are about time—time to make another trip to the courthouse, time to learn the advanced features of your software, or time to re-write a story or two.

Giant Leaps. Giant Leaps build upon Baby Steps and Next Steps and require significantly more effort, but are steps that professional writers, editors or publishers would take to make the book the best it can be. You *can* take the Giant Leaps. You can write a compelling memoir and package it in a way that even the snootiest, uptown publishing house cannot tell is self-published.

Enough with the soliloquy—on with the show.

SECTION 1

The goal in this section is to give you enough of an understanding about how publishing works to make you comfortable with the decision to self-publish.

Baby Steps

Take a look at the stages of all publishing projects—planning, writing, production and marketing. Consider a myriad of ideas before honing in on your own publishing project.

Next Steps

Learn how traditional book publishing works, and discover how everything a traditional publisher could do for you, you can do quite easily for yourself.

Giant Leaps

Examine the tools you will need to make your way from bright idea to a book in your hands.

Chapter 1

Who Needs This Book?

You need this book if:

- You want to pass on your own story to future generations, and you do not know where to begin.
- You are a beginning memoirist, and you want to focus your efforts on what to include in your first book.
- You want to issue a private publication that only you or your immediate family members will see, so that you can write about living people without worrying about privacy issues.
- You want to share what only you have access to, such as one-of-a-kind photographs or letters, the family bible or heirlooms.
- You are an experienced memoirist, and you want to cut your publishing teeth on the experiences you have already written about.
- You want to become a better storyteller and start writing.

Rest assured. The skills you have developed (or will develop) as a memoirist will help you research some story aspects, and the questions you raise while you research will help you write more compelling stories. Together those skills will enable you to write a memoir that is a pleasure to read.

Keep reading. If you have bought this book, and have read this far, chances are good that you have stories interesting enough to tell.

Why Publish a Memoir?

With a little bit of storytelling knowledge, you can write your stories down and make your book available to family, friends or others. Modern publishing technology makes it possible. In fact, publishing is one way to assure the legacy of your experiences.

Not only will your family members appreciate knowing more about your life and their own their heritage, the hours you spent remembering and writing deserves to become an everlasting record of your unique story.

Where Do You Start?

Have you ever said to yourself, "I'll write a book when I finish the research?"

Many of us—yes, myself included—could pitch a tent at the National Archives and still not obtain every source we desire. There is always another graveyard to find or courthouse to search. At some point, you need to put aside the quest for every possible memory, and focus on a few—just long enough to write the stories down so that they are not lost.

Kirk Polking in his book *Writing Family Histories and Memoirs* describes a woman who entered a "Why am I a Writer?" contest. Her answer to that question was that she had read about a man who had always wanted to be an artist. After he had died, family found his house full of unopened pots of paint and empty canvases. On the day the woman read that story, she put pen to paper with the thoughts she had been saving up for that someday when she would be a writer.

For you, that day has come.

Chapter 2

Publishing Projects

Every publishing project, whether it is a memoir or the next blockbuster novel, goes through four stages—planning, writing, production, and marketing.

Planning

The first step in any publishing project is the planning stage, where you decide what type of book to write—how much to include or how little. If you think you must include every memory in a single volume, you do not.

In fact, I want discourage the data dump—purging your research notes of every available story and source into one enormous manuscript. It may feel good to see how much you already have. But once you start adding the images and the historical or social context, the project may become overwhelming.

In the next few chapters, I am going to help you pick a doable project and suggest material to make the book more interesting. Then, you will finish gathering the materials you will need to begin writing.

Writing

The writing stage is perhaps the most feared part of the publishing process. All writers face that first blank page. All writers have doubts. "What if I can't think of anything to say? What if I don't like what I've written? What if no one else likes what I've written?"

Anxiety about writing is normal. Thankfully, the writing stage is not all writing. For most authors, it is a writing and research stage. Research, for many of us, is a much more comfortable, more familiar place. Feel free to retreat into the comfort zone every now and again to gather material to strengthen your stories.

Be wary, however, of letting a small detour back into the research become an excuse to avoid writing. Eventually, you will want to finish the book.

Once the manuscript is complete, you must edit. Not even the most accomplished writer can produce a perfect manuscript in the first draft. Editing always means fixing typos and catching errors. Editing often means rewriting. Editing will make your manuscript better, more enjoyable for the reader.

Production

During the production stage, you will design the look and style of the book, and follow a set of rules to make the book easy on the eyes.

Production decisions include page layout, image placement, typesetting, cover design and final files. Fear not. There are ample tools to help you lay out the pages and make the images look their best.

During the production phase, you will decide whether to produce the book solely in print, whether an electronic or an online format may be better, or perhaps some combination of all three.

Marketing

Marketing is not necessarily about generating sales. It is a means of letting people who have an interest know that the book is available.

You may choose to give the book away to family members as gifts or conduct a private sale, so only close family members can obtain a copy. You may want to sell the book to avoid financing the entire production yourself. Or, you may have a book with broader appeal that would warrant a sales campaign.

Marketing a memoir is a long-term process because memoirs do not go out of style and should not go out of print. If you want to add new information, you can issue a second edition or publish a new book. The most important part of marketing is letting interested readers know that your book is available.

❧❧

None of these stages has nice, neat beginnings and endings. Occasionally, you may need to return to the planning to gather more information to make the writing easier. You may discover errors or missing elements while you are typesetting that require research or may initiate a re-write. Later, you may discover some piece of blockbuster information that will inspire a second edition.

No memoir will roll off the press complete or perfect. Times ticks on. New information comes to light. Expect it and publish anyway.

Chapter 3

Pick a Project to Publish

The most important consideration for your publishing project is that you can complete it. The challenge for you, right now, is to pick a part of your story that you are willing to focus on—perhaps to the exclusion of other parts—and narrow the scope enough so that the project does not become overwhelming.

In Chapter 7: Taking Stock, you are going to take a critical look at any writing you have already done, and decide whether what you have fits the project you have in mind, whether it will with a little more research, or whether an entirely different project may be best, for now. In the meantime, let us explore a few ideas in more detail.

Each of the books in this series was written with the genealogist or family historian in mind. You, however, may have a project idea is unrelated to any type of genealogical research. That is fine. Each of the book projects below has a corresponding guide book with information specific to each book type.

A Memoir

While it may seem a strange exercise for family historians to do research on yourself or your generation, telling your story should not be. A generation from now, your children or grandchildren will be interested in how you lived.

The following are ideas for writing a memoir:

An Aspect of Your Life. Pick a part of your lifespan to write about—childhood, teenage years, college experiences, married life.

Professional Life. Perhaps it is your education, preparing for a profession, or your work life that you would most like to write about.

Military Life. Even if you did not choose the military as a profession, tell the stories of your experience in the service—during peacetime or at war.

Remembrances. If you have greeting cards or letters that help tell your story, consider weaving those into a memoir.

Journal or Diary. If you have kept a journal or diary, expand upon what you were thinking at the time you wrote the original entries.

Travel. If you have traveled extensively, create a lasting journal of the places you have gone, the experiences you had, the people you met along the way, and the things you saw.

A Family History

What is the difference between a genealogy and a family history?

In technical terms, a *genealogy* begins with an ancestor and moves forward in time through his or her descendants. A *pedigree*, on the other hand, starts with a descendant and moves backward in time through the ancestors.

For our purposes, consider a genealogy a way to pass on your well-documented *research* (with or without a lot of narrative). A family history, on the other hand, is less a numbered lineage, but rather the *stories* of your family.

The challenge with any family history project is limiting the scope enough that you can tell the stories well. One consideration is the time period in which the chosen family lived. For your generation, you have personal knowledge of the people and can tell their stories from your experience. And, most probably, there are hundreds if not thousands of photographs for you to choose from to help you remember events in order to write about them and help illustrate the stories once they are written.

To write about the generation before you, you may know each family member, or you may need to consult other family members for their stories. For your grandparents' generation (and further back), you may not have as many people to consult or as many photographs to view. Once you get back beyond the Civil War era, you may not have any photographs at all. At some point in the past, you will be relying entirely upon research.

The following are ideas for planning a family history:

Start to Finish. Pick the ancestor you wish to use as the first generation. Describe the circumstances of that ancestor's entry into the family—not necessarily his or her birth, rather setting the scene for his or her early years. Follow the family through the number of generations you have chosen to include describing the events that affect most families—the births, schooling, marriages, professions, and deaths. Add the migrations, moves or turns of events that involved your family. Enrich the stories with enough social history so that the reader understands what it was like to live in the time and place your ancestors lived.

Photographs or Memorabilia. If you have inherited a box of photographs or memorabilia, plan your project around the people and events you find in that collection.

Letters or a Diary. Write about the people or person who wrote the letters or diary, weaving the actual text into the stories, or using the events described as the timeline for the book.

A Tragedy. Write about a defining event that affected the family, such as a natural disaster, becoming a prisoner of war, losing a fortune, or surviving the Great Depression or the Holocaust.

A Triumph. Triumphs are also defining events, such as suddenly becoming wealthy or famous, being elected to an important public office, and so on.

An Ancestor and the People Known to Him or Her. A book of this type could include parents, siblings, grandparents, children and grandchildren, cousins, aunts and uncles—essentially five generations—the two before and the two following your main character.

A Single Generation. If you would rather focus on an individual or a couple (e.g. your parents or grandparents) than a multi-generational family line, consult, *Publish a Biography: A Step-by-Step Guide to Capturing the Life and Times of an Ancestor or a Generation.* The difference is mostly in the level of detail required.

If you have done the research and are ready to write the stories of your family, you will find a detailed chapter on storytelling in *Publish Your Family History: A Step-by-Step Guide to Writing the Stories of Your Ancestors.*

A Genealogy

By my definition (above), a genealogy is a little less about writing and a little more about passing along your research to other researchers. Publishing your research is a valuable effort, in an of itself. If you have plenty of research to choose from, but are not quite ready to write the stories, publishing a genealogy will give you experience with the publishing process.

The following are ideas for planning a genealogy:

Every Descendant of a Single Ancestor. That may be your grandparents or the first immigrant. The more generations you go back, the more challenging it will be to ensure that the lines are complete.

Direct Descendants of a Single Ancestor. Include the siblings in each generation, but the detailed information only for your direct line.

Female Lines. Your mother and her mother, and her mother, and so on, as far back as you have researched.

A Surname Line. Beginning with the first ancestor of a given surname (a female), following her surname (male) line backward. Another section could include the wives of the male ancestors as collateral lines.

A Direct Line to a Specific Ancestor. Beginning with yourself, you could trace back across different surnames to a specific ancestor, such as an American President or a Salem witch (the kind of research to join a lineage society).

A Surname Study. Focus on a surname in a particular region (e.g. The Bakers of Campbell County, KY), within a national database (e.g. Revolutionary War soldiers or patriots), or across a complete record set (e.g. federal census records).

If you have done the research, but are not quite ready to write the narrative, you will find additional details about numbering systems and formal genealogical writing in *Publish Your Genealogy: A Step-by-Step Guide for Preserving Your Research for the Next Generation*.

A Local History

There are endless possibilities for writing local histories. All families have elements of local history in their stories, right? They attended local schools, worked in local businesses, joined community organizations, participated in local government, and lived in neighborhoods or rural communities.

The following are ideas for elements of local history to enhance your family history. Any of these ideas could become a local history unto itself:

Professions. Farming, mining, ranching, medicine, crafts, craftsmanship, banking, manufacturing, logging, science, technology, information, inventions, merchants, wholesalers, working conditions, etc.

Institutions. Schools, courts, military units, libraries, government agencies, fire departments, law and order, etc.

Associations. Sports teams, Masons, Odd Fellows, Boy Scouts, Girl Scouts, 4H, philanthropic, social, fraternal, activist, etc.

Religious Groups. Churches, synagogues, mosques, religious movements, religious colonies, etc.

Transportation. Freighters, wagon roads, railroads, stage companies, stations or airports, riverboats, barges, trails or roads, aerospace, aeronautics, etc.

People. Famous or notorious, leaders, office holders, women, children, what became of (e.g. a school class), the poor, ethnic groups, religious groups, etc.

Events. Natural disasters, on this day, during this year, anniversaries, economic depression, loss or gain of a major employer, politics, etc.

Architecture. Neighborhoods, downtown, building styles, building techniques, public buildings, historic homes, etc.

Transitions. Town into city, fort into town, farm into metropolis, etc.

Customs. Marriages, burials, holidays, celebrations, 4th of July, parades, rallies, expectations, manners, roles for men and women, expectations of children, economic class, etc.

Entertainment. Music, art, dance, theater, movies, plays, books, museums, carnivals, festivals, leisure, etc.

If you are considering writing a local history, consult, *Publish a Local History: A Step-by-Step Guide from Finding the Right Project to Finished Book.*

A Photo Book

There are some family stories best told by focusing on the photographs or illustrations with snippets of text to accompany the images.

The following are ideas for family photo books or pictorial histories:

Heirloom Catalog. Share family heirlooms in pictures by showcasing them in a book. This is one way to preserve the many historical items that belong to your family, even if they have been scattered across the globe.

Holiday Traditions. Maybe you have Christmas or other holiday cards or letters saved over the years that could accompany yearly pictures. Or, perhaps you have photos of other holidays celebrations that would make a good transition-through-time photo journal.

School Pictures. Starting in the 1950s, most school children had individual photographs taken each year as well as a class picture. Collecting the school pictures is one way to show what the family was doing every year across a decade or a generation.

Themes. Does your family have something in common? Eye or hair color? Freckles or jawline? Hobbies? Can you find a picture of different members of the family with their bikes, while skiing or fishing? Perhaps you have a collection of wedding photographs across many generations.

Travel Diary. If you have made the trip of a lifetime, or a trip to research your family's origins, show your family what the old country looked like through your modern-day experiences and photographs. You could also provide tips for other family members who wish to make the trip themselves.

Preservation. If you have a photo album or scrapbook made by one of your family members, preserve it by creating a more modern edition while adding stories gleaned from interviews or research.

Letters Home. Perhaps you have letters from a soldier written to those at home during a war, or from a student who traveled abroad.

Talents. Was your grandmother a knitter, or did she embroider or tat? Do you have examples of her work to show in a pictorial history? Perhaps your family's talent was acting or painting, scroll work or whittling, jewelry or quilting?

If you are considering a picture history consult, *Publish a Photo Book: A Step-by-Step Guide for Transforming Your Genealogical Research into a Stunning Family Heirloom*, for more details on image preparation in full color.

A Biography

A biography is different from a family history in that it focuses on an individual or a couple rather than trying to follow a family across generations. A biography requires a greater level of detail about people including where they lived, the era they lived in, what kind of schooling they had, associations they joined, and how they worked.

The following are ideas for family biographies:

Parent(s) or Grandparent(s). This book could be a tribute to a couple or an individual. These are people you may have the most information about, because they are people you know or knew well which means you can draw from memories as well as research.

Famous Ancestor. Whether famous or notorious, did your ancestor participate in a well-known historical event? Was he or she a professional athlete, or famous entertainer? Did he or she establish a town, or start a business?

Interesting Profession. Perhaps you had an ancestor who was a hatter, a furniture maker, or a smelter. Maybe your ancestor was an inventor who changed the lives of many people? Researching how an ancestor worked may be interesting to other people whose ancestors held similar jobs.

If you are interested in writing a biography, consult: *Publish a Biography: A Step-by-Step Guide to Capturing the Life and Times of an Ancestor or a Generation.*

A How-To or Instructional Guide

If you have conducted extensive research in any one aspect of genealogy or local history, share your expertise with others. Everyone can benefit when you help others avoid the pitfalls of conducting family or local history research.

The following are ideas for how-to books:

Tips and Tricks. Give snippets of advice for people who are new to an area of research. This is especially useful for new members of groups such as re-enactors, so they can catch up with the more experienced members quickly.

Process. Describe how to do something from start to finish. This is where your knowledge of an earlier time may help readers understand what their ancestors did and how they did it. How were houses constructed in the 17th Century? How did hunters keep enough food on the table at a western fort? How did Paul Revere make copper-bottomed pans?

Lessons Learned. Reveal the techniques that *did not* work in your research so others can avoid making the same mistakes.

Record Type. You may have experience in land records or military records, for example, and can help others use those records effectively.

Research Facility. Do you have shortcuts to help make the best use of your time at a major repository? Or, perhaps you can shine a light on a repository that few researchers know about.

Recording or Preserving Records. Do you have photography tips for taking the best travel or cemetery pictures to use in a family history book, or advice for best practices to preserve the family bible?

Location. You may have conducted extensive research in a particular location (city, county, state or country) and could create a guide to what is available there.

If you are interested in writing a how-to book, consult: *Publish Your Specialty: A Step-by-Step Guide for Imparting Your Research Expertise to Others.*

A Source Index

Recently, I heard a speaker state that only two percent of all the material that could be digitized has been digitized. So, good records extractions will be necessary for a long time to come. If nothing else, creating an index that makes a record set easier to use is a valuable gift to other genealogists or researchers.

There is no limit to the places where records are kept. To name a few: government (e.g. schools, agencies, cities, counties, etc.); company (e.g. mortuary, ditch companies, banks, merchants, etc.); associations (e.g. religious groups, Masons, Odd Fellows, service clubs, philanthropic clubs, community groups, sports teams, etc.); publications (e.g. journals, newspapers, etc.), transportation (e.g. trains, freighters, ships, planes, etc.), or cemeteries (e.g. headstone transcriptions, lot purchasers, burial certificates, etc.).

The following are ideas for records extractions:

An Index. If you are in the records, you may as well do a thorough job and collect every name, every subject, and every location. In addition to record sets, many 19th century local histories could use an index.

An Annotated Index. If you want to take an index one step further, you could add useful information such as the role each individual played (e.g. juror, judge or witness) and the date each event occurred.

An Abstract. Without going as far as a full transcription, you could abstract the basic points of court cases, probate files, or meeting minutes.

A Transcription. While your first duty is to do no harm to the archive that holds the records, you can write a transcription in a way that encourages readers to visit the archive to obtain copies of the original records, so that the collection does not become less valuable as a result of your transcription.

An Annotated Transcription. You may be familiar enough with the records, or the people whose names appear in the records, that you could add information (an annotation) to make the transcription more useful.

Preservation Plus Extraction. Some records are so fragile that they are difficult to use without damaging them. In this case, photograph the records to display them in the book in their original form, along with an index, an abstraction, or a complete transcription.

A Comprehensive Index. Consider indexing each source within a single collection (e.g. California gold rush participants in the Bancroft Collection), or across many collections to create a comprehensive index (e.g. Boulder Pioneers in the Colorado State Archives).

If you are interested in publishing a source index, consult: *Publish a Source Index: A Step-by-Step Guide to Creating a Genealogically Useful Index, Abstract or Transcription.*

Hybrid Projects

You may have a project in mind that does not fit neatly into any one category. Your book does not have to fit a mold. Be creative with some hybrid ideas.

The following are a few of the many possibilities for a hybrid family history:

Biography/Cookbook. While you write a biography, include a few recipes or family traditions sprinkled through the text.

Cookbook/Biography. Organize this one as a cookbook, but include some biographical information about the people who contributed the recipes, or how your family used the recipes according to tradition.

Biography/Professional Manual. You may have enough information about an ancestor's work or business to write a professional guide along with biographical information.

Photographic Timeline. Show how each family member fits into the photographic tree, or how they fit into the timeline of history.

Memoir/History. Use recollections from a memoir, letters or a diary, alongside the real-world history taking place.

Travel Guide/Family History. Let your family members follow your footsteps as you traveled to the homeland, along with information about the people who lived in the places you describe. Include travel guide information to help the reader make the trip, as well.

Perpetual Calendar. Include birth and death dates, anniversaries, graduations, immigration, travel—anything that puts family members on the calendar.

On This Day. Place historical events from your family history research or local history into a day-by-day collection.

Genealogical Gifts

While books are the most appreciated gifts according to reunion-goers, there are many other ways to give away your genealogical research as gifts.

The following are a few of the many possibilities for genealogical gifts:

Charts. You can create phenomenal family tree charts using software that makes it easy to upload your tree—fan charts, half-circles, full circles, or bow-tie charts. You can add photographs or background images, and information in as much detail as you desire.

Scrapbooks. There are books, clubs and stores devoted to creating amazing scrapbooks. If you can picture it as a pedigree, you can scrapbook it in a way that shows family relationships.

Photographs on Products. You can put a photograph on nearly anything—cakes, wall hangings, button covers, place mats, cups, mugs, and much more.

Cookbooks. Many companies specialize in producing cookbooks since so many groups use them as fundraisers. Use your next holiday or reunion to gather up the family's favorite recipes.

Card Decks. There are companies that specialize in playing card decks that you can create using photographs of your family. Sports cards are another idea along the same line.

Quilts. Quilting was one way to re-use scrap material and create a warm blanket before there was central heating. Quilting patterns can reveal something about your ancestors' ethnic heritage or the area where they lived. Other textiles such as tartans have similar meanings to family groups.

Replica Items. You may find a replica item of something your ancestors owned or could have owned that may be a meaningful gift. Look in historical museum catalogs for these items.

Slide Show. There is software to help you gather photographs and add captions for a slide show that you can distribute or place online for your family to see.

❧❧

Now that you have a great many ideas for turning your stories into a book, read about the publishing process to determine the easiest way to finish your book and make it available to interested readers.

Chapter 4

How Publishing Works

Publishing has two essential parts—production and distribution. Before you determine whether to publish your book in print, electronically, or online, think about how your audience will want to read the book, and how you are going to deliver it to them.

It is hard to go wrong choosing print. The upside is that nearly everyone can read a printed book. The downside is that printed books must be produced and distributed (shipped) which cost money. Thankfully, print-on-demand technology has made it possible to print and ship books one at a time. Gone are the days when you had to order hundreds of books to keep the cost of each book down.

Publishing in an electronic format is tempting because there is almost no cost of production or distribution. Books can be sent to the reader electronically. The downside to electronic formats is that not everyone wants to read a book on a computer screen, dedicated eReader or tablet.

Publishing online is also tempting because most people have access to the Internet. Anyone with a web browser can read the book. The downside is that Internet companies come and go, so if your book is sitting on the server of a company that folds, the book disappears with it.

What is the best option? You do not have to make a decision about this yet. You may choose to publish in more than one format.

Before we move on to production, let us look at each publishing option in a little more detail.

Print Publishing

Before print-on-demand made publishing easy for anyone, there were four ways to publish a book in print. There still are. You can write a query letter to interest a traditional publishing company, pay a vanity publisher, hire a book packager, or self-publish. Before you decide to self-publish, what follows are the more traditional routes to book publishing and how they work.

Traditional Book Publishers

There are more than a few types of traditional publishers. There are the big publishers, such as Random House. Random House is one of the remaining Big Five, and companies such as this one are looking for the next blockbuster. They are not likely to be interested in a memoir unless your stories are of interest to the general public. There are also smaller publishers, mostly niche publishers, such as Arcadia Publishing that specializes in local history books.

In order to get the attention of one of the big publishers, you may need a literary agent to make a pitch to the company for you. Writing a good query letter introducing yourself and your book may work with a smaller publisher. Most memoirs, unless you are well known or the book has a more general interest theme, will not interest a traditional publisher enough to offer you a contract.

Even so, if you have a great story to tell and can interest a publishing company, they will buy the rights to publish a version of your work (e.g. print, electronic, audio, foreign language, or all rights) in exchange for a royalty—a percentage of the sales price. Most publishing contracts are based upon the sales price rather than the retail price because so many books are sold at a steep discount to bookstores or book clubs.

When the book sells, the publisher is paid, and they will handle any returns. You will be paid approximately ninety (90) days after the publisher, to allow time for returns.

A well-known author can expect a royalty of about fifteen percent, a lesser known author about ten percent, and an unknown author something less than ten percent. For most authors, a small percentage of the sales price (your royalty) means you have to sell a great number of books to make any money. For most memoirs, this is not likely.

A traditional publisher will have total control over the physical production, distribution, and sales. The publisher will choose the cover design. Oftentimes, they will choose the title. Most importantly, they will control the content through the editing process. As the author, you will start the process, but once you sign a contract, and the manuscript is turned over, the publisher is in control.

If your book needs revisions or corrections, that will take place only after the initial print run sells out. For many books, the first print run never sells out. (One advantage to self-publishing using a print-on-demand printer is that you can make revisions at any time.)

A traditional publisher will decide how long the book will stay in print, and how long marketing will continue. For many books, once the sales slow, the marketing ends. (If you self-publish, the book will stay in print as long as you want it to.)

Vanity Publishers

Please do not enlist a vanity publisher to "publish" your book and "market" it to potential readers. In reality, these companies are offering to take as much of your money as you are willing to give them, and do nothing for you that you could not do cheaper. It is best to avoid these companies altogether. That goes for some author services companies, as well.

Book Packagers

Book packagers offer the different parts of the publishing process as services a-la-carte. If you do not want to handle the book cover design, for example, you could hire one of these companies to do so for you. You sign a contract for a specific service at a specific price. Book packagers can be helpful if you do not want to learn everything there is to know about book production, but still want a professional looking book.

Author Services

Author services companies offer many of the same services that book packagers do, as well as editing and marketing. Some of the biggest print-on-demand printers also offer author services. CreateSpace (www.createspace.com and its author services company BookSurge, www.booksurge.com), Lulu (www.lulu.com), and Blurb (www.blurb.com), offer packages of author services, such as copy editing, eBook conversion, layout, and cover design.

Most of the time, you will be able to do for yourself most of what they are offering to do for a fee. A better solution may be to find a local person—a book packager—who can design a cover or typeset the book for you at a fee you can negotiate, rather than accepting a package price for more services than you want or need from an author services company.

Caution: Author Solutions (www.authorsolutions.com—the author services provider of Penguin Random House via its imprints AuthorHouse, Trafford, Booktango, WordClay, FuseFrame, PitchFest, Author Learning Center, Author Hive, Xlibris, Palibro, Inkubook, Partridge and iUniverse) had a federal class-action lawsuit filed against them in 2013 alleging that they have been cheating writers out of their royalties and charging outrageous prices for services—for years. What follows are the names of companies that have aligned themselves with Author Solutions. Please avoid these vanity presses: Archway (Simon & Schuster), Partridge (Penguin), Westbow (Thomas Nelson/Harper Collins), Balboa Press (Hay House), Abbott Press (Writers' Digest), Dellarte Press (Harlequin). Many thanks to David Gaughran, author of *Let's Get Visible: How to Get Visible and Sell More Books* for helping fellow writers avoid trouble.

Self-Publishing

The best option for most memoirists is self-publishing. You are the publisher. You are in control of the whole process. You decide what goes into the book and how it looks. You control who can buy the book if there is information about living people you do not want out to the general public. You control the contents and the process. You also do most of the work. Fortunately, printing technology and software to create book layouts and electronic files has made self-publishing not only possible, but relatively easy.

Now that you have a better understanding of the role of the publisher let us take a look at some of the nuts and bolts decisions about print production.

Book Printers

Please use a book printer, not the local copy shop. Producing books one at a time at the local copy shop is not only expensive, but most copy shops do not have the kind of equipment to create books with permanent covers—either softbound (perfect bound) or hard-bound. The local copy shop may be good if your manuscript will only fill a booklet (under 48 pages) rather than a book, and if you only plan to print a limited number.

To create quality softbound or hardbound books, there are two options—print-on-demand or offset presses.

Offset Book Printers

Using an offset book printer has its advantages, especially if you can sell or give away a large print run. Ordering books in quantity will keep the price per book down. The downside is that you have to print and pay for a minimum number of books up front—often 250 or more.

Offset printing is best for books with custom sizes or books that require high-quality reproduction such as photography or coffee table books. High-quality, full-color books are often printed in Asia because the cost is lower, even with international shipping.

Print-on-Demand Book Printers

Print-on-demand (POD) book printers are exactly as their name suggests—you can print a single book when you need it. There is a wide variety of print-on-demand printers. The following is a representative example of what you will find.

Lulu

Lulu (www.lulu.com) is a POD book printer that also offers author and marketing services. Their business model assumes that you, the publisher, have no experience, so their website will guide you through the process step by step. Anyone can create a printed copy of a book through Lulu. The only downside is that there is no quality control during the process, and some people—mostly those in the book industry—may assume that your book is amateurish if you publish through Lulu. If you are not worried about selling the book except to friends or family, then there is no need to worry about where you have your book printed. The ease of using Lulu's website is an attractive plus.

Lulu is one of the few POD book printers with privacy options. At Lulu, you can make the book available only to you or by private web link to only those people you allow to buy the book. Publishing privately is an attractive option for proofing books and for keeping books out of the hands of the general public if they contain information about living people. If your memoir contains information that would make some readers uncomfortable, you have the option of publishing privately through Lulu.

Lulu also has an online bookstore if you want to make your book available for sale. Lulu's catalog also appears in other major online bookstores' catalogs. Both Lulu and the other bookstores will take a cut before you earn a royalty, if you print your book through Lulu but sell it through Amazon, for example.

At Lulu, your wholesale prices may be higher than at other POD printers. If you are selling the book to make a little money, investigate additional options.

CreateSpace

CreateSpace (www.createspace.com) is Amazon's POD printer. They expect you to know a little bit more about the process, so the website is not as easy to use as Lulu. CreateSpace will have a staff person review your book before approving it. Your book will not become available in the Amazon catalog without approval. Gaining approval can be a hurdle if you have unusual page numbering or something that makes the staff unsure of the quality of the work.

The upside is that your book will be available at the largest online bookstore on the Internet, and your wholesale prices will be lower at CreateSpace than at Lulu. Amazon's reach is enormous, meaning your book will be available literally around the world if you print through CreateSpace.

Lightning Source

At the far end of the scale is Lightning Source (www.lightningsource.com). Lightning Source is an Ingram Company. Ingram is the largest book wholesaler in the United States, and selling through their catalog means access to 30,000 wholesalers, retailers and booksellers in more than one hundred countries.

Lightning Source *only* works with publishers. They expect you have experience with the process.

At Lightning Source, you must have your own International Standard Book Numbers (ISBNs), unlike CreateSpace and Lulu—both offer free ISBNs. All books, including different versions of the same book (an eBook or a 2nd Edition) must have an ISBN. ISBNs are like the Social Security number for a book. ISBNs distinguish one book from another or a newer version from an older version. The benefit of a free ISBN is cost savings since a single ISBN costs $125.00. A package of 10 ISBNs costs $295.00; 100 ISBNs cost $575, and so on. The more you buy, the less they cost per ISBN. You can purchase ISBNs through the Bowker Company's Identifier Services (www.myidentifiers.com).

Note: If you use a free ISBN from your printer, that company will become the publisher of record, not you.

Lightning Source charges fees to establish and maintain each book in their catalog. There are also fees for every update or revision. In other words, you need a next-to-perfect manuscript and a properly-sized and prepared cover to use this service, unless you are willing to spend a lot of money in fees and proofs until you get it right. There is no hand holding through the process.

The upside to printing through Lightning Source is that your wholesale costs will be lower than other POD printers, and your book will be available to a vast distribution network of wholesalers, retailers and booksellers—including Amazon and Barnes&Noble.

Espresso Book Machine

The Espresso Book Machine (EBM) (www.ondemandbooks.com) takes print-on-demand a whole step further. They provide equipment to select locations allowing readers to choose a book and have it printed in about fifteen minutes while they wait. You will not find EBMs in every city, at least not yet, and in some states, there are few locations. EBMs offer some exciting possibilities, however. Think about creating a book with recipes or stories gathered during a family reunion and being able to deliver the book to family members a few hours later.

Print Production Basics

One of your first major decisions is whether to print the book in color or in black-and-white. The cover, of course, will be in full color since that will not cost you more, and color covers are standard across the industry. Color *interiors*, however, add significantly to the cost. At print-on-demand printers, if you choose a color interior, every page will be considered a color page, even if it only has black-and-white text on it. If the book is in color, it is color throughout. An offset printer may be able to insert color pages either as a section in the middle or select places throughout the book. Either way, the cost of full-color books is much higher than books with black-and-white interiors.

Consider that you may be able to create a 200 page, 8.5"x 11" book in black-and-white for around $7 wholesale. Whereas, a color version of that same book could run $80 or more. **Tip**: One way to give your family the stories in black-and-white and the photographs in full color is to print the memoir with the images in black-and-white along with a companion photo book for the best images. That way, you print the black-and-white book for $7 wholesale, along with a 20-page color photo book for $10 to $15—together, still cheaper than a full-color interior.

Interior Files

All books have interior files and cover files. The interior file will contain everything from the title page to the index, including the images. You will set up your manuscript in the physical size of the final book, called the trim size. The paper will be slightly larger than the final size so it can be trimmed off neatly to give the book a finished look.

The most common trim sizes are 6" x 9," 7" x 10" and 8.5" x 11." You can create a book of nearly any size, but if you will use one of these common sizes, the production cost will be lower and your options for printers will be greater.

Choose a trim size based upon how many pages there are in the manuscript, and how large you wish to display the images. When you are ready to create the layout, you should have an idea of whether your book will run 50 pages or 500.

The 6" x 9" or 7" x 10" size is nice if you think the reader will sit down and read the book cover to cover because these books are easy to hold. If the book becomes too thick at one of the above sizes, you can increase the page size to 8.5" x 11"— the size of a traditional piece of paper in the United States. This size is a little less comfortable to hold while reading, but ideal for a book meant for research, and has more room on each page to display images.

Cover Files

You will not create your cover file until you have chosen the trim size, the binding, and have the manuscript ready because the number of pages will determine the spine width.

Most printers offer the following binding options:

Hardbound also Called Case Bound. Hardbound covers consist of thick cardboard pieces covered in material, glued or sewn to the interior at the spine. You will have the option of a plain cloth cover, wrapping the cloth cover with a dust jacket, or a full-color, glossy paper cover—such as a textbook.

Softbound also Called Paperback or Perfect Bound. Softbound covers consist of thick, paper cover glued to the interior pages at the spine.

Lay-flat. Lay-flat is a more expensive option than softbound, but best for workbooks or cookbooks that need to lay flat for easy use.

Each of the following binding styles is disliked by librarians and bookstore owners because they do not have spines, so the book must be removed from the shelf in order to read the title.

Saddle Stitch. Saddle stitch books are laid out in two-page spreads, folded in half, then stapled at the spine. Standard 8.5" x 11" paper becomes a 5.5" x 8.5" book, or an 11" x 17" paper becomes an 8.5" x 11" book. The covers are created from thicker card stock placed on the outside of the collated pages before folding and stapling. Saddle stitch is best for books under 48 pages.

Side Stitch. In a side-stitched book, pages are collated; loose card stock covers are placed on the front and back, then stapled on the left-hand side near the edge.

Spiral or Wire-O. These books look like a spiral notebook. One problem with spiral or wire-o is that every time the pages are turned, they rub against the binding. Eventually, the pages will tear from the book easily.

For memoirs, softbound or hardbound is best. Either looks professional, has a nice spine so you can read the title when the book is on the shelf, and lasts longer than spiral, wire-o, or old-fashioned comb binding which is expensive and does not hold up well over time.

Final Files

Most printers will accept Portable Document Format (PDF) files. Once you have your manuscript looking the way you want it to, save it as a PDF and send it to the printer. (More about the mechanics of saving PDF files in Section 4.)

Print Distribution Basics

To deliver a printed book to an interested reader, the book could be sold through a bookstore—a brick and mortar store or online. You could distribute them yourself by selling them on your own website; print a bunch and take them to a family reunion or other gathering of interested readers; ask readers to send orders to you; or, use an online print-on-demand service where buyers could purchase a copy for themselves. These are all easy options for distributing printed books.

Selling books through a brick and mortar store is a little more complicated. Most bookstores order directly through one of the major wholesalers—Ingram (Lightning Source) or Baker&Taylor. To sell books to a chain bookstore, you must have an account with one or both of the major wholesalers. For a memoir, however, chances are that the trouble you will go through to obtain an account will not be worth it.

There are exceptions. If you are well known, or if you have the kind of story with widespread public interest, then traditional bookstore distribution channels may be an option for you.

Another exception is selling through a local independent bookstore. A local store owner may be willing to stock a few books bought directly from you, but expect this to be the exception rather than the rule. You may have more luck with a local museum shop where making small purchases from local authors is more common. Museum stores will purchase a few copies at a time, so give them an easy way to re-order.

Be aware of the expectations of booksellers. Wholesalers will expect up to a 50 percent discount, so they can make money and allow the end seller (the bookstore) to make a few dollars on the sale as well. You can probably offer a smaller discount to a local bookstore or museum shop, more like 20 to 30 percent if you are not using a wholesaler.

Then there is the matter of returns. Bookstores and wholesalers expect to be able to return books if they go unsold. Returns are an accounting hassle for you, not to mention that the wholesaler or retailer may send the book back years later, in no condition to re-sell, but expect credit for the return anyway. For small publishers, the only way around this is to sell books on a *non-returnable* basis. You may have to offer a bigger discount to induce the bookstore or museum shop to a non-returnable sale, but the greater discount is almost always worth not dealing with returns.

Electronic Publishing

Except for adult fiction, printed books still hold about ninety percent of the book market. However, people are reading more and more via dedicated eReaders and on other electronic devices such as tablets. On tablets, readers use an application (app) to display the book as the dedicated eReaders do. As smartphones, tablets, and other mobile devices become more widely used in schools and offices, electronic books will become even more popular. Electronic books are cheaper, mobile and easier to store.

Currently, there are three primary formats for electronic publishing—PDF, MOBI, and EPUB.

Portable Document Format (PDF)

Creating a PDF does not require a publisher or a distributor. PDF is a file type developed by the Adobe Corporation that solved cross-platform problems between computers. Before the PDF, sending a file to a person using a different operating system (PC or Mac) or software (Word or Word Perfect) meant that the recipient could not open or read the document.

You can convert almost any file to a PDF, and almost every computer comes with the free Adobe Acrobat Reader pre-installed. If your computer does not have Acrobat Reader, download it free from Adobe (www.adobe.com). PDFs can be opened and read on most electronic devices including tablets.

One upside to PDFs is the ease of creation. Most word processing and page layout software will save their files to PDFs. Saving to PDF keeps the page formatting exactly as you designed it. Everything will stay in place—the text, the pictures, and the captions.

A downside is that documents designed using 8.5" x 11" pages are easy to read on a computer screen or iPad, but may be almost impossible to read on a smaller device such as a mini-tablet or a phone. The pages are a fixed size, more like viewing a photograph than reading a text document. A better option for smaller devices is to use a format that allows the text to reflow, such as MOBI or EPUB.

MOBI and EPUB

Where electronic publishing gets a little more complicated is in the creation and distribution of different formats for different devices. There are two primary formats for eReaders or apps that imitate eReaders—Kindle's proprietary format MOBI and the EPUB format used by many other devices. Acting as your own publisher for these formats is not impossible, but not simple either.

Publishing for Kindle

The Kindle is Amazon's dedicated eReader. To publish for Kindle, use the Kindle Direct Publishing (KDP) service (kdp.amazon.com). You will be able to upload a Word document or a PDF, and Amazon will convert it to their proprietary MOBI format. Amazon will handle all sales and distribution. Readers will make their purchase through Amazon and download the book to their Kindle or a device with a Kindle app.

Amazon pays you a royalty based upon the book's retail price. In 2015, any book with a retail price under $9.99 will generate a 70 percent royalty, whereas books priced at $10.00 or higher receive a 30 percent royalty.

One nice feature of Kindle books is their ability to sync across devices, meaning that readers can switch from their Kindle to their tablet or smartphone and sync the files to maintain their place in the book.

Publishing for Other eReaders

While most word processing software will create a PDF, you may need special software to create an EPUB file. Since so many devices are using this format, it may become easier to create an EPUB in the future. If you have a Mac, Pages software will create EPUB files. Adobe InDesign will create an EPUB file on a PC, but the software is expensive. Microsoft Word will allow you to save your manuscript as an HTML file, and then you can use the free Calibre software (calibre-ebook.com) to convert an HTML file into an EPUB.

If you create your own EPUB files, download Adobe's free Digital Editions software (www.adobe.com). Use Digital Editions to preview how the book looks before sending it to readers or elsewhere for distribution.

Electronic Production Basics

Electronic books, like printed books, need an interior file and a cover file, but there are differences in how the files must be prepared—sometimes big differences.

Interior Files as PDFs

Setting up your manuscript for a PDF is almost the same as setting it up for print production. You can set the interior up as two-page spreads, so that the reader experiences the book the same way they would if they were reading a printed version, or you can set it up as a single page document without right-hand or left-hand pages. Single pages allow the reader to keep a single page on the screen that will make it easier to read on a device such as an iPad.

You can use a word processor or page layout program to create your PDF file, or you can use a presentation program such as PowerPoint or Keynote for the Mac. Word processors have the best spell and grammar checkers, but presentation programs may give you greater control over combining text and images. The slide sorter view, for example, lets you move information around much easier than cutting and pasting in your word processor. Page layout programs (albeit the most expensive software option) will give you the greatest control over both text and images.

Interior Files as MOBIs or EPUBs

Preparing a manuscript for conversion to MOBI or EPUB is, in some respects, easier than laying out and formatting a PDF for electronic or print production. Electronic books must be simple, and without a lot of complicated formatting because the look of an electronic book is controlled largely by the reader. The reader can adjust the type size to suit their needs so the text must re-flow within the eReader's window.

While it is possible for you to create a MOBI or EPUB file yourself, it may be easier to let an eBook aggregator or distributor create the file so that there are no glitches when the file is read by electronic devices.

Cover Files

While it is not necessary to include a cover file with your electronic book, many eReaders will show the cover in the device's catalog, and most eBook outlets will show a thumbnail. Make sure your title is readable in a small thumbnail.

Electronic Distribution Basics

How electronic books are distributed depends upon the format.

Distributing PDFs

Distributing a PDF is simple. You can send it directly to the reader in an email. Fortunately, PDF files can be optimized which makes the file small enough to send even long manuscripts with photographs and illustrations by email.

Another option is to post your PDF online for readers to download for themselves. You could send interested readers a link, or they could use a search engine to discover it. You could also create a website and post your PDF behind a password so that only paying customers can access it.

One downside to *selling* your book as a PDF, however, is limiting distribution to paying customers. There are tools that allow you to mark copies with the name of the original buyer so if the book is widely shared, you will know who made it available. Other tools allow you to lock the PDF from printing or to password protect the file. Practically, however, once you distribute your book in a PDF format, it may be re-distributed without your knowledge.

Distribution for the Kindle

Amazon distributes Kindle books. You can publish your eBook directly through their distributor CreateSpace (which also handles printed books) (www.createspace.com), or Kindle Direct Publishing (kdp.amazon.com), if you plan to publish only in the Kindle format. Right now, Kindle holds a majority of the eBook market through either its dedicated reader or through the Kindle app available for tablets or smartphones.

Distribution for Devices Using the EPUB Format

Hundreds of different devices use the EPUB format. If you can create an EPUB file, you can distribute the book yourself, much the same way as you would a PDF file (above). There are also hundreds of distribution outlets for EPUB books including:

- iTunes (www.itunes.com)
- The Android App Store also called Google Play (play.google.com)
- Google Books (books.google.com)
- Kobo (www.kokobooks.com)
- Smashwords (www.smashwords.com)
- Gumroad (gumroad.com)

These online bookstores sell electronic books, acting as a wholesaler between you and the end user.

Rather than dealing with hundreds of online bookstores, consider using an aggregator. Aggregators charge a fee, but they will prepare your manuscript for distribution across multiple platforms making sure the file passes the standards tests for different devices. They will also prepare the file for the many apps that mimic eReaders such as the Nook app or the Kindle app.

Aggregators will handle sales through the different electronic book outlets, take a percentage as their sales commission and pay the rest to you as a royalty. The following are all eBook aggregators:

- First Edition Design Publishing (www.firsteditiondesignpublishing.com)
- Bookwire (www.bookwire.com)
- Ingram (www.ingramcontent.com)
- INscribe (inscribedigital.com)
- Smashwords (www.smashwords.com)
- BookBaby (www.bookbaby.com)

Distribution of Other Electronic Files

Services such as Gumroad (gumroad.com), allow you to upload your electronic file(s) to their servers. Gumroad accepts audio, video or zipped bundles, if you have more than one book available or want to include an audio file along with your book file. To sell your book, place a link on your website taking viewers to Gumroad to buy it. You price your book; Gumroad keeps a percentage as a hosting and processing fee; they pay you the rest. In essence, Gumroad is taking care of the credit card processing and electronic delivery. Once the item is paid for, the buyer will receive a download link.

Distribution to Groups

If you want to sell books to an organization in quantity, for example, you can use Amazon's Whispercast service (whispercast.amazon.com). The organization will create an account and send an invitation URL to its members. If the member accepts the invitation, the organization buys a copy for that person. After the member receives the book, Amazon charges the organization's credit card for the sale. This would work for a family reunion, by pre-selling books during the reunion, setting up a bank account with a debit card on behalf of the group and using the funds collected to pay for books through Whispercast.

Global Distribution

One of the biggest advantages to publishing electronically through one of the major distributors such as Amazon's Kindle Direct Publishing (kdp.amazon.com), or Barnes & Noble's Nook Press (nookpress.com), is that they will make your eBook available to people across the globe. There is no negotiating of foreign rights or dealing with a foreign publisher to distribute the book on another continent. If you have family members or other interested readers across the world, publishing electronically may be a good option for you.

Distribution by Gift Card

Enthrill Books (enthrillbooks.com) enables you to use a pre-activated gift card allowing the recipient to download your book either in the EPUB or MOBI format. You could take the pre-activated cards to a book signing, for example, to sell or give away to your audience.

Distribution to Libraries

One final consideration is placing your book with the major genealogical collections across the country and into the local libraries anywhere your family once resided. While most libraries still focus on print books, they are coming around to the idea of purchasing licensing rights for eBooks. The electronic format would allow the library to lend the book to patrons with eReaders. OverDrive (www.overdrive.com), is one of the leading digital distributors of electronic books to libraries, schools, and some retail outlets. If you are interested in selling your eBook to libraries, check out the publisher services on their website.

Online Publishing

For those of you who may want to make your book widely available and are not interested in selling it, publishing online may be a good option. There are a couple of ways to do so. You can use an online book publisher (Google Books), or you can act as your own publisher by using online publishing tools such as blogging software, website builders, social media or on a genealogical website featuring family trees.

The difference between an online book and an electronic book is how it is delivered. Online books and electronic books are both in an electronic format. An online book stays on a server somewhere where readers can use a web browser to access the book via the Internet. An electronic book is more likely to be distributed to a reading device such as a Kindle, Nook or smartphone.

The upside to publishing online is that anyone with Internet access can find and read your book. Many of the options below cost nothing to set up and use, although, you are completely at the mercy of the host as to whether your site stays up and running. If the company folds, your free site folds with it. Another option is to pay for your own website which will give you more options for the look and feel of the material or whether you want to sell the book rather than give it away. But, you must continue paying the hosting fee or the site will come down and your book with it.

The following are options for publishing a book online:

Online Book Publishers

Google Books is one of the only online book publishers I have found to date, meaning that they sell books meant to be read via the Internet using a web browser. Google Books allows readers to choose between PDFs formatted exactly as the publisher formatted the book, or read through a proprietary browser platform that presents the book in side-by-side pages as if reading a printed book. Google's browser-based software also gives readers the option of reading the book like other dedicated eReaders. The reader can change the type size or the font, and the book text will reflow. If you want to publish a book through Google Books, sign up through their Google Play Books Partner Center (play.google.com/books/publish/).

Amazon offers something similar allowing readers to purchase a book for their Kindle, also allowing them to access the book from a web browser through the Kindle Cloudreader software (read.kindle.com). The experience of reading a Kindle book online is similar to reading from the Kindle device itself.

Publishing a Book by Blog

Blog is short for web log. Blogging software allows publishers to post new content easily and quickly. If you can use email, you can blog. The process is similar. You will use a headline to alert the reader, and the body text to tell the story and display images.

The difficulty of publishing a book on a blog is organizing in a way that the reader understands what to read in what order, and keeping the segments short enough to avoid scrolling (and scrolling and scrolling).

Publishing a Book Using Social Media

Facebook (www.facebook.com) is the most popular social media site right now, although it has not always been, and may not be in the future. The appeal of Facebook is that it is so easy to connect with other people (family members) interested in reading your material. The downside of using something such as Facebook to deliver your book's content is that each post can be only so long, shorter, even than blog posts. You will be delivering your book in little dribs and drabs. Facebook may be a better place to obtain additional stories from family members while you are writing, more so than playing host to your finished book. (You will find more detailed information regarding publishing by blog or social media in *Set Yourself Up to Self-Publish: A Genealogist's Guide*.)

Publishing a Book on Your Own Website

If you create a website to publish your book, you can install blogging software such as WordPress, use a dedicated online genealogy program such as The Next Generation (TNG) (lythgoes.net/genealogy/software.php), or more traditional HTML coding using any number of HTML editors (website building software) such as Adobe Dreamweaver (www.adobe.com).

If you use web-based genealogy software such as The Next Generation (TNG), you may have trouble publishing your stories as a book *per se*, because the software is not meant for book publishing, it displays family trees, photographs and source information as a website. TNG offers "featured articles" that can hold large volumes of text, as well as a "histories" feature for short stories linked to individuals within your tree.

If you create your own website and use an HTML editor to build it, you will have complete control over how the site looks, and how you will organize your book as web pages.

Publishing a Book Using a Wiki Platform

Wikis are user-generated content that can be edited directly using an ordinary web browser. A wiki is a great opportunity for collaboration with family members to keep family information up to date, but it is also an opportunity for malicious users to spread misinformation or to delete a lot of hard work. The power and the bane of wikis is the ability of anyone to contribute.

Publishing a Book with a Genealogy Service

Neither the paid genealogy services Ancestry (www.ancestry.com), or MyHeritage (www.myheritage.com), nor the free service FamilySearch (www.familysearch.com) (or any of the other genealogy-based search sites) were designed as book publishing platforms. Many offer tools to attach stories and photographs to individuals within an online family tree. Publishing your book in this way is similar to publishing on a social media site—short snippets rather than a beginning-to-end book.

Note: FamilySearch, Ancestry, and MyHeritage have book or booklet publishing options that use your online tree to create printed books. When investigating the process, I found that the cost was much higher than using a print-on-demand printer, and the options for what to include or exclude was a bit clumsy, at least at this point. If you are going to create a print version of your research, it is worth the effort to use a dedicated book printer.

Online Production Basics

If you publish online, preparing your manuscript is relatively easy. Although, how you prepare it depends upon where you are going to place it on the Internet. Let us start with Google Books since they are the exception to the rule, and then we will look into making your book into blog posts or web pages.

Files for Google Books

If you publish online through Google Books, you can upload both a PDF version and an EPUB version, so the reader can choose whether to view the book exactly as you have it laid out, or as flowing text they can control through Google's browser-based platform. PDF and EPUB are the only two file formats Google Books accepts for upload. They will also accept a printed book and scan it for you, making it possible to create a new eBook out of an older, out-of-print title.

Google Books uses thumbnail-sized cover files in their online catalog.

Files for Blog Posts

While you can organize your material as a complete book on a blog, you must organize in a way that lets readers know how to follow the stories one after the other, and split the manuscript into short segments (posts) to keep scrolling to a minimum.

Each post requires a headline and body text, similar to composing an email. Blog posts can include images and captions. You can also add keywords to categorize each post so that readers can find the blog using a search engine.

Readers familiar with feed reader programs can subscribe to your blog so that they are notified every time you create a new post.

You can use your book cover image as a part of the blog's header so that it is always visible no matter which post the reader is viewing.

Files for Social Media

Publishing to a social media site is similar to publishing to a blog. Posting to a blog or social media keeps your short snippets in one place with the latest post at the top. The older posts will move down as the new posts appear.

On social media, if you create a page (sometimes called fan page) dedicated to your book, readers can come to that page to see everything you have posted, similar to visiting a blog, but if readers are "following" your page (i.e. they have "liked" it), then the snippets will be delivered to the reader through the newsfeed on their own pages.

For each post, use a headline to catch the viewer's attention as they skim their newsfeed (the posts coming in). Place the text in the body, and add images. Some social media platforms allow you to caption each image, and "tag" the people in the image. Tagging is similar to adding a keyword to the image. It helps people find the image using the search feature on the social media site, or by using a search engine.

Use your book cover image in the header area or as the profile image so that every time you post, the book's cover is shown in the little icon next to the post. Facebook uses square profile images, and book covers are longer than they are wide, so you may have to add a bit of white space on either side of your book cover image to make it square. Otherwise, it could be cut off at the top and bottom when displayed.

Files for a Website

Creating your own website gives you a lot of flexibility for how and what you make available to readers.

Web pages can hold text, images, video or audio files and contain links to other resources on the Internet. To publish your book as a website, use an HTML editor to create a page for each story or chapter and navigation links to help the reader move from story to story logically.

Keywords are used on web pages the same way they are used on blog posts to help the search engines find the web page. HTML editing software and most website building tools online offer a way to include keywords in the metadata for each page.

Use your book cover image in the website's header, or alongside the text on the home page.

Files for a Genealogy Service

Most genealogical websites where you can build an online family tree have a way to attach stories to individuals or groups.

Ancestry provides two ways to attach stories to people in your family tree. One method is to use the story view settings. Ancestry uses the documents you have linked to the person to suggest a storyline, and gives you the option of adding text and photographs to the story view page. Another option is to add stories directly through the media gallery section where you can also add images, video or audio.

The process is similar on FamilySearch. You will add stories in the "memories" section of your family tree where you can also add a picture.

At MyHeritage, each individual in your tree has a page where you can add biographical information and media files (photographs) or links to video files.

Cover files are a little more difficult to place at one of these online options, unless you want a book cover image attached to an individual.

Copy and Paste Text Cleanly

The easiest way to prepare text for any online option is to copy and paste from your word processor. However, many word processors add code for formatting features such as margins, fonts, font size, bold or italics. These codes do not always translate cleanly to email, blog posts or websites. Word processors use an 8-bit environment for formatting, while many of the tools of the Internet use a 7-bit environment which can cause conflicts. What you can end up with is unexpected characters in your text, mostly where you expect punctuation to be.

For example, this is what happens when a quote is copied from a Word document into an email:

From Word: "Jacob's intended return ..."
Copied into email: "Jacob@s intended return ..."

One way to avoid these unexpected ASCII characters is to copy the text into a plain text editing program such as Notepad first. Notepad will remove all formatting, leaving a plain text (.txt) version of whatever you are copying and pasting. The plain text version can then be used in an email, a blog post or a website without any unexpected characters surfacing.

Create Web-Friendly File Names

Tools of the Internet also prefer standard filenames. So, file names that are acceptable on your local computer may contain unexpected characters when posted online. For example:

Local file: Jacob Wilson's will.pdf
Online becomes: Jacob%20Wilson%20s%20Will.pdf (depending upon the server settings)

For clean file names, avoid punctuation except for periods and use underscores for spaces. Either of these file names would be fine, for example:

Jacob.Wilson.Will.pdf
Jacob_Wilson_Will.pdf

Online Distribution Basics

If you publish online, you have largely determined how the book will be distributed to the reader—on a blog, a website or within a social media platform. You do not have to distribute it; the readers will come to the book. You need only take the steps necessary to help readers find the book online—good, descriptive keywords, great content, and a willingness to get the word out.

༄ ༺

What is the easiest way to prepare a book and distribute it at the least cost? That would be a PDF. As long as the PDF is designed for easy reading on the screen, the book can be distributed by email. For some readers, a PDF is perfect. If they are used to reading on screen or a large format tablet such as an iPad, they will appreciate the PDF. For others, print will always be preferred.

What, then, is the easiest way to prepare a book for sale? The easiest way is to create an eBook and use an eBook aggregator to convert it to the different electronic formats for you. The aggregator will also submit the files to the various sales outlets online, collect the sales price minus the online bookstore's fee, and pay you a royalty from the sale. Creating an eBook is simpler than creating a book for print because there are a few simple formatting and image placement rules to follow. The reader can change the font or type size to suit his or her needs, so the formatting must remain fluid. There is a fee to have an eBook aggregator prepare and submit your manuscript, but for those readers who are used to a dedicated eReader, this option will delight them.

Publishing a book online and in print are a bit more challenging than publishing PDFs and eBooks.

Publishing online has organizational challenges, but most options are without cost. Online publishing has the risk of all other electronic products—obsolescence. If the company hosting your website folds, or the social media site becomes unpopular, or your blog is lost in a server crash, the book is lost.

The best, most permanent way to preserve your memoir is to publish in print. A book printed today, given the technology and materials, should last one hundred years or more. If preserved well, a modern book will last much longer. In the event of natural or personal disaster, giving a few copies of your book to the major libraries around the country will preserve your research and writing for generations to come.

Chapter 5

The Right Tool for the Right Job

To make your way from idea to finished book, using the right tool for the right job will save you time and frustration.

In a perfect world, you would use an organizational tool to set up the table of contents and organize your notes, a word processor to draft your manuscript, an image capture program to scan documents and other printed materials, an image editor to crop, size and alter images, a page layout program to typeset the book so that it reads and looks its best, and backup tools to keep your manuscript and image files safe from disaster.

In general, organizational tools are not the best place to format text correctly, word processors are not the best place to lay out book pages, and page layout programs are not the best word processors.

Realistically, you may not want to invest your time and money in all of this software. You may not need to. What you do need is an understanding of the rules of readability for books; and either, the willingness to learn how to create a layout, typeset the text, and prepare images in the software you already own, or recognition that the software you have will not do the job well. If the latter is the case, you can engage professional help or invest in software better suited to the job.

Organizing

In the preliminary stages, you may want software to keep you organized. Scrivener (www.literatureandlatte.com/scrivener.php) is a powerful organizing tool to gather your notes, pictures, video clips, or thoughts. It is available for both PC and Mac.

If you use an outline, the left-hand panel shows your outline in a menu that you can use to rearrange files, and expand or collapse depending upon what you want to see while you are working. You can split files into pieces to create a more detailed outline.

If you organize in a more visual way, you can see your notes, organized on a cork board. If you want to keep your sources attached to each note, you can do so either in the body of the text or off to the side in a panel designed to document source material.

At any time, you can move notes from one place to another using the drag and drop features in the cork board or outline, helping to organize your information into a cohesive whole.

Other organizing software includes: Microsoft OneNote (www.onenote.com) and Evernote (evernote.com). Both of these organizing tools have the advantage of being available on your desktop and by app on mobile devices with the ability to sync files. I use these apps to add notes or ideas when I am out and about, but when I am in the office writing, I use Scrivener to organize.

Word Processing

At some point, move your notes from an organizing tool into a word processor. Whether you are at the stage to add formatting, or you are still writing and want to collect your material chapter by chapter, a word processor is a better tool than organizing software to create a complete manuscript.

Word processors are ideal for creating eBooks. Unfortunately, most word processing software falls short when creating layouts and correct typesetting for print books because they lack the sophistication to create the best-looking pages.

Word processors often hyphenate incorrectly or add space between words to avoid hyphenating that can create rivers of white or blank areas through the type. Word processors do not have nearly the kind of control over how tight or how loose text is typeset that also can result in dense or dark areas of text on the page. Most word processors do not have as much control over margins, columns and text wrap around images, as page layout programs do.

Unfortunately, page layout software can be expensive, so you may opt to layout and typeset your final manuscript in your word processing software. If you do, be prepared to learn about the advanced features. Fortunately, some word processors have helpful time-saving features to create a table of contents, an index, and footnotes, for example.

There are numerous word processing programs available including:

- Microsoft Word (office.microsoft.com)
- Pages for Mac (www.apple.com)
- Word Perfect (www.wordperfect.com)
- OpenOffice Writer (www.openoffice.org)
- LibreOffice (www.libreoffice.org)
- Google Docs (docs.google.com)

Microsoft Word has become the standard among book designers and packagers, professional editors, some eBook aggregators, and online resellers. For book designers and book packagers, Word files can be imported directly into more sophisticated page layout software without much trouble. For editors, Word has a "Track Changes" feature that allows you to see and accept or reject an editor's changes. Most eBook aggregators prefer Word files because they can convert the file for the requirements of the different eBook readers easily. And, some online resellers will accept Word files from which to create print and electronic books.

Page Layout

When typesetting print books, you will achieve the best results from a page layout program. The two major powerhouses are:

- Adobe InDesign (www.adobe.com)
- QuarkXPress (www.quark.com)

Pages for the Mac (www.apple.com) was designed as a word processor but has many of the same features as the best page layout programs.

Page layout programs are designed to put the finishing touches on book-length manuscripts using the same tools professional typesetters use. These programs also can handle full-color books and, for the time being, are best for converting word-processed text into good looking eBooks in the EPUB format used by many eReaders.

PDF is another popular electronic format, and page layout programs create beautiful PDFs with settings to create the appropriate file sizes and quality for printing, emailing or posting online.

The biggest advantage to using a page layout program is the control you have over where items are placed on the page in relationship to other items, the ability to create precise text formatting styles (rules) for different needs, and the flexible layouts possible with master pages with different grids for different page styles.

The sophistication of these programs is a big step up from even the best word processors. Unfortunately, most page layout programs come with both a hefty price tag and a hefty learning curve. For some, using a book designer or packager to take your final manuscript from as good as a word processor can do, to as good as a New York publisher could do, may be a better tradeoff than buying and learning a page layout program.

Image Capture

There are two ways to turn a printed photograph or document into a digital image—you can photograph it, or you can scan it. For items such as photographs pasted into a scrapbook, heirloom objects or photographs with textured surfaces, re-photographing the item may give you the best results.

For most flat items, however, scanning will give you a good digital image. Producing a good, print-ready scan will save you time and effort later.

There is more information about scanning in Chapter 8: Scanning and Optical Character Recognition.

Image Editing

The best way to prepare images in the correct physical size and resolution is to use an image editing program.

There are hundreds of image editors, including online tools, free downloads, apps for mobile devices, pre-installed software, and those designed for professional photographers. One of the best is Adobe Photoshop. For most people, the consumer version called Photoshop Elements (www.adobe.com) will do everything you need to complete your book project.

Illustration

While it is possible to create a book cover in a word processor or a page layout program, to create the best-looking images and type, you may want to use illustration software, also called vector editing programs. The most popular among graphic designers is Adobe Illustrator (www.adobe.com).

There are many others available, including:

- CorelDraw Graphics Suite (www.coreldraw.com)
- Xara Designer Pro (www.xara.com)
- Inkscape (www.inkscape.org)

Illustration programs are another case where the cost of buying the program (and the time required to learn it) may be better spent hiring a cover designer.

Utilities and Backup

While you are writing, make backups—frequently. You never know when your hard drive will crash, or some other calamity may come your way. One way to create on-going backups is to use one of the cloud services such as:

- Carbonite (www.carbonite.com)
- MyPCBackup (www.mypcbackup.com)
- Mozy (www.mozy.com)
- SugarSync (www.sygarsync.com)

If you keep good backups and something happens, you can always retrieve the most recent backup of your manuscript once you are up and running again.

If you also want to share files with family or editors, think about using a file sharing service such as:

- Dropbox (www.dropbox.com)
- Hightail (formerly YouSendIt) (www.hightail.com)
- Box.com (www.box.com)
- Google Drive (drive.google.com)
- Microsoft OneDrive (onedrive.live.com)

These services are perfect for sharing copies of your manuscript, even if the file is large. Do not keep your only copy on one of these services, however, because anyone who shares the folder with you has the power to delete it.

The most secure place to keep backups is in the cloud, or on a portable hard drive, stored away from your home in a safe deposit box.

⤬⤬⤬

How many or how few of these tools you utilize is up to you. You may find that the right tool for the right job is easiest. Or, you may prefer hiring someone to handle the tasks you would rather not tackle. Thankfully, most memoirs are successfully published without spending a king's ransom on software or professional help.

Section 2

The goal in this section is for you to review your plans and gather anything else you may need before you begin writing.

Everyone should:

- Identify your target audience—the people for whom you are writing the book.
- Take stock of where you are and what you still have left to do.
- Read the chapter on scanning and OCR.
- Read the tips for conquering writer's block.
- Make completing your book project a priority by scheduling time on your calendar to devote to it.

Baby Steps

If, after conducting a research review, you are ready to proceed with the writing, draft a good outline, and start. If the task of digitizing your images feels overwhelming, look for a scanning company to help you.

Next Steps

After your research review, plan an additional round of research to fill in any holes or answer any questions you may have. Expand your list of characters to your extended family if you plan to write about them. Digitize your images and organize them in files by subject, family or time period. Visit historical or living history museums to spark your memory of times gone by.

Giant Leaps

After your research review, plan an additional round of research to gather any social history or historical context to help you write using historically accurate details. Expand your list of characters to friends, neighbors and colleagues if you plan to write about them. Digitize your images, organize them and add historical or modern-day images. Take research trips back to "the old homestead" or your old "stomping grounds."

Even though it may seem that I am suggesting you retire and devote your life to writing your book, I am not. I want you to be realistic about the preparation phase, however, because it can take longer than the writing.

Because this section has so many tasks, there are additional Baby Steps, Next Steps and Giant Leaps within some chapters.

*In this section, when I refer to characters, I always mean real people—not fictional characters.

Chapter 6

Identifying Your Target Market

Your target market—who you are writing for—matters. According to *Elements of Style*, "The true writer always plays to an audience of one." To keep your perfect audience in mind as you write, place a photograph on the wall or near the desk as a constant reminder.

Having a clear idea of the people who will appreciate your book will influence what to include and what to leave out. If you write to meet your audience's needs and expectations, you will naturally answer their questions, and use the images and events needed to make the stories engaging.

You also may choose to *leave out* stories if they would be embarrassing to living people. That is not to say that you should shy away from what actually happened, only that a touch of tact may be in order when telling those stories.

Who is Your Audience?

Your family, of course, is the natural audience for your book. Your immediate family, probably some extended family, even distant cousins may be interested because of their relationships with people in the book.

Even though you should write primarily to satisfy the curiosity of your core audience—your family—most books have more than one natural audience.

Genealogical Researchers

Genealogists who are researching family from your area, or want to know what your town was like when you were growing up may be interested in your stories.

Local Historians

There may be researchers or hobbyists interested in the era you are writing about to give them an idea of what life was like in the local area in days past.

The General Public

Your story may appeal to the general public—stories that are representative of a generation's experience during WWII, for example, or broader issues such as poverty, civil rights struggles or entrepreneurial successes.

Museum Shops

If your stories would interest local people, then a museum shop may be interested in selling your book.

Libraries

While many libraries are happy to accept a donation of your book, to convince the library to buy a copy, show a significant tie between your stories and the library's location or region.

Bookstores

Bookstores are great places. As a bibliophile, I love bookstores, but the pressure on bookstores is to move inventory. Unfortunately, memoirs, even those with broad, general public appeal, are a risk for bookstores unless you, the author, are well known. Unless you can generate traffic into the bookstore, do not count on bookstores to sell many of your books. There are ways to entice interested readers through the bookstore door, but that discussion is later in Section 5: Getting the Word Out.

While you are researching and writing, consider what your target market(s) may need to get the best experience while reading your book.

What Does Your Audience Need?

The goal while writing is to spend your energy making the book the best it can be, given the time you have to finish the research and write the book. Give the reader everything he or she needs to understand the action, feel an emotional tie to you and the other people you write about, believe that the stories occurred as you have relayed them, and experience what you did in days gone by.

Subject Matter

How much information you include will depend upon the number of events you will describe. The level of detail is up to you and how much research or recollecting you are willing to do.

Format

The format or style of a memoir, typically, is a more lengthy narrative than a picture history, for example, where the emphasis is on the photographs. Whether you tell your story as a beginning-to-end chronology, by time-period, by subject, or in short story snippets is up to you.

Documentation

There may be elements of your memoir that you will want to document with source information because some readers may expect to recreate your research steps, and some readers will use your evidence to evaluate the credibility of the book. For example, you may want to include footnotes to help explain elements of your recollections that do not fit neatly into the narrative. How you choose to document your experiences, however, is up to you. You may choose a format that is easier to accomplish than one of the more rigorous genealogical styles.

Images

If you have photographs to illustrate your stories, family members will certainly want to see them. If you do not, it may be worth a bit of research to find someone who does. I once found a portrait of an ancestor hanging in a museum. In that case, it was certainly worth the phone call to ask.

Images help guide readers through the story. Maps are a good example of this. While you may know exactly where your office was, for example, younger members of your family may not.

Illustrations can help readers imagine skills, places or events they are unfamiliar with, such as what a typical inner-city tenement looked like, how cattle were branded, or how machinery was used to create textiles, even if the illustration is only representative of your experience. Think of how many kids have never used a rotary phone. In addition, a beautifully illustrated book may be more appealing to a bookstore or a museum shop than a book with text only.

Index

An index is indispensable. One of the first things your family members are going to do is turn to the index to see whether or not they are in the book. Genealogical researchers will turn to the index to see if the place or the family line they are researching is represented. Additionally, librarians hesitate to stock books without indexes unless they are fiction.

Keep the following ideas in mind while you are researching and writing:

- How much of the story does the reader need to envision a complete and understandable picture of what is happening?
- How much detail is needed to make the reader feel as if they are experiencing what you were experiencing?
- Could an image clarify what is difficult to describe?
- For those who may want to do additional research based upon your book, what level of documentation will be the most helpful?

What Will You Need to Tell the Stories?

The next step is to figure out what *you* will need to tell the best possible stories.

Action

Events are the building blocks of good stories—the situations you faced. In order to keep readers engaged, the story has to keep moving. You may choose to tell your stories as vignettes or as a start-to-finish chronology. Either way, building a timeline of what took place, where events took place, and to whom, will become the backbone of your book.

Characters

One of the best pieces of writing advice I have ever read is this:

> The story is not what happens; it's to whom it happens.
>
> **—Peter Rubin and Gary Provost**
> *How to Tell a Story: The Secrets of Writing Captivating Tales*

Rubin and Provost have it exactly right. There is no reason to keep reading if the reader does not care about you and the other people in your stories. Your biggest challenge may be to learn enough about the other characters you will include to describe what kind of people they were—not just what they did or how they did it—but how they handled triumphs and struggles, and what that says about them as people.

Description

The best stories make the reader feel as if they are experiencing what the characters are experiencing. Your challenge is to either recall or add enough detail about the time period(s) and the place(s) described in your stories in order to give the reader a feel for the era and the location.

Detail

You must get the details right. There is a bit of a fudge factor for what you are able to recall and what you cannot. However, the credibility of your book depends upon historically accurate details. It is one thing to leave out a significant detail, it is entirely another to include a detail that makes the story seem untrue.

❧❧

Your next step is to conduct a research review. A research review will help you organize what you already have, and develop a plan for gathering what else you may need before you can begin writing.

Chapter 7

Taking Stock

The reason to stop and take stock is to evaluate and organize what you have—whether you have already written a bit or whether you have not, but plan to use items in your possession to spur memories or whether you will need a little research to bring out some details. More importantly, taking stock will help you create lists of what you do not have so that you can form a plan focused solely on the information you need for this book and not to wander into other interesting projects.

If you are starting from the beginning and you have not written anything, or perhaps you only have photographs or a couple of scrapbooks from which to begin, keep reading. You may be surprised by what you do have. Taking stock will let you know what you may need to gather in order to tell vivid, robust, well-rounded stories.

Each story contains the following elements—the people, the events, the places, and the context in which the events took place. After you assemble each story's parts, then you can analyze that you have and what you may lack.

Identify the Characters

Even though you are writing your memoir, you may or may not be the main character in each of the stories you will tell. So, the first task is to identify the cast of characters. Most stories have a main character(s). Along with the main character(s) are often central characters who had influence on your main character(s) and supporting characters who were present but played lesser roles than main or central characters. The best storytellers are those who can describe people in a way that makes readers feel something for the people in the story.

Identify the Events

You may be wondering, out of the tens of thousands of individual events in your life, which one to write about? One way to start thinking about events is to create a timeline in chronological order. Even if you are writing in self-contained vignettes, creating a timeline may help you remember additional events.

There are a multitude of methods for creating a timeline to help you analyze effectively what you already have and discover what you still need. Building a timeline will force you to organize your thoughts for what you will write about. Then you can determine whether or not you need additional research to help you tell the stories.

We will investigate the technique of creating story arcs later in Section 3: Writing. Think of story arcs as episodes of a television show. Story arcs in your book will be similar. You can tell the longer story by stringing together shorter stories where events come to a conclusion followed by new events. At the same time, ideas or themes will carry through the shorter stories to provide continuity for the longer story. A timeline will help you see the story arcs.

To create a timeline, I use an Excel spreadsheet because I can add columns for information that does not fit neatly into any one category. A spreadsheet is a simple, visual way to expose holes in a sequence of events.

The following are three websites where you can create a timeline:

- TimeToast (www.timetoast.com)
- Tiki-Toki (www.tiki-toki.com)
- Dipity (www.dipity.com)

While there are not quite as many mobile apps that create timelines, there are a few. Check out:

- iTunes (www.itunes.com)
- Android App Store also called Google Play (play.google.com)

Historical timelines featuring U.S. or world history may help you explain the historical context of the events you will describe. Check out:

- Wikipedia's Timeline of United States History (en.wikipedia.org/wiki/Timeline_of_United_States_history)
- The American Memory Timeline at the Library of Congress website (www.loc.gov/teachers/classroommaterials/presentationsandactivities/presentations/timeline/)
- The World History Timeline at TimeMaps (www.timemaps.com/history)

Although it may be helpful to look at major historical events, local events are much more likely to have a direct impact on you and the other people in your stories. You may find a timeline created by a local historical society describing community events or you may have to create one of your own by reading a few good local, business or unit histories, if you are writing about your military experience.

While you are building your timeline, ask yourself the following questions about each event, as a reporter would when covering the news:

Who

Who participated or was present? Are those other people among your cast of characters? Should they be? What roles did the other people play in the event? Did the event have an affect on people who were not present?

What

What happened during the event? What other events led to (preceded) and were a consequence of (followed) this event? What social customs surrounded the event? What significance does the event have for you? What made you remember the event? Was the event significant enough that a record was made of the event? Did someone take a photograph, issue a license or certificate, or record it in some other way? Where else could the event have been mentioned (e.g. a newspaper or magazine)? Would the event have been mentioned in someone else's personal account (e.g. letters, journals or diaries)?

When

What was the date and time of the event? How long did the event last?

Where

Where did the event take place? What do you remember about the place as it existed on the date of the event?

Why

Why did the event take place?

How

How did the event take place? What forces combined to spark the event? What steps were taken during the event?

For now, add any event you think you will include in the book. Record your questions, the answers, and any further questions raised while evaluating each event. Keep a separate timeline for social history or historical context (more about this shortly). You can add those details to your events timeline once you have a better idea of which events you will actually include in the book.

Social History

Social history is the history of daily life, and can provide rich details for storytelling. You may have an abundance of social history in your home. Each of the following items may help stir memories. While you are taking stock, be on the lookout for the following:

Personal Papers. Letters, diaries, journals, recipe cards, scrapbooks, greeting cards, birth announcements, wedding invitations or funeral cards. Look for anything that may have been written, compiled or saved as a remembrance.

Photographs. Get out the photo albums, look through the slides, and collect the negatives. In the next chapter, we will spend some time on the details of getting good scans. For now, gathering them all up, identifying the people, and organizing by either people or events is a big enough job. While you are looking through them, though, see if you can also spot evidence of social history—the way people dressed, a new car, houses or land, a barn or farm animals. See what you spot in the background. It may be more information than you think.

Newspaper Clippings. Look for obituaries, birth, wedding or engagement announcements, feature stories or advertising. Advertising can be a quick, visual way to remember what fashions and prices were like "back in the day." You may find newspaper clippings loose or within other bound volumes such as bibles, photo albums or scrapbooks.

School Records. Gather up anything school related, such as report cards, diplomas, academic achievements, group activities, club or sports awards, theater or music programs, personal or class photographs, and yearbooks.

Business Records. Look for anything that may indicate how you were employed or conducted business, such as employment records, pay stubs, account books, store ledgers, client lists, professional guides or books, licenses or certificates.

Military Service. If you served in the military look for your service records, discharge papers, uniforms, commendations, medals, photographs, or identification papers.

Religious Records. Religious institutions were often the place where ceremonies were recorded, such as baptisms, confirmations, weddings, deaths or burials. You may find a certificate of the event. Also look for bibles or other religious texts, evidence of religious education, religious magazines or bulletins, general magazines or newspapers.

Association Records. If you joined any associations, look for handbooks, costumes, awards, jewelry, rules or bylaws, group photographs or membership lists.

Court Records. Court records are rich sources of juicy stories. If you have spent any time in the courthouse, look for court rulings or judgments, lawsuits, probates, divorces, and civil or criminal cases.

Administrative Records. Look for any papers filed with a government clerk or other administrator such as deeds, taxes, licenses, voter registration, or auto registration. Your first auto registration may remind you of what you were driving at age sixteen.

Collections. Are you a collector of things, such as stamps, coins, spoons, salt and pepper shakers, images, statuettes or photographs? There is almost no limit to the things people collect and where they may have gone to add to their collections. Are your collections a source of a good story or two?

Enthusiasts. Are you a fan? Did you keep photographs of stars, autographs, tickets, posters, playbills, albums, memorabilia, or sports jerseys?

Ephemera or Memorabilia. Ephemera is a catch-all term for items that were meant to be temporary such as tickets, menus, playbills, posters, or advertising. Memorabilia is a slightly larger category that may include items such as snow globes, travel posters, postcards, souvenirs, reunion books, mugs, or t-shirts. Have you kept ephemera or memorabilia from different events?

Any of these items should spark memories of daily life, your activities and who the people associated with those activities were.

Family Traditions

Examine your family traditions. Family traditions can be a rich source of memories and stories. It may be interesting to try to figure out from *where* in your family's history each tradition came, and how those traditions may have changed over time. Figuring out *which* family traditions came from your ethnic heritage is going to be interesting because so few of us are 100 percent this or that. And, it can be difficult to distinguish which traditions are ethnic, and which are religious, regional, or unique to your family.

Examine how your family celebrates holidays and special occasions. What activities take place after a baby is born? What is done (or not done) during weddings or funerals? How often does your whole family gather together?

What type of food is served at each holiday? Write out a menu of the meals you remember from holiday celebrations in the past and see if there are any trends. Have you asked other family members if they have recollections of holiday celebrations or family recipes?

Is there a family business? Even if there is not a brick and mortar business, is there a type of job that people in your family tend to do? Do you come from a long line of teachers, shop owners or farmers?

Are there heirlooms that represent traditions in your family? Do you have quilts or knitted items? Do you find unique textile patterns in the things that have been passed down? Do you have furniture that came from a particular region? Are there hand-crafted items unique to a particular place?

Does your family hold reunions? What activities take place during reunions? Does your family meet at a place of significance? What kind of food is served? You may find completely different recipes for a reunion potluck than you would for a holiday celebration.

What stories have older relatives told you? Through how many generations have the stories been passed down? Write those stories down and ask other family members if they have heard the same stories. You may be surprised how many versions of the story are out there among the cousins.

Families are not the only source of traditions, either. You may recall traditions associated with your place of work or your occupation, associations you have belonged to, schools you have attended, or the military, if you served.

Historical Context

Adding historical context to your memoir may help the reader understand why events happened the way they happened, but it can also be a little bit tricky. Major local, regional, national and even world events may have influenced why events occurred in your life—or they may not have. It is important to be realistic about how events impacted you and the people in your stories. Living through World War II as a kid in America was a completely different experience than living through it on the Bataan Peninsula, for example. Chances are good that local or regional events will have the greatest impact while a few national or international events may have played a role.

As you are taking stock, look for areas where a bit of additional historical research could help you tell your own story in a more vivid way using historically accurate details. And, look for places where giving the reader a bigger picture view could help put your own story into context.

The Story in Pictures

Most memoirs will benefit by adding images. Not only do they help break up daunting pages of dense text, they help give the stories context. While you may be intimately familiar with a place or an era, your reader may need visual clues to put the pieces together. Think about how many kids have never seen, let alone used, a rotary phone.

Photographs

In a memoir, photographs are a must. One issue you may run into is that the further back in time you go, the fewer photographs you may have. Keep an eye out for those photographs that are one-of-a-kind or rare and include them in the book, even if they bear the dents and scars of time. Your family will likely appreciate those photographs the most.

Once you start writing about the stories that took place within the last twenty years, you may have too many photographs from which to choose. In this situation, use the critical eye of a photojournalist to pick out the best photographs. Photojournalists look for *the* photograph that sums up the story and often it is the emotion in the picture that makes the difference.

Look through your photographs for the following: good photographs of the central cast of characters at different ages; photographs that help distinguish siblings (height, weight, hairstyles, paired or group photographs); and photographs of biographical details (lifestyle, hobbies, pets, profession, room arrangements, celebrations, or travel).

Leave out any photographs of sensitive subjects or embarrassing situations. For some relatives, it is bad enough that a photograph exists, but to include an embarrassing photograph in your book may be a step over the line. Leave out photographs that are badly over- or underexposed, and those with distracting backgrounds unless you are willing to digitally alter these photographs to make them usable.

Make a list of what you *do not* find, as well. Are there heirloom objects that should be photographed under studio conditions to look their best? Are you missing a picture of one of your siblings? Do you have wedding photographs for each married couple? Are there decades between pictures of some individuals? How about school pictures?

The process of sifting through photographs serves three purposes: one is to help you remember events and details to include in your stories, the second is to choose photographs to include in the book to help readers best understand your stories, and the third is to compile a list of photographs you want, but do not already have. Chapter 8: Scanning and Optical Character Recognition has advice if you need to alter photographs in your possession digitally. Chapter 9: Developing a Research Plan has tips for obtaining permission to use stock photography or historical photographs, having photographs taken by a professional, or taking new photographs yourself.

Documents

Many memoirs include document images of one type, or another. The challenge is choosing documents that will be the most meaningful to the reader or will help tell your stories in the most convincing way.

Consider including these items as images: business cards, advertisements or letterheads; yearbook pages; city directory listings; memorabilia; letters or journal pages; land records that have hand-drawn lot lines; wills and inventories; birth, marriage, christening, or death records; pension records; passport files; ship's passenger lists—essentially anything interesting for the reader to see.

Illustrations

There are times when an illustration conveys a clearer message than either a document or a photograph. The following are a few examples:

An Ancestor Chart. If you want the reader to see where you fit into the family, or who descends from whom quickly, a multi-generation ancestor chart may be the easiest way.

Timeline. A timeline is an effective way to show small bits of information in a logical way. You could show the birth of each child or your military unit's participation in different battles, for example, using a timeline.

Diagrams. An architectural drawing, for example, may help give readers an idea of what your old house looked like if you do not have a photograph of it. I particularly enjoy artists' renderings of what a place may have looked like, or how buildings may have been constructed in the past. Diagrams are also a good way to demonstrate how something was done in the past that may not be done the same way today. Think of how many kids have never put up a canvas tent with wooden poles.

One caution about using illustrations for the sake of having something to look at on the page—it is worth your time to find a good image to illustrate an old technique, for example, or to have a good image created by an artist rather than settling for a low-quality, ClipArt image.

Maps

Maps are an easy way to help readers get their bearings. Some of your readers may not be familiar with the settings you are describing.

Context maps can help readers understand, in general, what part of the state or country you are referring to in the story. The map of Kentucky shows Bath County up in the northeastern part of the state. The second map shows the relative distance between Bath and Caldwell counties, giving readers a general idea of place and distance.

A map can also help the reader find a location to visit. The topo map shows the roads leading to the cemetery, marks where the cemetery is, and shows the topography—all helpful information for a visit.

Maps help describe movement from place to place as you would if you were describing a battle scene, for example. A battlefield map would help the reader visualize where the opposing forces met, how far troops had to go from one battle to the next, and so on.

The possibilities for including maps are nearly endless: plats, roads, historic, political, battlefield, migration, topographical, economic, climate, coastline, survey, nautical, soil, trails, and so on. If you cannot find a map of exactly what you need, you can create one using Google Maps using the My Maps feature

Road map showing directions for readers to follow.

County map showing Bath County, KY

County map showing Bath and Caldwell Counties

59

(mapsengine.google.com). Google Maps has a generous Terms of Use agreement that includes creating and sharing individualized maps with proper credit. Make sure you read the Terms of Use before including a Google Map in your book.

Gather a list of places readers may need to see a map for context, clarification, or to visit for themselves.

Art and Objects

Look at the artwork and heirlooms you have. These objects can spark memories or may have interesting stories of their own.

Make a list of the items in the possession of other family members. When approaching them for information about heirlooms, be clear about your intentions—that you want to get a good photograph so that readers can see what your grandmother's china looked like—not that you have any designs on the object(s) yourself. The same advice goes for asking to use family members' photographs or portraits for your book.

Artwork and objects deserve a special mention because these items should be photographed not scanned, so they will display well. You will find information about photographing these items in Chapter 9: Developing a Research Plan.

Write a Bit

While you are creating a timeline and thinking through the details of each story, write a short bit about each. This exercise is similar to a good warm up stretch before running. You do not need to worry about the quality of the writing at this point. Even if you write only a synopsis of each, you will be writing and giving yourself a quick reminder of what took place that will be useful later.

There are good tools for recording little bits of writing so that you can not only keep track of them, but rearrange them easily once you start writing the manuscript. In particular, I like the following software:

- Scrivener (www.literatureandlatte.com/scrivener.php)
- Evernote (www.evernote.com)
- OneNote (www.onenote.com)

OneNote and Evernote also have application versions that you can download to a tablet or smartphone so your notes are available to you even when you are away from your computer.

❧❧❧

Taking stock of where you are in the project and what you have to spark memories or write about should be fun. There are no rules about how much you need to do each day or each week as long as you keep the project moving forward. If you have a trunk full of photographs, start with a few dozen. Accomplish what you can in an hour and come back to the rest later. If you have a filing cabinet full of information you have been meaning to review—get it started, a few sheets at a time.

And write. When you look at a photograph or evaluate a document, write a little bit about it. When you find a great illustration, write about it. Google your grandma's china pattern, and write about it. Put a picture on Facebook, write a little about it, and ask your cousins to comment. Write about what you see, what you do not, and the questions it may raise that you would like to answer later.

The biggest problem I see with people who are starting a book project is becoming overwhelmed. It is easy to do, even for an experienced author. If you are busy with other activities and only have fifteen minutes a day to devote to the project, so be it. Do your fifteen minutes and go on to other things. Those fifteen minutes will add up over time.

If you make out a plan, and put the pieces of your plan onto your calendar, you greatly improve your chances for getting what you intend to accomplish, actually accomplished.

This is the time for making good notes about what events you plan to write about, which events may take a bit of research to include, and what objects or images you should look through before you begin writing.

At the end of your research review, you should have:

- A list of characters (main and supporting)
- A timeline with events listed
- A list of social history items to use for details or illustrations
- A list of events that put your stories into historical context
- A list of images
- A list of the items you want to ask your family about
- A list of holes that you could fill with a bit of research
- Simple, written summaries of each item you have examined

If you choose to conduct research, Chapter 9 has suggestions for ways to fill in any gaps you have in your recollections, to locate items of social interest, and to add details from any historical events that shaped your story.

Chapter 8

Scanning and Optical Character Recognition

Many memoirs use images—photographs, documents, maps and more. If you have many images to scan, it pays to begin by learning about your scanner and scanning software. You will save a lot of time and effort making your images ready for print if you get a good scan from the start.

Scanning Basics

From the scanner's point of view, there are only three types of items it can scan—reflective items (photographs or documents), negative transparencies (film negatives), or positive transparencies (slides). Because the scanner will treat each of these types differently, you may need different software settings or different equipment to obtain the best scan.

The goal while scanning is to create an image large enough to look good in print, at the size you want to display the image. Once you have the largest scan you will need, you can scale, downsample or resize the image for other uses such as a website, an electronic book, or to share on social media.

Scanners

There are many different types of scanners including dedicated flatbed, all-in-one, photo, film, slide, hand-held, and microfilm/microfiche. Each has advantages and disadvantages.

Dedicated Flatbed Scanners

For most book projects, a dedicated flatbed scanner is what you need. The major scanner manufacturers such as HP, Epson, Canon or Xerox (among others) include software, most of which will work for your book project. Some dedicated flatbed scanners are designed to scan photographs primarily, so the software may include Digital ICE (digital image correction and enhancement). Most photo-priority flatbed scanners allow you to make corrections to the image as it is scanned.

Not all dedicated flatbed scanners are equipped to scan transparencies, either film negatives or slides. Transparencies require a dual light source and an adapter to hold the film or negative during scanning, allowing the light source to shine through the transparency. Because of the small size of the transparency (usually one inch square or less), the software must be able to scan at much higher resolution to obtain a print-ready digital image. (More about resolution shortly.)

Film or Slide Scanners

Dedicated film or slide scanners have no glass between the light source and the transparency to prevent distortion. These scanners also use a cool light source to keep from warping the film or slide, and the software included will be capable of high resolutions. Some of these scanners have a feeder for 35mm film strips or a stacking tray for slides. If you have older, large-format negatives, you will need a flatbed scanner with adapter trays to hold those negative sizes.

Hand-Held Scanners

Hand-held scanners (or wand scanners) are convenient, but often it is difficult to produce a good scan if your hands are not steady or the object is not perfectly flat.

One hand-held scanner I like, however, is the FlipPal (flip-pal.com). This mini-scanner was designed with the researcher in mind. It is small, light-weight, and is approved for use in repositories such as the National Archives. Even though the surface area of the FlipPal cannot scan a full piece of standard U.S. paper in a single scan, the software that comes with the FlipPal has a stitching function to put documents back together after they have been scanned in pieces. The one disadvantage to the FlipPal is how little control you have over making corrections as the scan is being made. It is a trade off—the ease and convenience of being able to scan photographs or documents where you find them, versus producing the best scan possible. Better to obtain the image while you can and make corrections in your image editing software later.

Microfilm/Microfiche Scanners

You may run into a microfilm or a microfiche scanner while conducting research. Many Family History Centers and libraries across the country have them. It may be more convenient to save your scanned images as PDFs while you are researching because they are easy to read on your computer later using the free Adobe Acrobat Reader software. If you know, however, that you want to use an image of a document, obtain a higher resolution JPG (.jpg) while you are at the library. Take both. Look for the settings in the scanning software to change back and forth from JPG to PDF.

Most word processors and page layout programs will not treat a PDF the same way they will a JPG. Most will not allow you to place a PDF directly into a document. You will need an image editing program to convert the PDF to a JPG, PNG (.png) or TIFF (.tiff).

All-in-One Scanners

For those of you who own 3-in-1 or 4-in-1 scanners (scan, copy, print, fax), the scanning software that came with the machine may be fairly rudimentary. Dedicated flatbed scanners tend to come with better software including:

- SilverFast (www.silverfast.com)
- VueScan (www.hamrick.com)

You may purchase this software as stand-alone products. You may find that once you have better software, an all-in-one will do what you need it to, as long as you do not have transparencies. In my research to date, I have not found a 3-in-1 or 4-in-1 scanner that includes a transparency adapter.

Resolution

First, let us be clear about some terminology. You may see the acronyms dpi and lpi and ppi used interchangeably. They are not exactly the same, however. Dots per inch (dpi) is an old printer's term that refers to the number of horizontal dots per inch in a halftone. If you look closely at a photographic image in a pre-digital-era newspaper, you will see the dots used to make up the photograph. Printing dots was a clever way to simulate the effect of a solid image. Commercial printers used the same technology to produce magazines, maps or brochures.

Lines per inch (lpi) is another way to measure the number of dots per inch in a halftone, although this is a vertical measurement. The more lines per inch, the sharper the image. Magazines have more lines per inch than newspapers.

Pixels per inch (ppi) is the proper way to describe resolution in the digital era. If you zoom in to a digital photograph closely enough, you will be able to see each pixel. Pixels are square, whereas dots are round. The higher the number of pixels per inch, the higher the resolution in the image, and the better it will look when printed.

What resolution you need depends upon the physical size of the image you want to display, and how you will display it.

Scan high and use low, meaning that you want a scan that is as big physically—in inches—as you will display in print. Most books are (physically) 8.5" x 11" or smaller. If you subtract room for margins, about the biggest image you will need is 8" x 10." If you go wild with the print size for a coffee table book, you may need a larger image.

For print, the resolution must be at least 300 ppi for photographs. Line art (think handwriting in a document) may look better at 600 ppi because the edges of the lines will be crisper.

Many of the older photographs you will encounter may be physically small. It was not until the 1990s that photography became so much cheaper. Today, you can buy a poster-sized print for less than what a small school portrait cost in the 1940s.

Take a 1" x 1.5" slide or school portrait as an example. In order to create a proportionally equivalent 8" x 12" digital image at 300 ppi, the final file size must be 2400 x 3600 pixels (8" x 300 ppi and 12" x 300 ppi). If you are scanning a 1" x 1.5" slide, in order to end up with a file at 2400 x 3600 pixels, you will need to scan at 2400 ppi (1" x 2400 ppi = 2400 pixels wide and 1.5" x 2400 ppi = 3600 pixels long).

A common pre-1950s photograph size was 3" x 4.5," so let us use that as an example. If we want to use a photograph that size in print at 6" x 9," then we will need a final file size of 1800 pixels x 2700 pixels. In order to achieve that resolution, you must scan at 600 ppi (3" x 600 ppi = 1800 pixels wide and 4.5" x 600 ppi = 2700 pixels long).

If you are planning to acquire images from a stock photography company, a library or an archive, ask for the image resolution needed to print at 300 ppi in the physical size you want for the page or the book cover.

There may be other uses for your photographs at much lower resolution, such as an eBook, to email to family, to post on social media sites or to an online family tree. As long as you start with an image large enough to look good in print, scaling down is easy with good results. Scaling up is not. An image that has been scaled up may look fine on the screen because your computer screen can only display an image at 72–96 ppi. A scaled-up photograph may look fine in your word processing program viewed on a screen, but pixelated or blurry when printed.

There is also a difference between scaling a photograph and stretching it. Your word processing program will allow you to take an image, insert it into the text, and then adjust the display size by pulling the corners. Pulling the corners is not scaling the photograph; it is stretching it. Stretching causes even worse results in print than scaling the image up to a larger size.

Scaling a photograph means opening it in an image editing program and changing the physical size of the image. You will achieve far more consistent results on the press if you scan the image to the correct size first, and then place the image into the layout in the correct size and resolution.

File Size

Do not over-scan your images, either. To keep the file size of the final book manageable, create images at a size that will look good in print, but not any bigger. In other words, scan your image so that you could print an 16" x 24" photograph to use as a marketing piece (the biggest use you may have for the image), but adjust it down proportionally before placing it into your book layout.

To adjust the image down proportionally, determine the final size you want the image to be on the page, for example 3" x 3.75," and use your image editing program to make the physical size of the image smaller.

What you do not want to do, is place the largest size image into your manuscript, and squeeze it into its final size by dragging the corners. Dragging the corners will make the physical size smaller, but it will not alter the file size. If your original image is 8" x 10" at 300 ppi, it will have a physical size of 2400 pixels x 3000 pixels. If you squish those pixels closer together to make them fit into a 3" x 3.75" space, your resolution will go up from 300 ppi to 800 ppi (2400 pixels divided by 3" = 800 ppi and 3000 pixels divided by 3.75" is 800 ppi).

Print publication requires a final image resolution at 300 ppi. Use your image editing program to reduce the physical size of the photograph to 3" x 3.75" which is a proportional reduction, while maintaining the resolution of 300 ppi, giving you a final image size of 900 pixels (3" x 300 ppi) x 1125 pixels (3.75" x 300 ppi).

Color Depth

Color depth affects file size. The greater the color depth, the more color possibilities there are and the larger the file size. A black-and-white image (e.g. a printed document) has only 1 bit of color depth because there is only one color—black. The other color, white, is the paper color. A black-and-white photograph is made up of shades of black—an 8-bit black-and-white file would contain 256 shades of gray. A 24-bit color file could contain up to 16.7 million colors and so on up to 36-bit and 48-bit files.

Scanning a photograph to display on the side of a bus, would need as much color information as possible because the image is so large, and too little color information can cause banding rather than smooth transitions between shades.

Many of the newer scanners offer greater than 24-bit depth. The biggest difference between 24-bit and 48-bit scans is in the file size. Reserve the 48-bit setting for scanning negatives and slides. Anything you want to scan for a printed book (and even less so for an eBook or digital file) can be scanned at 24-bit color depth and look great. There is no need to over-scan color depth.

Color Density

To achieve the blackest blacks and the whitest whites—the greatest possible dynamic range for color in your images—you may want a scanner that captures the greatest image density, not necessarily the greatest bit depth. Be forewarned, however, the higher the image density, the higher the cost of the scanner, and realistically, unless you are planning a high-end, glossy photo book, the end results on the page will not be any better.

Color Space

Color space matters to some printers for some print jobs. Chances are good that you will not have to mess much with the color space during your book project, but, just in case, here is a quick explanation of what color space means.

RGB

Computer monitors and other digital screens use the RBG color space (red, green, blue). RGB is also fine for printing photographs. RGB is preferred for images in eBooks that will be displayed on digital screens. The most common file format for RGB images is JPG. When you are scanning photographs, it is acceptable to scan them as RGB images and save them as JPGs.

CMYK

The CMYK color space (cyan, magenta, yellow, black) is necessary to use an off-set press and print in full color. Cyan, magenta, yellow and black are the four process colors that are combined to create full-color images. For most books, you do not need to worry about the CMYK color space. It is acceptable to leave your images in their original RGB color space when creating your final file. Let the printer convert the images to CMYK based upon the equipment they have, to generate the best results.

Grayscale

Become familiar with the grayscale color space. For books with black-and-white images in the interior (forget the covers for right now, almost all covers will have full-color), convert your images to grayscale before you place them into the layout. Another reason to do this is to see how the image will look when printed in black-and-white. Not all color images make good black-and-whites. If there are not enough shades of gray, the finer details will be lost.

Convert black-and-white originals to grayscale. It is possible to scan directly into grayscale, and some scanners have good grayscale settings. Most of the time you will achieve better results if you scan black-and-white photographs in full color, and then use your image editing program to convert the image to grayscale.

Bitmap

The bitmap color space is one that you may use, but infrequently. On occasion, you will find that a document or line drawing is easier to read if scanned as a bitmap. The bitmap color space only contains black and white; there are no shades of gray. The scanner will force each pixel in the image to be one color or the other.

Sometimes, especially if there is a noisy background on a document, the type or handwriting is clearer when scanned as a bitmap image.

File Formats

Digital image file formats are either compressed or non-compressed. A non-compressed format will retain the most information and will create larger file sizes than a compressed format.

TIFF or RAW

Two non-compressed formats are TIFF (or TIF) (.tiff or .tif) and RAW (.raw). RAW image files can be especially large because they are not compressed in any way. To compare, an image taken in my 16 MP (megapixel) camera and saved as a TIFF is about 5 MB (megabytes) in size, whereas the same image saved in RAW format runs 16 MB or more. Saving images in the RAW format is an option in high-end cameras. Some scanning software will create RAW files, but unless you are planning to use your image on the cover of a high-end magazine, there is no compelling reason to create RAW files while you scan.

JPG

The most common file format for photographs is JPG (or JPEG) (.jpg or .jpeg). JPG is a compressed file format, and yes, you will lose information every time you open, alter and save the file, somewhat like making a photocopy of a photocopy. But, unless you alter the file hundreds of times and then blow the photo up to something large enough for the flaws to become obvious to the naked eye, do not worry about whether you scan and save your photographs as compressed or uncompressed files. Save them as TIF or JPG, whatever is easiest for you to use with your image editing software.

Producing a Good Scan

Before you begin scanning, clean the glass on the scanner. Unless there are smudges, compressed air or a good microcloth will do the trick. If there are smudges or fingerprints, use a good glass cleaner. Read the instructions for your scanner to make sure an alcohol-based glass cleaner is safe. Then, spray the cloth, not the scanner glass and clean the glass often. Small specks of dust will show up in the scans (magnified if you are scanning film or slides) and it takes much more time to fix the dust particle flaws in your image editing program, than it does to eliminate them from the scanner.

Do not damage originals in order to scan them. Do not cut them or try to make repairs, and please *do not* clean the photograph unless you know what you are doing. Any effort to alter the surface of a photograph can damage or destroy it. If you are in doubt, seek the help of a photo restoration company. If you have delicate photographs, it is always safer to re-photograph, than to put them on the scanner exposed to a strong light source.

Photographing a Photograph

The trick to photographing a photograph is to use a macro setting on your digital camera that allows the lens to be close to the photograph while keeping it in focus. Fill the frame with the photograph to take as large an image as possible.

Keep the angles consistent so the photograph does not become distorted in the digital image. Place the photograph on a level surface (wall or table) and set the camera up to shoot straight on. If the camera is angled in any way, the original photograph will not look square in the new image. You can fix distortions later in your image editing program, but you will save a great deal of time if you take a good photograph to begin with.

If your old photograph has curled or has warped, introduce a little humidity before unrolling it. I have had good luck with my own photographs by steaming up the bathroom and taking the photograph into the bathroom away from the faucet where the hot water is running. I have only tried this on modern photographs (less than 50 years old). I would not attempt this on any photograph made before modern fixatives were used. If you are at all in doubt, take the photograph to a photo restoration company for help before you begin. Never try to force a photograph to unroll. Once the emulsion on a photograph cracks, you cannot undo the damage.

For photographs that uncurl easily, placing a piece of non-glare glass over the top may help to hold it down while you photograph. Even non-glare glass can yield reflections, though, so watch for flares from light sources such as lamps, overhead lighting or windows.

If you are not a steady hand, use a tripod. In fact, a tripod with a scientific arm that allows the camera to point straight down, is the easiest way to obtain great digital images of photographs or documents.

Scanning Slides or Film Negatives

Before you scan slides or film negatives, use compressed air to clean them. If you remove a slide or negative from a plastic film sleeve or run a microcloth over it, static electricity can attract even more dust. Be careful not to use the spray air too close to the slide or negative because of the moisture that comes from the spray.

Scanner Software

Get to know your scanner and its software. Locate the feature that allows you to change the physical file size and resolution while scanning. It will not take you long to be able to calculate what you will need to achieve a 300 ppi resolution for images at the maximum size you will display them in your book. Remember to scan high, use low. It is better to create an image that is bigger than what you will ever need and scale it down to fit the page, than to scan an image too small and scale it up to size.

Some scanning software features will correct image flaws while scanning. Some software has good automatic settings for color, contrast, brightness, sharpness, and saturation or neutralization. Others do not. Experiment with a few flawed images to find out what your software is capable of correcting well.

Save Time Scanning

Most scanning software allows you to preview the image before you scan it. In the beginning, this feature will save you a lot of time having to look back and forth between the scanning software and your image editing program to make sure you captured the image you wanted in the scan. After a time, especially if you are scanning the same types of items that are also the same size, you may be able to skip the preview to save time. The trick is to keep similar items together, the black-and-white photographs, for example, or the images with fading tints.

While it is tempting to place as many photographs on the plate as possible and scan them all at once as one big photograph, avoid this. Not only will you spend more time turning them into separate photographs later in your image editing program, but the scanner will take readings across many different photographs which will give the automatic correction settings a difficult time determining what should be corrected. The results are often bad scans.

Some scanning software allows you to batch scan everything on the plate with separate settings for each item. This feature will save time because each object on the plate is being analyzed and scanned individually.

The straighten and flip settings can save time. Even if you place a photograph on the plate perfectly, closing the lid may cause it to move. Allowing the scanner to straighten the photograph will save time. Same for flipping photographs—especially flipping slides and film negatives. It can be difficult to slip the slides and film strips into the holders exactly the right way each time. Look at the preview, and then let the scanner turn the image right-side up or flip it on the vertical axis to make the scan match the direction of the original.

Photographs

While it would seem that scanning photographs will have fewer challenges than other types of material, it all depends upon the type of photographs you need. If you have the time, consider scanning everything you have and creating backups on external hard drives or DVDs just in case. You never know when originals will be lost or damaged.

Older photographs that have curled over the years can yield Newton Rings when scanning—distortion caused when there is distance between the photograph and the glass. If a photograph is particularly delicate, taking a new photograph of the old photograph is always safer than putting it on the scanner and exposing it to an intense light source. If you cannot re-photograph the item, look for a studio photographer who has the right setup and lighting to do so.

Occasionally, scanning a black-and-white photograph in full color will leave tinges of yellow, cyan or magenta in the picture. You can use your image editing program to eliminate unwanted tints. Or, try scanning in grayscale to see if you achieve a better result.

If your book will contain only black-and-white images, it may take some experimentation not only with your scanner, but also in your image editing program to make each photograph look its best when printed in black-and-white.

It was popular for a time to print photographs on textured paper so that they looked more like a painted canvas. These photographs (mostly from the 1970s) can be a challenge to scan because the texture can cause shadows on the scan. Taking a new photograph may be a better option.

Matte prints often scan with fewer streaks or glare than glossy prints. Modern glossy prints are not as difficult as older glossies mounted on thick paper, such as those from instant cameras such as Polaroids. If you see streaks in scanned images from glare off the glossy print, taking new photographs may be easier than fixing the digital images.

When a digital image is printed on uncoated paper, such as what will be used on the interior pages of your book, dot gain (ink absorbed by the paper) causes photographs to become darker than expected. You may need to lighten the shadows and mid-tones of photographs in order to make them look their best in print. This is true whether the photographs are in black-and-white or color.

One way to create a digital image from a slide is to scan it; another is to project it onto a screen and photograph it using a digital camera. While the projector version works quite well for images that will be shown on a computer monitor, often the result in print is flat, soft or dark images that do not look as good as if you had scanned the slide directly. If a slide is particularly important to you and you cannot produce a good scan, print the slide at the size you need for the book, then scan the new photograph. Printing slides is an expensive option, however, if you have more than a few vital slides.

Documents and Illustrations

For the most part, documents and illustrations (line art) are easier to scan and achieve good results, than photographs. Line art such as lithographs look best when scanned at 600 to 1200 ppi to keep the edges and lines crisp. Many of these images will be black-and-white, so scanning as bitmaps (BMP) that forces the image into black-and-white, may give you the best results. If the line art is in color such as a logo or sign, scan in at least 24-bit color depth to keep gradients smooth. Scanning at lower bit depths may cause banding in the colored areas.

One challenge may be the paper the item is printed on, however since thin paper can allow printing on the reverse side to show through. If bleed through is a problem, one option is to photocopy the originals using light settings to lessen what shows through, and then scan the lightened photocopy using settings that make the document darker.

Using Optical Character Recognition

Most scanners come with optical character recognition (OCR) software. While it may be tempting to OCR documents or passages from printed sources so that you do not have to transcribe each and every one, be careful with the results. The software works best with printed, standard font text (nothing script-like or hand-writing-like) in point sizes between six (6) (very small but still readable) and 72 (about 1 inch high) on laser or inkjet quality print or better.

Mocavo (www.mocavo.com) the online genealogy search engine, is experimenting with OCR that works on handwriting. They are the first, and they have not perfected it yet. You will not find commercially available scanner-based OCR software that can help you with handwritten documents just yet.

No matter how sophisticated your OCR software, you must proofread the results. It is difficult for the software to tell the difference between a "1" that looks like an "l" that looks like a "]."

The easiest OCR programs to use are those that let you correct the copy while the software is creating the text. Many of the best programs show the image in one window with the text results in another window side by side so that you can look at the original as you edit.

If your scanner did not come with OCR software, OmniPage (www.nuance. com/for-individuals/by-product/omnipage/index.htm) consistently receives high accuracy ratings and is easy to use.

Maps, Newspapers, and Memorabilia

If you have maps, newspaper clippings or memorabilia, such as a theater program that was printed using halftones (bunches of little dots rather than a solid image like a photograph), you may have some challenges when scanning items printed on older presses.

Halftones may create moire patterns (common in black-and-white images from newspapers) or rosette patterns (common in color images due to the CMYK colors used on the press). The result of scanning may be images with irregular areas, or areas that are much darker or lighter than other areas.

A special feature in some scanning software allows you to de-screen as you scan. Software that comes with a de-screening feature will have the following settings for different types of print: art print (175 lpi), magazines (133 lpi) and newspapers (85 lpi). You will achieve the best results with the setting closest to what was used to create the original image on the press. Sometimes de-screening can soften an image too much. Sharpening can help restore the edges.

If your software does not have a de-screening feature, try scanning at a 45-degree angle. Turn the object so that it is not straight up or down (90 degrees), but at an angle (45 degrees) on the plate. Another option is to scan at twice the size you are planning to use in the book, and then downsize the image so that the dots or dot patterns are not so obvious.

Objects

It is much easier to photograph objects, such as heirlooms, against a neutral background than it is to scan them. It is almost impossible to make a teacup look good sitting on a scanner. Instead of scanning dog tags, a uniform, needlework, or a picture in its frame, take a photograph.

For less than $50, you can buy a small studio lighting kit that sets up as a two-foot square box, with neutral backgrounds of several different colors, a couple of lights, and a table-top tripod. For around $200, you can buy a similar studio lighting setup to photograph larger objects such as quilts or furniture.

Art

Photograph artwork rather than scan it, especially if the art is in a soft media such as pastels or charcoal. Pencil sketches can smudge. Oil paintings or watercolor paintings can be a challenge because of the texture of the paint or the unevenness of the canvas.

Film Negatives and Slides

The biggest issue with scanning film negatives and slides is cleaning them before you scan to minimize the dust and particle debris in the digital image and scanning at high enough resolution for your planned use.

A standard 35mm negative is not square. It measures approximately 1" x 1.5" or at a 2 x 3 ratio. If you want the digital image to fill an 8.5" x 11" page, you will need a digital image of 2550 pixels (8.5" x 300 pixels) by 3300 pixels (11" x 300 ppi). So, the resolution for a 1" x 1.5" 35mm film negative is 2550 ppi. The ratio of standard American paper at 8.5" x 11" is not quite 2 to 3, however, so your scan at 2550 ppi will be perfect across the 8.5" top, but too long for the 11" length. Even when you adjust for the margins, cropping may be necessary. If you are thinking about printing from your digital image and want a good 12" x 18" print, scanning a 35mm negative at 4000 ppi will work.

Curled filmstrips can result in blurry scans. If necessary, the individual negatives can be cut and mounted into slide mounts, but once you cut the negatives, they can no longer be printed at a standard photo lab. You will need a specialty lab that often charges more. If you are going to cut a filmstrip, make prints first.

Scan film negatives with the emulsion (duller side) down. The emulsion side should be closest to the glass on a flatbed scanner. You can tell if you are looking at the emulsion side if the film numbers along the edge are backward.

Before you scan slides, check to see if your scanning software has adjustments for different slide types. Kodachrome slides, for example, should be scanned on a Kodachrome color setting for best results. If you have no idea what type of film was used to create your slides, you may have to play with the color adjustment settings to create the best digital image during the scan.

Tip: Although it may be tempting, once you have finished scanning, never discard the originals. Newer scanners may do a better job in the future, and digital images can be lost or become corrupted.

Enhance, Repair, Retouch

Even if you achieve great scans, you may want to open each image in an image editor to take a look close up. Before you place any image into your layout, fix flaws, sharpen softly-focused images, adjust the contrast, or crop to enhance the composition. Repair damage from bends, breaks or mold on the surface. Restore the faded color. Fill in the scratches and correct over- or underexposed areas.

There is controversy surrounding editing or enhancing images that alters *in any way* the historical accuracy of the image, because you are using the image to tell your story which should be historically accurate. Having said that, there is no reason not to repair or retouch photographs so that they look their best.

When does restoration become alteration? That is a matter of opinion, but I think it is fine to use a little grain reduction to make a person's skin look smooth and beautiful, or to remove red-eyes, or to whiten teeth. It is fine to crop an image to enhance the composition, or to merge two images to create a more complete picture of what a place looked like. I know I am stepping into controversial waters here, but it is acceptable to remove distracting elements from the picture even if it alters the historical accuracy of the photograph a bit. I am not advocating that you digitally cut out your ex, or blur the face of a family member you do not like. Oftentimes, however, amateur photographers take pictures without paying attention to the background, resulting in images that appear as if a telephone pole, for example, is growing from a person's head. I find it historically acceptable to remove the telephone pole.

There are many options for editing your digital images. Most computers come with simple image editing software pre-installed. There are also many websites or photo sharing sites that offer image editing tools. Some of them, such as Pixlr (pixlr.com) or Picasa (picasa.google.com), have impressive features. There are also apps by the dozen for tablets or smartphones that edit, enhance or create funky artwork from digital images. Another option is to buy a stand-alone image editor such as Corel PaintShop Pro or Adobe Photoshop (the full version is pricey, but Photoshop Elements, the consumer edition, is not).

Before you alter any digital image, make a copy and keep the original scan in a safe place. Work off the copy in case you make an alteration that you regret.

This book is not the place for a complete primer on digital image restoration. Consult, *Digital Restoration from Start to Finish* by Ctein or other works on digital photography repair and retouching.

Anyone can learn to make simple adjustments to damaged photographs. If you are not interested in learning how to make complex repairs, a photo restoration firm can make your damaged images look almost new. Save this step for the images that are so faded or so broken that fixing them yourself may be nearly impossible without a lot of investment in time and effort, because digital restoration can be expensive.

Final File Preparation

The first step in the final preparation of your digital images is to create a backup that can be stored somewhere safely off-site. A backup drive, a flash drive or a DVD can be given to another family member, or stored in a safe deposit box. It breaks my heart every time there is a natural disaster, not only for the lives that are lost or endangered and the property destroyed, but for the memories that cannot be recovered in a tangible way.

At this stage, you may not be ready to choose the final images for the book. You may have far more images than what you could possibly use, so the next step is to implement an organizational system that makes sense—not just for this book project, but for future projects.

For some, naming each digital image with the subject and approximate year will make sense. I have too many photographs to spend my time naming each image individually. I would rather keep folders within folders. I keep images of families together, meaning that pictures of children will appear in the parent's file folder, but once the child is an adult, he or she receives his own folder. I organize by last name, then first name so that the file folders alphabetize well. I also keep dated folders of events such as vacations or holiday celebrations so that there is a folder for each family Thanksgiving by year, for example.

I also keep originals in folders and work only from copies. I give my copies different file names with an indicator of what type of correction I have made. As an example, a file that has been color corrected will have its file name changed from IMG2036.jpg to IMG2036cc.jpg. That way, the files still alphabetize together, but I can tell without having to open the file which is the original and which has been altered.

Consider adding borders to keep images with light skies, for example, from fading into the page, or adding photo corners to make the images look like they are in a scrapbook. There is no need to apply any final touches, however until you are ready to place the images into the page layout.

Share

While you are scanning, share with other family members. Sharing will build interest in the book and may encourage family members to reciprocate with their photo treasures.

Send a few interesting images by email, post them on Facebook or Twitter, or add them to your family tree online. If you have a smartphone, send a few by Snapchat or Instagram. Create a few albums or slideshows at websites such as Photobucket (photobucket.com) or Flickr (www.flickr.com).

Sign up for one of the multitudes of online picture sharing sites such as Snapfish (www.snapfish.com), Shutterfly (www.shutterfly.com) or DotPhoto (www.dotphoto.com). Then send an announcement that you have created a photo album for family to see or order copies.

Create interesting gifts for purchase on sites such as CafePress (www.cafepress.com) or Zazzle (www.zazzle.com). If you are planning a reunion, photo gifts are popular.

You can even design fabric using photographs at websites such as Spoonflower (www.spoonflower.com) or Fabric on Demand (www.fabricondemand.com).

Learning a few simple techniques for scanning your images will give you an abundance of options for how to use them, and will guarantee the images will look their best in your book.

ఎൗഴ

If you find yourself overwhelmed by the prospect of scanning an abundance of family photographs, film negatives or slides, you may want to engage a scanning company to help you.

Working with a Scanning Company

Contact one of the many companies listed on the Memory Preservation Coalition's website (memorypreservationcoalition.org). The coalition is a non-profit group dedicated to helping individuals preserve, protect and archive documents and photographs.

One idea I particularly like is having a scanning service come to you. Scangaroo launched this idea. The company has since been acquired by Gen-Arc Digital Estate Scanning (www.gen-arc.com). They use mobile scanning labs to come to your home so that your important photographs, documents, scrapbooks or video never leave your possession. They also offer cloud-based digital asset management meaning you can store your documents and photographs so that they can be accessed for years to come (assuming the company stays in business).

Another option is to contact FamilySearch about their Worldwide Photo Scanning and Preservation Initiative. The Mormon Church has teamed up with Kodak and E-Z Photo Scan (ezphotoscan.com) to equip a few of their Family History Centers, their central library in Salt Lake City as well as a center in Riverton, UT with high-speed, high-resolution scanners. Look for one of their "photopalooza" events or find out whether the Family History Center in your area offers photo scanning.

There are also local companies who can scan photographs, or convert older forms of analog film into modern digital video. A company that specializes in memory preservation, however, may be better than the local photo shop.

National Archives Standards

Before you hire a scanning company, ask whether they follow the guidelines prescribed by the National Archives for handling your photographs or delicate documents. You would not want an item damaged by careless handling.

File Size and Format

Make sure you have the images scanned at the largest size you will need to make a reprint or to include in your printed book. You may have images of different sizes to scan, so if you want all digital images large enough to create a full-page image in your book or a large photo reprint, be specific about that requirement.

Be clear about what file format (JPG or TIFF) you need. Most scanning companies will return files as JPGs. Unless you have a compelling need for TIFF images, JPGs will work for a printed book, an eBook, and any use you can think of online.

Bound Items

Ask about scanning photographs that are glued into photo albums. Photo albums often require special handling in order to scan, so these items may cost more. If your photo albums are bound or such that they will not lay flat on the glass for scanning, ask whether the company could re-photograph, or whether they have the kind of equipment used to scan open books. Book scanning equipment may be better for the uneven surfaces in a scrapbook than a flat, plate scanner.

Slides and Film Negatives

Ask about scanning slides and film negatives. Make sure the slides or film will be scanned at a resolution high enough to create a digital image large enough for your biggest need. Often slides and negatives are scanned at a standard 4000 dpi resolution which will yield an image of 3622 pixels by 5320 pixels for the average slide that measures 23mm x 34mm. This image size is large enough to produce a photograph of 12" x 17" at 300 dpi, which is large enough for most book projects unless you are planning an oversized coffee-table book.

Video Transfer

You may have other media that you want made into digital images or transferred to a modern DVD—VHS, VHS-C, 8mm, Hi8, Super8, mini-DV or other formats.

Most film- or tape-to-digital video transfer is done at a standard resolution, and the transfer is done in one piece—the length of the original film to a single video clip.

If you need still digital images from your video, work with the technician to create a list based upon time stamps. You also may need to ask for frame-by-frame images over several seconds in order to obtain the best still from video where the subjects are moving. Obtaining multiple images may cost a bit more, but is more likely to generate one usable image than a single attempt.

If you need stills at higher resolution, that process is more difficult because the film must be marked and stopped in order to adjust the resolution upward. The technician will likely make the complete transfer, then rewind the film and start and stop at each place where you requested a digital still from the film. Again, this may cost a bit more, but if you need a high-quality, high-resolution digital image from a family video, it may be worth the money.

Restoration or Retouching Services

Ask about photo retouching services. Most scanning companies offer basic retouching services, and some offer advanced retouching services for photographs that are badly faded or damaged. For most old photographs, even a bit of dust and scratch removal, color correction, sharpening, saturation adjustment or over- or under-exposure correction is well worth the trouble and expense. Much of this, however, can be done in your image editing software. If the photograph requires extensive digital restoration, such as fixing tears across people's faces, or removing color shifting caused from mold, expect to pay more. If the only photograph you have needs major restoration, the cost may be less important than having a restored, usable image.

Write a Formal Proposal or Contract

Write a formal agreement detailing the work you want to have done, the cost, when you are to deliver the items to the company (or the date the company's scanning equipment will come to you), and when the scanning will be complete. Include the file type and how the images will be given to you—thumb drive, external hard drive, archival DVD, through a file sharing service, or in permanent cloud storage that you can access at any time.

⁂

The primary goal for scanning is to create a digital image large enough and at the correct resolution to look good in whatever format you plan to use it. Once you have a print-quality digital image, you can reduce the image size for other uses such as sending by email or posting on the Internet. A secondary goal is to preserve photographic memories and documentary evidence. Preserving your images is important, but try not to let the task of scanning sideline your book project. For those of you with hundreds or thousands of images to scan, it could.

Chapter 9

Developing a Research Plan

In this round of research, gather as much information as you need to flesh out the details of your stories—including facts based upon documentary evidence, but also any pertinent social history and the historical context that influenced the events in your life.

Why go to this trouble? Because books with accurate details are more respected, and stories with rich details are more engaging to read. Besides, having a pile of research with historically accurate details will make writing the book easier. One caution while conducting research, though. The object of your research is to help you remember, not to replace your memories with more colorful people or events. If you catch yourself thinking, "I don't remember it that way," stop and write down your memories before you continue on with the research. That way you will have your own recollections recorded before they are enhanced or changed in any way.

Baby Steps

If you prefer to write your stories just as you remember them, then by all means skip this chapter and get started. If you would like to bring out a few more details, then a little bit of research can not only help you write, but also help you remember.

Fill in any holes in the biographical information regarding the people in your stories using genealogical research. Pick the low hanging fruit first. Gather as much as you can from research you can do a little bit at a time online. Search the major genealogical databases to fill in missing records.

For details regarding local places or events, search the local history collections in the card catalogs of libraries in the areas where you once lived to see if there are any written histories about the area at the time you were there if you have moved around. Google Books (books.google.com) and WorldCat (www.worldcat.org) should help you turn up written histories, as well. Oftentimes, you can download a free PDF copy of an out-of-print title. If you cannot locate a copy to download or at a nearby library, use the interlibrary loan service at your local library to request a copy from another library.

Next Steps

Consult the manuscript collections of local, regional or state archives for additional original source material as well as eye-witness accounts of other people who may have experienced the same events you did. Visit museums to fill any holes in your memory about what life was like back then.

Giant Leaps

Take a research trip to the location(s) of your stories to make an exhaustive search for documentary evidence that you were unable to access online, or hire a professional researcher to do so for you. Consult scholarly articles or books written by experts in the social history or historical context where you have remaining questions.

The rest of this chapter contains tips for collecting as much factual evidence and visual representations as you may need to tell great stories.

Before You Begin Any Research

Let us step back to the book project for a moment to make sure you have a clear idea of the scope of the project, because you will not want to spend time researching elements that you will not use for this book.

Do you have a clear vision of the project? Think about writing the introduction. The reader will want to know who the players are, the events, the time period, and the place(s) you will cover. The introduction is where you will explain your vision of the project to the reader and set the stage for the stories to come.

Before you can explain it to your reader, however, you have to be clear about it yourself. About how long will the book be? Are you writing about your entire life, or just one aspect of it? When you took stock, could you answer all of these questions? Or, will you need this round of research to make a final decision? If you do, that is all right.

Try not to get too bogged down by expanding the project unnecessarily. In this round of research, gather enough material to write cohesive stories.

Preliminary Organization

Even the best-researched book is unreadable if not well organized. You do not have to tell each and every story play-by-play from start to finish, but you do have to tell them logically so that the reader can follow what is happening.

Look at the following ways to organize a memoir. It may give you a few ideas, not only for how to tell the whole story, but what additional research you may need in order to tell it.

Chronologically

Organizing from the past to the present makes the most sense to readers because it follows a natural timeline. What happens in the present or the future is often influenced by what has happened in the past.

Reverse Chronology

It is possible to tell your story from the present to the past. Reverse chronology can be tricky and requires more planning than other organizational styles.

By Family Member

You could keep your recollections of different family members in different sections—a chapter for each parent, each sibling and so on.

By Topic

You could tell stories about different aspects of your life by subject, such as family life, school stories, best friends, work experience, military duty and so on.

Randomly Organized

You can tell stories as vignettes. This is a common way to start writing down your recollections.

It is not necessary to determine what organizational style you will use for the final manuscript if there is research you think you will need to tell your stories. Thinking about *how* you could organize could generate additional research ideas.

Fill any Gaps in Your Memories by Research

There are a few common areas where memoirists find holes or gaps in memories—names, common life events, exact dates and location details.

Names

Have you ever looked at an old photograph and wished you had written down the names of each and every person in the photograph while you could still remember their names? It happens to all of us. Could you locate another person in the photograph who may have a better memory? Could you use social media (i.e. Facebook, Instagram or Pinterest) to ask for help identifying people in the photograph?

Do you have complete names or only initials for some people? Before the 1970s, it was common in newspapers, for example, to use only the initials of individuals or the formal married names for women. A bit of basic genealogical research can help with names. For example, marriage and death certificates often have complete names, as do wills and probate files. You may find an index of this type of information at a Family History Center located at the nearest Mormon Church or at a local genealogical library.

Common Life Events

While you were filling in your timeline, did you accounted for common life events such as attending school, learning a trade or profession, working (establishing a business, working for one, serving in the military), or joining groups (religious, social, philanthropic, or sports teams)?

It is easy to skip over life events that seem ordinary. Ordinary, that is, until you start thinking about the things that took place during school, or at work, or while you were hunting for a job.

In your timeline, do you have a line for each year of your life? You may not have an event to write about for each year, but a line for each year will help you visualize how much time elapses between the events you are currently planning to write about. Other stories may occur to you as you write, or as you fill in holes in your timeline.

Dates

Exact dates are not always easy to remember, except in the case of major milestones such as birthdates or anniversaries. For other events, whenever possible, obtain complete dates.

Locations

In some stories, the location can play a role as big as a central character. In others, location is only a background for the action taking place. One of the biggest challenges in describing places is to make sure you are describing the place that existed at the time of the story and not the modern version that you are more familiar with now.

While you are taking stock, see how much detail you can remember about places you lived or worked. Are you able to describe what you saw every day? Can you remember what kind of sounds and smells there were? What was the terrain like? What was the weather like at different times of the year? How imposing was the place? Did you live miles from the nearest neighbor, along a sleepy suburban street, or in a crowded apartment?

It is important to get the location details right. You will not want to describe yourself sacking groceries at the Krogers if it was actually the Piggly Wiggly, or driving a Mustang before that line of cars was introduced. These are easy errors to make that could harm the credibility of your stories.

Be careful, also, when describing places that are so familiar to the general public that the places take on characteristics making it difficult to describe them without using clichés (e.g. The Brooklyn Bridge, Mississippi river boats, Army barracks).

Take Care of the Housekeeping

While it is possible for you to relate your stories just as you remember them, if you conduct a bit of research to help with the details, those little bits of research should be well-documented. Your memoir will be more respected, if you do. As you research, put your citations in order, guard against any inference of plagiarism and gather any permissions and usage fees you may need to pay in order to use materials belonging to others.

Citing Sources

Create good citations as you go. Decide how you will cite each piece of factual information in your book. Include the name of the article, book, image or document, and the location where you found it so that other researchers can weigh the strength of your sources and recreate your research steps, if necessary.

I do not recommend waiting to create citations until you are ready to add footnotes or endnotes to your book. At that point, the task will seem daunting. It is better to figure out what method you want to use now, and stick to that method as you write and perform any additional research. There is no need to decide whether you will include your sources as footnotes or endnotes yet, as long as you have the citations ready to work with when you start writing.

For some genealogists, the mere mention of the Elizabeth Shown Mills book, *Evidence Explained*, sends some family historians into fits of pique, but she offers a way to document every conceivable source type systematically. Friend, fellow genealogist (and a good gentleman of Kentucky), Kirk Woosley Patten, likens formal citations to setting a formal table. He explains that "once you understand where everything goes, you never have to guess which utensil to use." I agree, but I also shudder at the thought of having to correctly pick out the lobster fork. Formal citations may cause you the same anxiety. Thankfully, there are ways around a strict adherence to formal citations without compromising the scholarship of your book.

Many of the online genealogy websites where you will find documentary evidence of events also give you the citation information. Take a look at how the top genealogy sites—FamilySearch, Ancestry, and Fold3—provide citation information. Each cites sources in a slightly different way, but you have all of the information you need to cite your sources properly.

The two major formulas for proper source citation are *The Chicago Manual of Style* or *Evidence Explained* by Elizabeth Shown Mills.

The Chicago Manual of Style type:
1. 1800 U.S. Census, Second Census of the United States, New York, Essex County, Crown Point, pg 192-A, line 7, Daniel Smith household; NARA microfilm 1804, roll 1.

Evidence Explained type:
1. Daniel Smith household, p. 192-A, Crown Point, Essex County, New York; Second Census of the United States, 1800, vol. 2, New York: Clinton-Green Counties; Manuscript Schedules of Decennial Population Census, 1790–1870. Records of the Bureau of the Census, Record Group 29, National Archives, Washington, D.C. [Evidence Explained (2007), p. 238].

Here is a third option.
2. "**beguiled ... rifling around in the past**": Alice Munro, *The View from Castle Rock* (New York: Knopf, 2006), p. 347.

I found this example in David Laskin's book, *The Family*, (New York: Viking, 2013), p. 342. The book is well documented. He and his publisher have chosen to place their source citations in endnotes rather than in footnotes, and although they do not strictly follow either formal style, it gets the job done.

There is software as well as downloadable templates that make creating good citations easy. If you have not discovered the software *Evidentia*, now may be the time. This software leads you through the process—first choosing your preferred style as either *Evidence Explained* or *The Chicago Manual of Style*, then giving you a template in the chosen style for most of the common sources used to document a family history. They also work for a memoir. There is also a way to create a template for any additional sources that do not fit the existing templates.

If you are determined to create citations in a unique way, the following are the basic elements necessary for a good citation:
- Who created the source
- What the source is
- Where the source was created
- When the source was created

- How to find the source (where the source is held or where you saw it as a digital image)
- The form (original, a copy such as a microfilm or a digitized original)
- Why the source is useful

For a complete explanation of these elements, consult *Mastering Genealogical Proof,* by Thomas W. Jones. Consult Robert Raymond's article, *Citation Baby Steps*, in the FamilySearch wiki online for more information about why effective citations are necessary.

Plagiarism and Copyright Reminder

Avoid using another writer's words—no matter how beautiful they are or how tempting they are to repeat.

Facts and ideas cannot be copyrighted, but the way they are expressed belong to the author from the minute the words are recorded. The most common form of plagiarism is inadvertent. If you repeat more than three words in a row or use words in a distinct combination or with a distinct emphasis copied directly from another author, you must give that author credit.

Note: Writing a memoir without trying to make money does not absolve you from plagiarism or copyright violations. Give credit where credit is due and ask permission to use written words, images or illustrations that do not belong to you, even if you plan to change them in some way. A derivative of an original belongs to the copyright holder as well. If an original is not yours, ask permission.

The following are good, general sources of copyright information:

- The Pocket Copyright Guide for Publishers by Laura N. Gasaway.

- The Writer's Legal Guide, 4th Edition by Tad Crawford and Kay Murray
- Authors, Copyright and Publishing in the Digital Era by Francina Cantatore
- The Copyright Handbook: What Every Writer Needs to Know by Stephen Fishman

A good source for information about copyrights and genealogy is Judy Russell, the Legal Genealogist (www.legalgenealogist.com).

Permissions and Usage Fees

You may encounter repositories or collections that require permission to transcribe or display images of source materials in their possession. The terms of use and fees vary from repository to repository, so it is important to check before you make an image or a transcription an integral part of your book.

Oftentimes, permissions are nothing more than citing your source in a particular way acknowledging the repository or collection. In many cases, if you explain the nature of your book and that you are not planning a commercial run of thousands of books, you may be able to get fees waived.

Gather any permissions you may need, and keep a good record of any fees that you may need to pay. As you write, you will be able to evaluate whether it is worth the fee to include the image or source in the book.

Biographical Details

Stories are all about people, but it can be difficult to remember all of the people who may have played a role in an event from years ago. Some basic genealogical research can help with this. Take a look at some of the commonly used sources for genealogy, such as the census records or a city directory. The reverse listings on a city directory would give you the names of every neighbor near your old home. Looking at the names above and below your family on the census would also give you neighbors.

Fleshing out the biographical details about each event's central characters may also reveal who *else* may have had a role to play during an event. A good cast of characters is a useful tool going forward with your research—a tool that should grow and become more detailed with every new thing you find.

Timeline Events

Take a look back at your timeline(s). Do you have each of the common life-cycle events accounted for, such as schools attended, profession studied, work history, religious affiliation, land purchases, court cases, taxes paid, associations joined or hobbies?

While you research, keep your timeline(s) up to date. As you discover new information, it is much easier to update the timeline(s) as you go, rather than trying to organize an even larger pile of research later.

Locating New Sources

In order to gather enough material to write stories full of rich detail, it is time to take a headlong dive into the biggest genealogical databases on the Internet. Even if you have consulted Ancestry, FamilySearch and MyHeritage (among others), new sources are added daily. It pays to take another look.

Because not everything you may want to gather is online, make a list of locations to visit (or have someone visit for you), followed by a list of social and local history questions you have and where you should find the answers.

During each of these steps, watch for images to help tell your stories visually. You may as well gather the images as you go.

Another important housekeeping task is to keep your citations current. Creating good citations should be old hat from your research review. Keep up the good work during this round of research, so you do not have to repeat any steps to locate or flesh out citations when you should be writing.

If you are an experienced genealogist, what follows may be familiar to you. If it is, skip ahead to the section about adding social history.

Online Research

It is not necessary to search every possible genealogical site on the Internet. In fact, that approach could delay the publication of your book by years.

Start with a search for each of the central characters in the biggest genealogical databases available. The following sites are primarily for researchers in the U.S. and Canada. If you are researching from the U.K., Europe or Australia, the major sites such as Ancestry may have a satellite site, but other major search sites for your location may not be listed here. The *GenealogyinTime Magazine* puts out a list of the 100 most popular genealogy websites each year based upon usage. You may find more appropriate sites to your search in their list.

Leading Free Sites

The items followed by an asterisk are free but also have a paid option.

- FamilySearch.org
- Findagrave.org (now an Ancestry company)
- AncientFaces.com
- Mocavo.com (now a FindMyPast company)*
- CyndisList.com
- JewishGen.com*
- BillionGraves.com (now a MyHeritage company)
- Jewish News Archive—archive.jta.org
- US Genweb Project—usgenweb.org
- US Genweb Archives—usgwarchives.net
- SteveMorse.org
- EllisIsland.org
- GenealogyTrails.com
- DAR.org*
- Interment.net
- DeathIndexes.com

Leading Subscription Sites

- Ancestry.com
- MyHeritage.com
- Geni—Geni.com (now a MyHeritage company)

- Archives.com (now an Ancestry company)
- Genealogy.com (now an Ancestry company)
- GenealogyBank.com
- Fold3.com (now an Ancestry company)
- Newspapers.com
- NewspaperArchive.com
- WorldVitalRecords.com (now a MyHeritage company)
- GenealogyToday.com
- FindMyPast.com
- FamilyLink.com (now a MyHeritage company)
- HeritageQuestOnline.com (available through a library subscription)

Most of the subscription sites offer a free two-week trial. You may want to block out some time so that you take full advantage of the trial period to see what each of the paid sites has to offer in the research for this project. While it may be tempting to see how many of your own family lines you can find at the same time, try to stick to what you need for this book to keep the project moving forward.

Use the Search Engines

One final word about searching online—your efforts will not be complete until you use the search engines such as Google or Bing to search for the people, places and events in your book. Using search engines to look for people can be frustrating until you learn a few tricks to narrow the results of your search. There are good tips and tricks for conducting efficient searches in *Google Your Family Tree* by Daniel Lynch, *50 Google Hints, Tips & Tricks for Online Researchers* by David Bradford (available free on Rootsweb through Ancestry) or *Google Genealogy Style* by Kimberly Powell (genealogy.about.com).

The National Institute for Genealogical Studies (www.genealogicalstudies.com) offers a recently updated course entitled *Google for the Wise Genealogist* by Gena Philibert-Ortega that is excellent. Many of the tips for Google also work on Bing, Yahoo!, Ask or search engine aggregators such as Dogpile.

Repositories List

Start a list of repositories you want to visit or have someone else visit on your behalf (e.g. courthouses, libraries, archives or private collections). If you are unable to take a trip to do the research yourself, there are both professional and amateur genealogists who are willing to do research for you. For more information about hiring someone, see Working with a Professional or Personal Historian or Genealogist below.

Within your repositories list keep the title, author and call number of every item you want to search at each repository. If you find a book at more than one repository, put the book on the list for each place. You never know when a book may have been lost or misplaced. Leave a place to add new sources you run across while at the repository, and keep a log of what you were expecting to find, what you found, and what you did not find so that you know to keep looking.

Library and archives staff can be helpful since they may be more familiar with the items in their collection than you are, and can point you to sources you may not have considered.

The National Archives and Records Administration (NARA)

NARA (www.archives.gov) is the U.S. depository for records compiled on behalf of the Federal Government. View filmed records at one of the regional NARA centers. Other records such as the census records and many land records have been digitized and are available through one of the major genealogical databases. The most requested records from NARA are military service records, immigration and naturalization records, passport applications, land records and bankruptcy records. But NARA has much, much more. If you are unable to travel to the main facility in the Washington, D.C. area or to a regional center, a professional researcher who specializes in gathering records at NARA can help you.

State Governments

State government records may be found at a state archive or within governmental agencies. Examples of state governmental records available for research are: local military units or national guards, vital records (births, deaths, marriages and divorces), state courts (appeals courts and the supreme court of the state), penitentiaries, business incorporations, health and agricultural agencies.

Not every state has a statewide archive. Illinois, for example, keeps some records at their central facility in Springfield but also has records spread out through their Regional Archives Depository.

Local Governments

Local governments are also a rich source of records. Local governments include cities, counties, school districts, water and sewer districts, fire and police protection districts as well as the local courts. You may find records by city, county or township including: board minutes and proceedings, land deeds, mortgages and tax sale records, poll books, voter registrations, early naturalization records, civil and criminal court cases, coroner's inquests, school and probate records.

Before searching for records, establish whether the borders of the counties changed during the time when your event occurred. Software such as AniMap (goldbug.com/animap/) shows county border changes, as does the Newberry Library's Atlas of Historical County Boundaries (publications.newberry.org/ah-cbp/).

The National Association of Counties has a nice database of counties along with addresses for each county's courthouse or administration building plus links to county websites (www.naco.org/counties/pages/findacounty.aspx).

Discovering the location of older local records may be a challenge. Some local governments keep all of their records; others give the older records to a university or local archive. The only way to find out is to call and ask. Retention policies change over time. What is precious to one administration may be "clutter in the way" to the next.

Many local government records have been filmed and may be available at a local library (or through interlibrary loan), or available through one of the major genealogical websites. FamilySearch.org has an incredible list of film available. You can have film sent to a Family History Center in your area, and to a few public libraries.

Local Libraries

There are many databases of public libraries available online including the Find a Library feature at WorldCat.org (see the online libraries section below). Check the catalog of the local library wherever you have resided. Even the smallest library may have a good local history collection and may be the only place where you will find limited-edition or privately published histories of the area. You may be able to borrow these books through interlibrary loan, or if they do not circulate, you may be able to call the reference librarian and describe what kind of information about the area you are interested in and ask that they copy the pages that would be helpful to you.

Many local libraries also have collections of yearbooks or newspapers from local schools that could be helpful in recalling classmates from long ago.

University or College Libraries

Oftentimes individuals will leave their personal and business papers to their alma mater for inclusion in the school's archival collections. Or, local people, even if they did not attend the school, may choose to leave their materials to the local college. Check the catalogs of any local college, university or community college in the area where your ancestor once lived. You may also find well-researched masters or Ph.D. theses about the local area in the university library.

College or University libraries also keep items such as yearbooks, and many of your classmates may have donated their own papers to the school. It pays to search the online catalog by name.

Online Library Catalogs

Worldcat.org is the largest online library catalog in the world. A helpful feature on WorldCat is the repository location feature. When you search for a book (or article, DVD or CD), it will locate that item and tell you the closest libraries that have a copy of the item. It is worth signing up for a free account so that you can keep lists of books or articles, so you do not have to repeat searches. WorldCat also has a "Find a Library" link that will give you a list of public, school, corporate, academic, or specialized libraries within a city, state, province or zip code. Some of the specialized libraries will be helpful for social history research or adding historical context. Another source for finding libraries is PublicLibraries.com. This website has a searchable database of public, college, presidential and state libraries.

Archives

Archival material such as personal letters or journals, may be the most helpful materials for gathering the kind of detail to make your stories believable and interesting. The "rumble of a twelve-pound mountain howitzer" is more engaging than "the sound of a cannon," right?

WorldCat is also expanding as ArchiveGrid to include archival material from around the world. ArchiveGrid (beta.worldcat.org/archivegrid/) is similar to the old National Union Catalog of Manuscript Collections (NUCMC) on steroids. NUCMC still exists through the Library of Congress (www.loc.gov/coll/nucmc/).

Online Libraries

Many institutions are making out-of-print materials available as electronic books. You can find them for sale in print at online bookstores such as Amazon.com, or as free electronic downloads at sites such as Google Books (books.google.com) or HathiTrust (www.hathitrust.org)—a consortium of research institutions that have made millions of titles available as digital books.

Some universities are also making books available electronically, good news if you are looking for one of the many county histories written in the late 19th or early 20th century. Some of these "mug books" as they are called (because people paid to have information included about themselves) are useful when researching a location.

William Filby's *A Bibliography of American County Histories* is also a helpful resource for locating local histories.

Archive.org, the Internet Archive, deserves special mention since it has the WayBack Machine—an archive of billions of web pages. If the information you seek is on a website that has been taken down, a copy may still exist on the WayBack Machine.

Many of the records to help you write your book are available online, but not all. Some research must be conducted on site—the old-fashioned way.

Add Social History

Adding social history will help you define your characters and tell your stories with vivid detail. Social history is more about *how* people lived rather than where or when. Social history provides context and not only makes your characters more interesting, it can make your descriptions of events more interesting, as well.

The following are categories of social history you may want to look into during this round of research:

Heirlooms. What items do you, or other family members have that been in your family? Household goods? Books? China or silver? Jewelry? Watches or clocks? Clothing or quilts? Some of the rarest items in Americana museums are the everyday household items or utensils because so few still exist. Everyday items were used, worn out or broken and thrown away. Household items are sometimes the closest connection we have to members of our close family.

Household. Who was in the household? How many family members were in the household and when? Were there young children coming along after older children moved away? How many generations lived together? Were there friends, boarders or servants along with the family? Who were the neighbors?

Home. What type of house did your family have? How was it built and by whom? What type of furniture did you have? How big was the house? What was the floor plan? How was each room used? Did the house have plumbing and electricity? Was there central heat? Did you use fireplaces or stoves to heat the house? What type of fuel was used?

Ethnic Heritage. Even though America is the world's great melting pot, many of us maintain pieces of our ethnic heritage. Look for ethnic differences in language, customs, cooking, clothing, music, theater, building styles and the way holidays or other special occasions are celebrated. Are there obvious ethnic influences in your family traditions? Have they changed over time?

Customs. Birth, marriage, and death have customs that differ by location, ethnic influences and era. Did births take place at home? Who would have attended the birth? How many pregnancies were typical for women in your mother's or grandmother's era? What was the infant mortality rate? How did couples meet? What was courtship like? How were marriages celebrated? Did couples honeymoon? What was a typical age at marriage? Was it different for men than for women when you were growing up? How were burials handled? What happened during a funeral? What customs or laws governed inheritances? Are there unusual names in your family? Were names passed down from generation to generation?

Beliefs. Religion, superstition, education, politics and social standing influence beliefs. Beliefs affect the decisions we make. Could beliefs have influenced events in your life?

Health. What kind of illnesses were common? Did people in your family live to be old? Were there any siblings who died young? What kind of home remedies were used?

Religion. What was your family's religion? Did that change over time? What religious beliefs did the family follow, or not? Did you attend services regularly? Who was the head of the church? Did anyone in your family hold a leadership role? What type of music did you hear? What messages were given during sermons? What other social activities were associated with your house of worship—weddings, funerals, church suppers, revivals?

Politics. Did you or your family participate in the political process? Did you or anyone in your family run for office? Who was the first woman in your family to vote? In small towns, you may be surprised by how many of your older family members or ancestors held offices. Think beyond who was mayor. There were roads overseers, school district superintendents, fire department members and utility organizers and builders. Looking through the records in your hometown may be quite revealing.

Education. How much schooling did you and your family members have? What was being taught? How did you get to school? How long was the school day? Did you bring lunch? What type of lunch? Did you use a lunch box or a bucket? How did you carry your books? What circumstances influenced the school year? Who were the teachers? How big was the schoolhouse? How did the children dress for school? What were the after-school activities? Did you play school sports? Did you participate in music programs or act in the school play?

Social Standing. Did your family's social standing affect where you lived? Did it affect the associations you joined or the people you knew? Were there customs your family adhered to because of their social standing?

Economic Standing. How well did your family live? Was every day a struggle, or were you well off? Were there times of plenty and times of want? Did your family's economic position affect decisions you made personally?

Employment or Profession. Did your family have a business passed down through the generations? What type of schooling or apprenticeship did someone need in order to practice the family profession? How many times did you change jobs and why? Who else worked with you? Who were your customers? Who were the wholesalers? What other businesses did your business use? What techniques did you use? What made businesses thrive or fail during that time? What other economic influences affected you job or business? Did an invention revolutionize the business or eliminate the need for it? How were you paid? Did you earn a salary? Did your business supply goods or services on credit to members of the community? How were the bills paid?

Roles. Who was the primary bread winner in your family? What was expected of women and children? Did that change over time or due to circumstances such as war? Did the women or children work? In what kind of situation? At what age were children considered old enough to work when you were growing up? What were common childrearing practices? Who cared for the sick or the aged? Who handled the family finances?

Entertainment. What type of leisure activities did you have? How much leisure time was there? Did you play music? Attend concerts? What was the popular music of the era? Did you or your family own musical instruments? Did you play games or sports? Was there a theater or playhouse in the area? What was the community's attitude toward entertainment? What kind of art did you see locally? What did you read? Did you own many books? What were the popular magazines of the time? What were the blockbuster novels? Did your family go on vacations or travel? Did they visit resorts or go camping? Were there popular local destinations or did they travel abroad? What did you pack in your suitcase? How did you get to your destination?

Holidays. What holidays did you celebrate? Are the holidays the same as they are today? Are the customs the same? What type of food was served? Who participated? Did the whole family gather for each holiday? Why or why not?

Neighbors. Who were your neighbors? Did they live in the next apartment or a few miles away? How close were neighbors? Did the kids flock to one or two households? Were there persnickety or difficult neighbors?

Neighborhoods. What types of businesses were in the neighborhood? Did you live in an area with other people with the same ethnic background? What kind of social or religious influences were there? How established was your neighborhood? How old were the houses? What housing styles were present?

Animals. Did your family own work animals? How were they cared for? How were they marked or branded? Was the family's brand registered? Did you have animal shelters or barns on the property? Did you have domestic pets? Did you raise animals for sale? What type of market was there for animals?

Building Styles. Did your family build their own house or barn? Most building styles are influenced by what building materials are available in the area. Ethnic preferences also affect building styles. Barns built by Germans look different than barns built by Swedes. Your family's ethnic heritage may have influenced the building style they chose. A good reference of building styles is *A Field Guide to American Houses* by Virginia McAlester.

Clothing. How did you and your family members dress? How many sets of clothing did you have? How practical were the styles of the day? What kind of clothes were worn for special occasions?

Transportation. What type of transportation was available in your area? Were there trains, boats, barges or cars? Were there street cars? Did your family own a car or a motorcycle? Did the kids have bicycles? How else did you get around town or back and forth to school?

Cooking. What type of diet did your family have? Who did the cooking? How did they cook? How much time was spent cooking? How did they shop or grow food? What was on a typical household menu? Do you have recipes from earlier generations? What were your favorite or least favorite homecooked dishes?

Communication. How did your family keep in touch with other members of the family? Do you have letters or journals? Did your family have a telephone? Did the town or area have a newspaper? How often was the newspaper published? How else did you get news?

Inventions. What inventions changed how you lived or worked? How long was it between the time a new gadget came out and your family got one?

Relocation. Did your family move from one place to another? From one country to another? How did they move? Did one member of the family move first? Did they all move together? Were other family members left behind? Did the family ever return for a visit?

There is a lot to think about in terms of social history, but thinking about these things will likely help you better describe events in your life.

Where to Locate Social History

To study social history, you will use many traditional genealogical sources. To gather good, detailed information consult eyewitness testimony—through interviews, diaries, journals and letters; expert research found in academic books and journals; museums where artifacts of daily living have been preserved; and memorabilia or ephemera—those items meant to be used and thrown away.

Manuscript Collections

I have discussed the value of WorldCat and ArchiveGrid in finding manuscript collections. These search engines can also be used to locate letters, diaries, journals or other community history appropriate to your research. Do not limit your search to personal accounts, either. Business records can give you an idea of what it was like both to own a business or to be a customer of the business.

Every archive is different. Some archives keep only original sources created by governmental institutions while others keep personal papers. It pays to search major and local archives.

Oral History Collections

You may want to consult an oral history collection if members of your community have been interviewed. The Oral History Association (www.oralhistory.org) has a good list of links to oral history collections across the country. Probably the greatest collection of oral histories is Stephen Spielberg's Shoah Project hosted at the University of Southern California (sfi.usc.edu).

Scholarly Articles

Journals address nearly every historical niche, and the people who write articles for these journals are experts in their fields. You may find the physical journals at your local university and some public libraries. Most universities have access to JSTOR's online collection (www.jstor.org). One category not often consulted for well-researched material are the thesis collections of colleges and universities. Even though not all theses are published, their bibliographies are often treasure troves of original source material.

Museums

One of the best ways to remember the experience of how people lived during a certain era is to visit a historic house, living or open air museum of that time. There, you can get a feel for the size of the living space, items that were in the home and, in some cases, the land that surrounded the home. There are museums for nearly every type of living space from ships that transported people to the new world, to tenements in the inner city, to sprawling plantation homes. The trick is to find one from the right era, in the area where you came from since building styles varied so greatly from place to place.

Another way to experience an era is to attend a re-enactment. Re-enactors pride themselves on their ability to create exact replicas, and they often create temporary museums using items such as WWII-era military tents or clubs filled with era-appropriate items.

Collectors clubs and their events are another source of temporary museums. There are collectors clubs for farm equipment, automobiles, costumes—name it; there are people who collect it. When they gather together to show off their collections, you will have an abundance of objects to look at, and enthusiastic experts to answer your questions.

Inns and hotels are additional sources of period information. Think of these structures as working museums. Some have been restored to their original look, although most have modern conveniences such as indoor plumbing and electricity. Nor will you likely have the experience of sleeping in a feather bed, as most inns and hotels opt for modern mattresses. In order to restore their buildings accurately, however, many inn owners have become experts in period furniture, building techniques and other information in which you may be interested.

Look for specialized museums if you want to get an idea of how your older relatives worked. There are too many types of specialized museums to name them all here, but consider some of these possibilities: school house, transportation, medical office, agricultural, newspaper office, courthouse, mining, and railroad depots.

Art museums may be a source for landscape paintings that could show you what your area looked like before photographs were available in your parents or grandparents generation. Art is are also a source of images of period dress or events, such as battle scenes.

A good source for finding historical museums is the *Directory of Genealogical and Historical Societies, Libraries and Museums in the U.S. and Canada*. If your local library does not have a copy, ask that they purchase it.

Many museums, if they do not also have a full library, have a collection of books and journals to help the staff answer questions about their collection. These highly specialized collections could save you countless hours of research. Ask if the museum has a working bibliography of their books and journals, or a list of their archival items. Make an appointment with the staff member who has expertise in what you are researching. He or she may know of additional sources.

Ethnic Associations

Use the search engines to find associations or journals that honor your ethnic heritage. Some have active memberships and websites devoted to the history of immigrant populations and the customs that make each culture unique. Many ethnic societies maintain libraries, archives or museums, as well.

Neighborhoods

Look for a history of your old neighborhood(s). You may find that archaeologists or field historians have studied the area. You may find a neighborhood association that maintains a website, or that has historical information about the neighborhood. Has the neighborhood been declared a historic district? The National Park Service maintains a database of buildings on the National Register of Historic Places (nrhp.focus.nps.gov).

Religious Institutions

Houses of worship are not only rich sources of original documents, they often keep a local library for congregants that may include more than religious texts. It is common to find histories of the institution written on anniversary dates, such as centennials, sesquicentennials or bicentennials.

Search Engines

Use the search engines to find niche sites to help answer specific questions. Try searching for "coal mining in 1940s Pennsylvania" or "wedding gowns in 1950s rural Ohio." You never know what you may find. Check out demonstration or re-enactment videos on YouTube; hard to find books on Google Books or the HathiTrust; and the incredible collection of digitized images at the Library of Congress.

Cyndi's List (www.cyndislist.com) is a collection of active links to websites of interest to genealogists and includes many links to places to search for social history. Use the search engine on her site, but also browse the list of links within the category you are interested in. You may discover search terms you have not considered.

Specialty Books

Many modern specialty books are full of social history such as cookbooks, travel guides, business or industry histories, histories of events or tragedies, and institutional or neighborhood histories. The two largest publishers of this type of material are:

- Arcadia Publishing (www.arcadiapublishing.com)
- The History Press (www.historypress.net)

Publishers Global (www.publishersglobal.com) Publishers Global has a directory of publishers by subject including military and history publishers.

eBay

eBay is a rich source of ephemera and archival material. I never know whether to be sad or glad when archival items come up for sale on eBay. I guess it is better that the material be sold to a collector who will preserve it, than not. Search for items on eBay that may pertain to your family, the area where your family comes from, or the era you are researching. If you cannot afford to purchase the item(s) of interest, perhaps the seller would give permission to use their photographs.

Setting up an eBay email alert is simple and helpful to ongoing research. Create a free eBay account and sign in. In the big search box enter a term you are interested in (e.g. horton family new york) and hit search. Click on the button at the top of the results labeled "+ Follow this search." Your search terms will be saved, and you will have the option to receive a daily email showing you the results.

To help narrow the listings, use the categories in the left-hand navigation bar. Adding dates will also narrow the results. For example, I have searches running for Colorado for each year from 1859 through 1876, the territorial period. If you were to add "Colorado 1859–1876" to your search rather than individual listings for Colorado plus a single year, the search results would only return an item that had the whole phrase "Colorado 1859–1876" in it exactly. That could limit your search too much. It is better, in this case, to have a greater number of individual search terms than one covering a range of years.

Family Heirloom Exchange

The Family Heirloom Exchange (www.justajoy.com) is a subscription website linking family members to antique dealers who have heirlooms with known family ties. You may find pieces of your family's social history online.

One of the challenges of investigating the social history of your family is not in how hard it is to find it, it is how easy it is, and how much of it there is. I could easily become distracted on Google Books or eBay for days. The best advice I can give you is to avoid the temptation to become a collector. You do not need every possible book or item available before you begin to write. Use the tools above to answer specific questions, rather than an excuse to go fishing or collecting.

Include Historical Context

Placing your life's events in historical context is as much about placing the event and the people involved in the event within the community as it is analyzing what historic events may have changed the course of your life.

To write about yourself within historical context means to understand not only the era in which you lived (much of which is social history), but the place(s) where you lived. Along with the location, it means researching the politics and events that affected *how* you lived. It means investigating the forces in the economy that determined how *well* you lived.

Research the Locations

The following are a few places to gain information about your neighborhood, town and area:

County Histories. County histories are a good place to begin. Search the online catalog of a library in the area. Most library catalogs allow you to search either by keyword or subject. Using the subject category may return a better list. Look for a history written during the time you was there. You may find lithographs or photographs in the book that will help you describe the area. Google Books (books.

google.com) and the Internet Archive (www.archive.org) are also good sources of county histories available to read online or for download.

City Directories. Browsing through a city directory from the right years is another good way to remember what was there when you were there—the neighbors, the schools, the businesses. City Directories often have street maps. While it is easier to find a city directory for larger towns, some directories include the rural areas nearby. Ancestry.com has a good collection of digitized city directories, although many thousands are available on microfilm through:

- The Family History Library (www.familysearch.org)
- The American Antiquarian Society (www.americanantiquarian.org)
- The Library of Congress (www.loc.gov)

Bird's Eye View Maps. Bird's eye view maps were popular in the early 20th century and if you can find one with a publication date close to when you lived in the area, you can get an idea of how the town was laid out, what buildings were prominent, and the terrain. Your memory of your neighbor as a child may not have included how the larger community was laid out. The best sources for these maps are:

- The David Rumsey Map Collection (www.davidrumsey.com)
- Art Source International (rare-maps.com)
- eBay (www.ebay.com)

Fire Insurance Maps. Starting in 1867, the Sanborn Company made fire insurance maps of more than 12,000 cities and towns to help insurance companies assess the risk of insuring buildings. There are many digitized Sanborn maps available online, and major universities and libraries also have collections of these maps. The Sanborn maps will give you an idea of what each building was constructed of and how many structures were on the property (barn, carriage house, garage, or coal bin).

DVD Extras. Modern day filmmakers often go to great lengths to achieve historical accuracy in their films, and often the DVD extras will describe their research or how they created different aspects of the film. If a film was set in your area during the correct era you are researching, watch the DVD extras, as well as the commentary tracks, for background information. Although I would not use films as the only source of location research, there is something to be said for being able to see the 'old town' again to spark memories.

Places Where You Lived

In addition to reading about the communities where you lived, your readers will likely want to know more intimate details, such as what your home was like. Was it made of clapboard or brick? How was it furnished? Were there rag rugs on the floor and quilts on the beds? Was there a fireplace or a furnace? Answering these kinds of questions will give you an abundance of detail. *Houses and Homes: Exploring Their History* by Barbara Howe, Delores A. Fleming and Ruth Ann Overbeck is an excellent study of the role that homes play in local history.

Deed, tax, and homestead records along with plat maps can help pinpoint where your home was and give you details you may not have known about the property as a child.

Places Where You Worked

The place where you worked is the other location where you spent a great deal of time. Details of your work life may be as interesting as details of your home life. What was your first job? Did you ever work on a farm or in a factory? What local conditions influenced what businesses developed or died? Did you own the business or were you an employee? What products or services did the business sell? Who were the customers? What was it like to spend a day or a shift in the workplace?

Look at the newspapers of the era for ads touting the places where you worked. Search a local archive for items with the company's logo and sales brochures, or a local museum for examples of product packaging.

Specialized, living, or open air museums may be the best way to re-experience what it was like to work as did in days gone by. If the museum has docents or re-enactors, see if you can spend a day doing what you did back then. Try your hand at operating the machinery, pressing the linen or cooking the meals.

In addition to your workplace, consider a little research on the places you went to school, shopped, attended religious services or other public buildings in the community such as the local courthouse.

Community Events

Get reacquainted with the politics of the time and the area. What were the political issues of the day? What was newsworthy?

At this point, include any event you think may have had an impact. Later, we will take steps to make sure that you do not include events merely for the sake of including them. It is much easier to winnow down too much information once you begin writing than to stop and conduct another round of research.

Read What You Read Back Then

One of the best ways to become acquainted with local events as well as how people spoke, thought and felt in the past, is to read the newspapers and magazines that people read then. These may be the books or newspapers your parents or grandparents read while you were a child.

Newspapers

Reading a local newspaper will give you a good feel for the language of the era, albeit sometimes a bit flowery or over-dramatized by today's standards.

Look at the headlines. Headlines then, as headlines today, are designed to attract the reader's attention and tend to follow the hot news. The headlines will help you fill out your timeline with historical context.

The best part of early or local newspapers is often the gossipy type of news about the comings and goings of local people—who has come to visit whom; who is taking a business trip; who has returned with what kinds of goods—fabulous stuff for authentic detail.

Take a look at the advertisements. The ads are much more about social history than historical context, but they will give you an idea of what items cost, what goods were available locally, and what kind of items your family may have had to scrimp and save for in order to purchase.

Of course, do not forget the obituaries. Before the modern era when newspapers began to charge for obituaries, the newspaper often had a reporter assigned to write nothing but obituaries. A lot of family information can be packed into a few short paragraphs, albeit subject to the whims and misinformation given by the person who wrote it.

To find out whether there was a newspaper published in the town or area where your ancestor lived, consult the U.S. Newspaper Directory, 1690-Present, found at the Chronicling America section of the Library of Congress website (chroniclingamerica.loc.gov/search/titles/). The Library of Congress also has a large number of digitized newspapers available. If you want to know more about a specific paper or about the early newspaper industry, consult *The History and Present Condition of the Newspaper and Periodical Press of the United States*, produced by the Census Office of the Department of the Interior. This book is available as a free download at Google Books (books.google.com).

The following free sites have links to digitized newspapers:

- The Ancestor Hunt (www.ancestorhunt.com/newspapers.html)
- Elefind (www.elefind.com)
- Google News Archive (news.google.com)
- Old Fulton New York Post Cards (fultonhistory.com/Fulton.html)
- Australia's Trove (trove.nla.gov.au/newspaper)

There are also many local or state-wide newspaper preservation projects. Consult the area's major universities as well as the state historical society, as they often either have original copies or microfilm copies of newspapers significant to the area. The Ancestor Hunt (www.theancestorhunt.com/newspapers.html) also has a state-by-state list of historic newspaper projects as well as helpful articles on searching historic newspapers.

There are several subscription websites devoted to newspapers where you can either search by name or keyword. The name search can be frustrating, especially if you are searching common names. Use the advanced search features that allow you to narrow the search by date and location. Use the keyword search, especially if you lived in a town near where the newspaper was published. Local newspapers often carried columns of information from surrounding towns as a regular feature.

The following are the leading newspaper subscription sites:

- Newspapers.com
- NewspaperArchive.com
- GenealogyBank.com
- PaperofRecord.com

One of the best features of the subscription newspaper sites is the ability to search across multitudes of papers. Keep the date ranges narrow to limit the number of results.

Magazines

Finding an era-appropriate magazine often is more difficult than finding a local newspaper. There are not nearly as many digitized early magazines as there digitized newspapers, but there are a few universities undertaking magazine digitization projects.

One of the best ways to get an idea of what your parents or grandparents would have been familiar with, or events they may have reacted to, is to read what they read. While national magazines are helpful in following major events or subjects such as fashion trends, finding a local newspaper can provide priceless, personal information about your family and the people they knew.

Follow the Money

If you want to understand how well your family and neighbors lived, investigate what was happening in the region or country that could have affected the economy and thereby the choices people made. Economic booms and busts are often the reason people left an area or flooded into others.

How did people in the area make a living? Did they trade with other local communities or only among themselves? How did they conduct transactions—in cash, barter or on credit? What inventions or circumstances influenced the way people made money? What economic forces were the drivers, either upward to booms or downward to busts?

One of the easiest places to start researching economic events is on Wikipedia (www.wikipedia.org). They host a page for each decade that includes science and technology (including new inventions), commerce, and notable misfortunes such as natural disasters and epidemics. There is also quite a bit of social history on these decade pages, including literature, theater, music, sports, fashion, and art.

Did Your Family Move?

Did your family make substantial moves? To a different region? A different country? In most cases, people were either pushed from one place by difficulty or conflict or they were pulled to another place by opportunity.

How did your family get where they were going? Did you come from overseas or from down the block? Did you move out of town or into town? Did other members of your family move with you—uncles, aunts, cousins, grandparents? Did transportation change over your lifetime? The experience of making a move is rich storytelling material. If you were too young to remember, luckily there are many first-hand accounts of what it was like to travel by steamship, river boat or barge, or by train. Transportation museums are another good source of information about how people made a move.

The kind of details you will get from researching social history and historical context will help you tell your stories well. Along with the written details, a few good images are a must.

Get the Graphics

In this round of research, gather the images to help your readers see the story you are telling. While you can imagine the color of your mother's hair or the clothes she wore while cooking, your readers will need you to help them imagine it too. If need be, use charts to show relationships and to help keep names straight. Use photographs of your family, friends or colleagues if you have them. Use illustrations to demonstrate concepts or maps to give directions, or show routes and distances. Gather any visual clues you think the reader may need to fully understand the stories.

Charts

Generation charts or pedigree charts are good visual references for readers who are not familiar with different branches of your family. Generation charts show three or more generations at a glance. Most genealogy software will produce a generation chart at the push of a button. If you want to fancy up the chart, you can add photographs or background pictures. You could also use third party software designed to make elegant, detailed generation charts. If you have a fancier chart with pictures or illustrations, offer it as a separate product (printed sheet or PDF) to people who are interested in the book.

For your book, however, keep the charts as simple as possible so that they are easy to read on a single book page. It is difficult to include more than four to five generations on an 8.5" x 11" page. You do not need to include full information if it will not fit, but include at least birth and death dates.

Another useful visual reference is a family group sheet showing a nuclear family—a couple and their children in the order in which the children were born. Genealogy software creates these charts, as well. The charts can be modified to show multiple marriages with all of the children (full and half-siblings), as well as the children's spouses. Family group sheets are another simple way for readers to see who belongs to the family at a glance.

Photographs

Include personal or candid photographs of as many of the central characters as you can. From your research review, you should have a list of images you want, but do not have. Reach out to your extended family, friends and colleagues. Ask other researchers. Look in local archives, newspapers or historical society collections. Search military history websites or museums. Try eBay. You never know where you may find a photograph.

Depending upon the story, you may want more than portrait photographs of the people, such as candids, group pictures, animals and pets. Unfortunately, most people do not take pictures of the scenes they see every day such as the rooms in their own homes, their offices, or of their cars—even today, when photography is so cheap. If the story takes place in the recent past, look for pictures of your home(s), business(es) or neighborhood(s). If your story occurs more than 50 years ago, you may find nothing but portrait photographs, and even those may be relatively few.

Historical Photographs

You may want to add images beyond your own or family collection to include historical photographs of the region or era. Even if you do not use all of the photographs you may find while researching in the book, they may be helpful to you when describing scenes.

Searching the Internet

While it is easy to locate images by using the "Images" feature on a search engine, the Internet is not the best place to find digital files with resolutions high enough to look good in print. For print production, you need an image at 300 ppi at the size you want to display it. You will need a higher resolution image than most of what you will find on the Internet because websites use images that have been down-sampled to 72 ppi for quick retrieval and display.

You can use the search engines to locate collections that contain the images you want, some free from copyright restrictions, others require a fee.

Locating Photograph Collections

Use the "Images" feature on Google or Bing to search for a location or an event. For example, I searched for the "Battle of Guadalcanal, WWII" and came up with dozens of digital images of that battle including one that came from the National World War Two Museum. Clicking on the link to the original image took me to the image, and from there I was able to obtain the address for the museum to ask for permission to use the image, as well as to obtain a better, higher-resolution version to use in my book.

Bing has an interesting feature on its Images page called "Image Match." By clicking on an image, then using the Image Match feature, the search engine will list other places online where that image exists. In this case, I found the same Guadalcanal image on the Library of Congress website in several varieties including a digitized version from color film, another from a color slide, and a black-and-white version, all with links to images with resolutions high enough to use in a book. The information about the image indicated that there are no known restrictions on publication. Good news, indeed.

Sources of Royalty Free Images

The following are websites where you may find photographs or illustrations free from copyright restrictions so that you can include them in your book without permission or fees. Proper attribution, however, is a must.

Library of Congress Photographs. Each image within the pictures collection at the Library of Congress (www.loc.gov/pictures/) has an indicator of whether the image has any known rights restrictions. The images in the American Memory Project within the Library of Congress are gathered from other collections, so be sure to check with the image's owner for permission.

Flickr: The Commons. Flickr (www.flickr.com/commons) is a photo sharing site that has a section of images that owners have agreed to allow others to use without copyright restriction. Flickr is also the host of many museum and archive photographic collections. Unless you find the image you want among The Commons, ask permission to use it.

Getty Images Stock Photos. While Getty (www.gettyimages.com/creativeimages/royaltyfree) mostly sells images, it has made a collection available without copyright restrictions. Please do not be tempted to use an image that is rights restricted, however, without paying for use. Getty is known for its hardball tactics to extract compensation if you use an image without permission.

Ancestry. Ancestry (www.ancestry.com) has a postcard collection consisting of thousands of images from around the world. Old postcards are a great source of location and event images.

Wikimedia Commons. Wikimedia Commons (commons.wikimedia.org) has millions of images without licensing restrictions contributed by the individuals who own them.

Again, proper attribution is a must.

Sources of Rights-Managed Images

Rights-managed images are those that you may license for use. The following are sources of low-cost, rights-managed images:

- Shutterstock (www.shutterstock.com)
- Dreamstime (www.dreamstime.com)
- MorgueFile (www.morguefile.com)

Historical Societies

Many local historical societies have photographic prints, slides or negatives in their collections that have not been digitized or cataloged online. The same is true of some local libraries. It pays to call and ask. Explain that you want the image for a memoir. If the institution will not make the images available to you without cost, negotiate the fee. You may have to pay only for the staff time to scan the image for you. You could offer to help scan images in return for waiving a fee. What the historical society may lack is staff to scan their images.

Ideas for Images

The following sites have millions of images of everything imaginable. If you need ideas, consult one of these sites.

ClickAmericana. Click Americana (www.clickamericana.com) has images covering every decade from the 1820s to the 1980s. ClickAmericana has such a good collection of images that you are certain to get a few ideas, and the site encourages sharing to Facebook, Twitter or Pinterest.

Retronaut. Retronaut (www.retronaut.com) describes itself as a photographic time machine. Retronaut has partnered with museums and archives around the world to create this digital collection.

Mountain West Digital Library. Mountain West Digital Library (www.mwdl.org) is a portal to the image resources of several historical societies and universities in the western states.

Panoramio. Panoramio (www.panoramio.com) is a user-generated Wiki site where photographers post their images. Panoramio is a good resource for modern photographs of the places your ancestors once lived. Ask for permission. Often, the photographer is flattered that you want to use the image and asks only for proper photo credit.

The sites above are also sources for images of people in period clothing; objects found in museums or full-color images of historic places. In fact, you may find better images taken with modern equipment, than historical photographs.

Digitally Altering Photographs

Most photographs could use a little touching up, to lighten areas that are a little too dark, sharpen edges or increase the contrast. Most image editing programs allow you to make these corrections easily. The corrections that are not quite as easy are those that help re-build parts of a damaged photograph or those that eliminate unwanted or distracting elements (see Enhance, Repair and Retouch in Chapter 8).

Color or Black & White?

Not all photographs look their best when reprinted in a book. You can test how each photograph will look by creating a digital scrapbook, of sorts, with all of the images you are considering. Use Lulu (www.lulu.com) to print a private book as a proof. That way, you will see each image as it will look printed in black-and-white so that you can reject some images or fix others that look washed out or too dark.

Taking New Photographs

There is no time like the present to take a few new photographs. Even if you do not use them in this book project, ask for updated photographs of the people in your extended family every so often.

Children have their pictures taken frequently, but adults have a nice portrait made only about once a decade, if that. Ask your family members to send you a recent photograph of each member of their families. They do not need to use an expensive portrait photographer. Plan a time when everyone can gather, and then find a friend or neighbor who can take a decent digital photograph. Take pictures of the entire family, as well as a few pictures of each person individually.

Asking for recent photographs can help open doors to other areas where you want help from family members, such as information, stories, or old photos.

Heirlooms

Photograph objects that are difficult to scan. If there are heirlooms spread throughout your family that you want to show in the book, ask family members to photograph them for you (if you are not in the area to do so yourself).

Small objects, such as china or jewelry, often look best when isolated in a studio box with a neutral background and good, even lighting. Larger objects may have to be photographed in place.

Good lighting is key to good photographs. In most cases, opening curtains for natural light or placing reading lamps to shine on the object along with proper camera settings will be enough light to take a good indoor photograph.

Artwork

Artwork, like other objects, is difficult to scan—easier to photograph. The key to photographing artwork is to make sure the camera is lined up in a way that keeps the image square, so that you do not create distortions—either narrower at the top than at the bottom, or narrower on one side than the other. You can fix distortions in your image editing program, although taking a good photograph to begin with will save time.

Research the artwork or heirlooms you discover. Readers may be interested to know, for example, that a desk that has been in your family for 150 years was hand-crafted in New England and brought by train to Wisconsin. Or, that your aunt has a complete set of dinnerware popular in the 1920s, sold in dime stores.

Location Photographs

While it is interesting to find good historical photographs or paintings that show an area as it looked while you lived or worked there, there are some instances in which a photograph of what the place looks like today would be appropriate as well. If you have both a modern and a historical photograph, consider creating a side-by-side composite for comparison. Search the website What Was There (www.whatwasthere.com). It pairs historical photographs with Google Maps.

While You Are on a Research Trip

If you are taking a research trip "back home," schedule enough time to take an abundance of photographs. Digital photography is cheap, so shoot away. You may not use all of them in this book project, but they will be available to you or other family members for future projects.

Bracket Your Shots. Most digital cameras will allow you to alter the speed or the aperture from shot to shot. Some cameras do so in a three-shot burst. By bracketing, the camera will use different settings to alter the amount of light in the photograph. By bracketing, you are likely to take at least one usable shot from the three-shot group without having to alter it in your photo editing program.

Take Establishing Shots. The best example I can give of an establishing shot is to take a picture of the sign at the cemetery entrance, and then a few shots of the view within the cemetery to give readers an idea of what the landscape is like. In a town, take a few photographs of the landscape as you come into the town, and a few of the town square and surrounding neighborhoods. Shoot whatever you think the reader will need to understand the general landscape.

Take Encapsulating Shots. An encapsulating shot is a complete picture. At a grave site, take a photograph of the entire stone. In the town square, take a shot of the whole courthouse.

Take Close-ups. On tombstones, take close-ups to make sure you can read names and dates when you get home with the photographs. Taking close-ups will also remind you to look carefully at the entire tombstone from all sides, so you do not miss anything. In town, take photographs of any historic markers. Shoot close enough so that you can read the marker when you return home.

Take Both Vertical and Horizontal Shots. You will not know how a photograph may fit best into the book's layout until much later, so shooting from both directions is helpful.

Panoramas

Panoramic photographs sometimes tell the story better than a single photograph can, and they are easy to create. If you want readers to experience how wide open the family homestead was, how close together the homes were on your family's street, or where buildings were in relation to other buildings, panoramic photographs are the way to go.

There are many image-editing programs, such as Photoshop (or Photoshop Elements) that will stitch together different shots to create a single image. It can be tricky to stitch together two historical photographs if the horizon lines or focal distances are different. Editing prior to stitching can help.

If you are taking new photographs to create a panorama, overlap the shots by about thirty percent. Do not change the focal distance while you are shooting the series, and try to keep the horizon line at the same position in the viewfinder as you shoot. If you are not a steady hand, a tripod can help with this.

For panorama purposes, I shoot a scene first going from left to right, and then repeat the series going the other direction. Sometimes, shots taken going one direction come out better than the other.

Most people take photographs according to long-established personal habits. We shoot from the same standing position, from the same distance, from the same angle or from the same direction (e.g. horizontal). Your book may be more interesting, however, with a few out-of-the-ordinary photographs.

Documents and Memorabilia

Your memoir could include a few documents so that readers can see for themselves the proof you have for your stories. Think about how you are using the real estate on the page, and whether what you are showing is so important that the reader will want to see it. Census records, for example, can be boring unless they show something extraordinary. You can add the information contained in the record as a part of the storytelling without having to show the actual census for each decade. If you are listed in the census at Buckingham Palace, however, that would be another matter.

The following are examples of documents your reader may be interested in: an ornate marriage certificate; a passenger list showing the name of the ship, its captain and your family; a land patent showing a map of the property; or a document with an ancestor's signature on it. Signatures are fabulous, because they are so personal.

Some items are considered ephemera or memorabilia rather than documents, but are welcome in a memoir, such as a letterhead from your business, a newspaper clipping, a funeral card, a playbill if you were in a show, your school report card, and so on.

The documents most handy for laying down facts for storytelling are not always the ones that readers will want to see, even if they are mighty interesting to the person doing the research. What should make the cut for the book are those documents that help tell the story *and* are visually interesting. In fact, photographs or illustrations may be better than documents for that purpose.

Illustrations

There are times when an illustration is better than a photograph. Think about how you use maps online today. If you want to see what a place looks like, you may prefer the street view (a photograph), but if you need to drive there, a standard street map (an illustration) would be easier to follow.

There are rich sources of illustrations online. The key, again, is finding files with sufficient resolution to look good in print.

You may find an image that is out of copyright, such as a line drawing or lithograph from a 19th century magazine or book. The trick is locating an original and producing a good scan or photograph. There are stock photography companies that also offer line art free, but in most cases, you must pay to use the image.

If you are looking for house plans, Architectural Designs (www.architecturaldesigns.com) has plans with photographs and floor plan illustrations as PDFs for download. These plans are for houses to build today, but are based upon historical designs. The floor plans in the PDFs may not be of sufficient quality for re-print, but you could re-create one as a simple pen and ink drawing to use in its stead.

Another option is to find an illustrator who can create original drawings. (See Working with an Illustrator below.)

Maps

Create a list of places for which a map may help readers get their bearings. As a part of your research, locating a map created at the time you lived in a place is an invaluable source of accurate information. Such a map enables you and your readers to see what streets existed, or how far the town extended, for example.

Fortunately, there are many places that have good map collections. Check with the major universities (e.g. Harvard and Yale), large libraries (e.g. Newberry Library and the Free Library of Philadelphia) and the local college or university in the area you are researching.

Historical Maps

The following is a list of good map collections online:

- Library of Congress Maps Collection (www.loc.gov/maps/)
- David Rumsey Map Collection (www.davidrumsey.com/)
- Perry-Castaneda Library Map Collection at the University of Texas (www.lib.utexas.edu/maps/)
- American Geographical Society Digital Map Collection (collections.lib. uwm.edu/cdm/landingpage/collection/agdm)

Modern Maps

A modern map can show relationships between places, how many different locations you lived, or how far your family traveled. Modern maps can be useful for this type of demonstration.

There are easily searchable modern maps at:

- MapQuest (www.mapquest.com)
- Bing (www.bing.com)
- Google (www.google.com)

Each has fairly generous Terms of Use that allow you to capture a screenshot of a map and reproduce it elsewhere as long as you are not using the map, itself, for commercial gain. Check the terms on the site before you spend too much time gathering maps as screenshots.

Google, Bing and MapQuest each offer street maps, topographical features, and satellite views. All three offer directions and information about local services such as restaurants, hotels, and local attractions.

Google and Bing offer GPS coordinates and closeup views—Google calls it Street View, Bing calls it Bird's Eye and Streetside. These features are helpful in determining what exists at a location currently. Not all areas are updated by Bing or Google frequently, so looking at the date watermarked on the map will give you an idea of how long ago the view was captured.

Google allows you to sign in to your Google account and create maps with your own map points, to save or share by email. They also offer developer tools to create your own maps and place them on your website or blog. The Community Walk feature allows you to create a map with personalized points, and add photos, videos, and comments.

Google Maps will give you the outline of an entire county by searching for the county and state. Since so much genealogical research is conducted county by county, showing an outline of a county with the cities visible may be helpful.

Bing Maps has a feature that is helpful when filling in missing location data from your research. Bing Maps will give you the county name if you have a city and a state, but do not know the county. The information will appear at the top of the map to the right of the centering tool as Country > State > County > City. If you put in Nederland, Colorado, for example, you will see: United States > Colorado > Boulder County > Nederland.

Screen Captures

Screen captures are not an issue if you are planning to publish only in an electronic form. They can be an issue, however if you want them to look good in print.

Your computer, whether a PC or a Mac, probably has a screen capture feature. On the PC, press Control + Alt + PrtScrn, then paste the image into another program such as Word or Photoshop. Unfortunately, standard screen capture software does not always create an image that looks good in print because the software is only able to capture what is on the screen displayed at 72 to 96 ppi.

To obtain the best possible screen capture, increase the size of an image displayed on screen by zooming in (Control+Shift+[+] on a PC), which makes the image bigger on the screen when you capture it. Ideally, you will end up with a screen capture at a size large enough to create a 300 ppi image at the size you want for the book. For example, if you were to capture an image on screen at 16" x 12" at 72 ppi, that would translate into a pixel size of 1152 x 864. The largest 300 ppi image you could create from that pixel size would be 3.84" (1152 divided by 300) x 2.88" (864 divided by 300).

SnagIt (www.techsmith.com/snagit.html) has been the industry leader in screen capture for years. It has the most options for gathering screen captures from different sources such as websites or video, and the ability to edit and enhance captured images. The cost is around $50, but if screen captures are important to your printed book, it may be worth the purchase.

Memoirs satisfy the curiosity. Not only will your family members be curious about the stories you have to tell, but also about what you looked like back then, and what your home(s), land or business(es) may have looked like. A simple pedigree chart can answer questions quicker than an entire chapter sometimes. A beautifully printed marriage license, your first driver's license or a certificate of achievement may delight your readers.

Use as many images as you think you need to tell the story. Leave out images if they are included solely to document facts. Seek out instead, memorabilia or ephemera that helps define the era, or maps that put the stories into context. If the book grows too big because it is beautifully illustrated, you can always split it into more than one volume.

Asking for Help

You should have an idea of what your additional research needs are, and what you may need help with—either from friends and family, other genealogical researchers, or perhaps the professional assistance of photographers, illustrators, researchers or companies who will help you make your images look their best.

Help from Family

Ask family members for anything that you think they can contribute to complete your research. Get the family legends down. Determine from where the heirlooms came. Locate the pictures. Find out who still has stuff.

Social Media

It is amazing how many cousins you can rustle up on Facebook, Twitter, or LinkedIn. Use the message boards on sites such as Ancestry.com where other researchers may be working on the same family lines. Look for blogs in your area of interest.

Private messaging features allow you to send a message that is only between you and one other person, more like sending an email than asking a public question. Privacy settings allow you to determine who will see the comments you make or the questions you ask. Even so, be careful how much information you share about yourself online.

Although you can post photos to most social media sites, there are dedicated photo sharing sites such as:

- Flickr (www.flickr.com)
- Shutterfly (www.shutterfly.com)
- DotPhoto (www.dotphoto.com)

Some photo sharing sites will let your family members download the digital images or order prints for themselves. Encourage family members to use the photographs you have shared. Holidays or family reunions are a good time to make use of the images. Besides, you may find your images coming back to you through talented or creative cousins in the form of scrapbooks, photo books or other photo-inspired gifts.

If you are not familiar with how social media can be used for family history, the National Institute for Genealogical Studies (www.genealogialstudies.com) offers a course in *Social Media for the Wise Genealogist,* or consult Drew Smith's book, *Social Networking for Genealogists* (albeit a bit dated, having been released in 2009), or Thomas MacEntee's eBook, *Staying Safe with Social Media: A Guide for Genealogy and Family History.*

Interviews

If you have not already done so, conduct interviews with family members who have stories to tell. Arrange for a visit and record each interview with a video or audio recording device. By recording, you will be free to participate without the pressure having to write everything down. Come prepared with specific questions, and make sure you ask questions that are open-ended enough to get your relative not only talking, but remembering. Bring photographs along. Asking a relative to recount the events seen in photographs is not only a good way to get an interview started, but the images may trigger additional memories.

There are many good guides for conducting interviews, including:

- Cynthia Hart and Lisa Samson, *The Oral History Workshop: Collect and Celebrate the Life Stories of Your Family and Friends*
- Donna M. DeBlasio, *Catching Stories: A Practical Guide to Oral History*
- Donald A. Ritchie, *Doing Oral History*
- Valerie Raleigh Yow, *Recording Oral History: A Guide for the Humanities and Social Sciences*
- *The Step-by-Step Guide to Oral History* (dohistory.org/on_your_own/toolkit/oralHistory.html)
- *The Principles and Best Practices Guide* on the Oral History Association's website (www.oralhistory.org/about/principles-and-practices/)

Help from Strangers

Reference librarians are my favorite "complete strangers" to ask if I need help with research. Many libraries offer an "Ask a Librarian" feature which is essentially an online chat between you and someone in the library who may be able to obtain quick answers to your questions.

Social Media

Mobilize an army of researchers at the click of a mouse using social media. Throw your question out on one of the big genealogical blogs and see if one of the blog's authors can answer you, or put you in touch with someone who can. See if a museum you are interested in or your old school has a Facebook page. Alumni associations and military groups are another good source to connect with old classmates or military colleagues.

Photo Sharing Sites

There are helpful photographers on Findagrave.com, Flickr.com or Panoramio. com. Oftentimes, a credit for taking the photograph is enough for the photographer to give you permission to use their photo.

If you cannot find exactly the right photograph online, sometimes you need only ask. If you want a photograph of a school you attended, for example, you may find a helpful stranger associated with one of the websites above, willing to make a trip over to the school to take the picture. The staff at the local library or historical society may also know of a volunteer willing to help you.

For the best results, be specific about what you want. Explain that the photograph will be used in a printed book, so you need a high-resolution image. If you need a photograph of a building with enough clear blue sky above it to accommodate your title and subtitle, say so. Ask for both horizontal and vertical images if you do not know yet what you need for the layout. You are more likely to receive exactly what you need if you are specific when you ask.

After getting what you need from a helpful volunteer, a nice thank you goes a long way. (This applies to family members as well.) Send a hand-written note or a small gift card for someone who has gone the extra mile for you.

Help from Experts

Experts can be helpful if you can sum up succinctly what you need and why, to get on and off the phone quickly, or to come to the point in a few paragraphs in an email.

If you need more than a quick question answered, schedule an interview. You must tell the expert why you are consulting them and what types of questions you want to have answered before they will agree to an interview. Most experts, will not allow you to waste their time dithering about. Prepare a list of questions before you make the call. You never know, the expert may be available right then if you are ready to go. Other experts may prefer you to send the questions ahead of time or to answer by email.

Expert advice can be invaluable and can cut your research time down dramatically. He or she may know of other resources available or other authorities who could help. Most experts in their field know which books are the definitive guides and which are best to gain background information. An expert should be able to explain the jargon common to their field of expertise to you in an easy-to-under-stand way.

Some experts will give you quick answers freely; others may charge for their time. Others may turn you over to a research assistant. With any expert you hire; it is worth the effort to negotiate. To get the best deal possible, it does not hurt to have a good counter-offer ready, or something that would suffice, say … a nice meal. You will not know until you ask.

Working with a Photographer

You may need photographs for the book that you are unable to take for yourself, obtain from family members, or from a helpful local volunteer. In this case, hire a photographer or license a photograph taken for other commercial uses.

Find the right photographer for the job. If you want a group picture of the entire family or candid photographs taken during a reunion or other gathering, find a portrait photographer—someone who specializes in people pictures.

If you need location photos, look for someone who shoots photographs for advertisements in the area. That photographer may have images not previously sold to clients that he or she would make available to you, for a nominal fee or photo credit. If the photographer has to go somewhere on your behalf, however, be prepared to pay for their travel time as well as shooting time.

Studio Photography

If you need good studio photographs of your heirlooms, consider using a profes-sional. A commercial photographer should be able to shoot objects in their own studios, or take their equipment to a location if the heirlooms are too fragile or too big to be moved to the studio.

Portfolio

Before you hire, ask to see a portfolio. Many photographers have their portfolios online, so you may be able to find exactly the right photographer before placing a call.

Fees

Ask about fees and whether they include travel, time at the location and any cropping or alterations before the photographs are given to you. You will not need prints unless you want them. Portrait photographers expect to make their money on packages of prints, although many photographers are willing to take a higher event fee in exchange for giving you the digital images outright.

Most event photographers will charge for the time they spend at the location, not by the number of images they take. Be clear about this, however. You will not want to pay for time and two hundred images you cannot use, just because the photographer took them. You also do not want the photographer to limit the number of photographs taken. Even with a good photographer, one-quarter to one-third of the shots taken will not be great photographs.

File Type and Resolution

Most photographers today shoot in resolutions much higher than what is needed for print production, so resolution should not be an issue. Ensure, however, that the photographer will deliver images in the largest resolution and size you need. In most book projects, that is the book cover image.

Location Images

If you want location shots, give the photographer the names of local landmarks. A good photographer will know to take shots from different angles, but it does not hurt to be specific. If you want a blue sky in the background in order to put your title in that space, say so. If possible, show the photographer a book cover with an image similar to what you want, so the concept for your cover is clear.

Capturing an Event

If the photographer is to capture a family event, be specific about the images you want. Give the photographer a schedule of activities and a list of the people you want to be photographed. You may need to provide a spotter—someone who is familiar enough with the family to point out who is who on the shot sheet.

Consider asking for establishing shots—shots of the location where the event is taking place. Ask for close-ups as well as group shots, candids as well as staged or portrait shots.

Make sure the photographer is familiar with the event location. Schedule a site inspection with the photographer to discover any lighting issues, obstacles or distracting backgrounds to avoid.

Deadlines

Set clear deadlines. Unless you have an upcoming family reunion where you would want the photographer to be present, wait until the manuscript is nearly finished to send a photographer to take location photographs for you. The only exception to this rule is if the time of the year makes a great difference to the quality (or subject) of the images. If you want a clear shot of a building, for example, you may want the photograph taken in winter.

Copyrights

Do not make a big issue about copyrights unless you are willing to pay more to make the photographer give them up entirely. Negotiate the uses you want for the photographs instead. If you plan to use the photographs for more than your book project, obtain the rights for other uses—on your website, in your eBook, on a family reunion t-shirt or journal cover, on photo souvenirs, and any other use you can think of. It is unlikely that a photographer will deny you any extended uses of photographs of your family. But, it does not hurt to be thorough.

Note: If you have permission to use a volunteer's photo for your book (from sites such as Findagrave or Panoramio), but want to use it for some of the extended uses listed above, ask permission from the photographer for those uses as well.

Payment

Ask about any extra charges, so there are no surprises and clarify how you are expected to make payment and when. Half of the total fee is common for a down payment to secure the booking, with the final half due upon delivery of the photographs. Ask about album fees, overtime charges, or any special handling of the images not included in the quoted price.

Cancellations

Cancellations can be problematic. If you have to cancel, be prepared to pay at least part of the photographer's booking fee unless you cancel well ahead of time. Unfortunately, there may be a reason for the photographer to cancel. To protect yourself, require that the photographer has a similarly qualified backup colleague to fill in, in the event of a cancellation, or that he or she pay any additional charges you may encounter in order to hire someone at the last minute.

Write a Formal Proposal or Contract

Use a formal proposal to indicate the photographs you want and how you want them delivered to you—on a thumb drive, an external hard drive, an archival DVD, or through a file sharing service. Make sure deadlines, and dates of events are clear. Include all prices and payment terms. State what uses the photographer is allowing you, and be specific about what happens if either you or the photographer cancel.

Working with an Illustrator

Working with an illustrator is a bit different than working with a photographer. Because of the artistic nature of the work involved, illustrating often takes far longer than taking photographs. If you want one-of-a-kind illustrations, build extra time into your publishing timeline.

Hire the right illustrator for the job. Illustrators have their own styles, although many illustrators can work in different media, such as pencil, pen and ink, or watercolor. Some illustrators create only computer-generated images. Find a style that you prefer, and then choose an illustrator who can create the images you want. Use the same illustrator throughout the book so that the style is consistent.

Portfolio

Ask to see a portfolio. Many illustrators have their portfolios online, or they can point you to other books they have illustrated. The illustrator may have worked on a book that is available commercially, and has an online preview.

Fees

Ask about fees and be specific about the size and resolution of the digital images you need. A professional illustrator should be able to advise you how their art-work will look best in a print publication, whether by scanning the originals or photographing them. There may be additional fees if the illustrator must engage a studio photographer to create a digital image of their art.

Deadlines

As with hiring other professionals, be specific about what you want and make your deadlines clear. Ask for a set price per illustration, and inquire about any extra charges, so there are no surprises. Clarify how you are expected to make payment and when. Illustrators often require payment in installments as the il-lustrations are in progress, rather than half before and the balance after an event as you would pay a photographer.

Copyrights

Copyrights may be a more complicated issue with an illustrator than with a pho-tographer. Because of the time it takes to create illustrations, illustrators may not be as eager to give up their copyrights. Negotiate any other uses at the same time you negotiate for your book. You may wish to use the illustrations on social media, on your website or in an electronic book. If you have a reunion coming up, you could use the illustrations on giveaway items such as t-shirts, tote bags or mugs. Negotiate the rights to use the illustrations in other ways or at least leave open the possibility for uses in the future.

Cancellations

If you must cancel, be prepared to pay at least part of the fee unless you cancel well ahead of time. If the illustrator cancels, you can expect a full refund of any fees you have paid. In your agreement, ask that the illustrator pay any additional fees you encounter as a result of his or her cancellation if you are up against a deadline to finish the book.

Write a Formal Proposal or Contract

Use a formal proposal to indicate the illustrations you want and how you want them delivered to you—on a thumb drive, an external hard drive, an archival DVD, or through a file sharing service. Make sure deadlines are clear. Include all prices and payment terms. State what uses the illustrator is allowing, and be specific about what happens if either you or the illustrator cancel.

eLancers and Freelancers

One place to find an illustrator online is to use one of the freelance services, such as Elance (www.elance.com), oDesk (www.odesk.com) or Freelancer (www.freelacer.com). At any of these sites, you will find illustrators listed under designers or graphic design and the person you hire may be from another country. You post the project details and your budget. Freelancers will bid on your project. You accept a bid from the person who offers the best price and has the portfolio you think is best. You will be able to see their ratings from other clients before you choose. They do the work. You approve the work or ask for revisions. They submit final versions, and you pay them through the website, not directly. The sites will take care of the funds transfer and any taxes that apply.

Another place to find freelance illustrators or photographers are at local schools. There are plenty of high school or college students who want to build their portfolios, and who may work for a recommendation or fees far less than a professional would charge.

Working with a Professional Historian or Genealogist

There are times when it pays to hire a professional historian or genealogist to help you finish your research. Although there is some crossover between the work that professional genealogists and historians do, before you hire someone make sure you have the right type of professional for the job. Genealogists tend to focus on establishing relationships, whereas historians tend to focus on location-based research.

Initial Consultation

The initial job consultation should be free. A phone call of 30 minutes or more is not unusual, but you should have your homework done before you call. In some cases, you may need to describe the research problem in detail in order to get a professional researcher's opinion of what it will take to obtain what you need and how much that may cost.

Portfolio

Ask to see examples of their previous work, and check the researcher out online at their personal website, and on social media sites. If there are no testimonials listed, ask for the names of a few previous clients. Look for credentials and certifications. In the U.S., membership in the Association of Professional Genealogists (APG) is a good indication of their experience. In the UK, look for membership in the Association of Genealogists and Researchers in Archives (AGRA).

Deadlines

Be clear about your expectations and deadlines. State how many hours you agree to pay for and the completion date for the work. If the researcher must travel to a repository, be prepared to pay for their time even if they do not find anything.

Fees

Fees vary greatly and you can negotiate. Shop around and get a sense of the going rate for researchers in the area. Clarify how and when you will make payment(s).

Ask about additional fees for copying or the use of a digital camera at different repositories. The researcher will expect you to cover these expenses. Spell out fees for travel. Expect to pay a retainer, and have the researcher explain how the retainer will be applied to the balance.

Research Report

Expect a full research report and that the researcher will maintain the copyrights to the report. If you want to use any part of the researcher's report in your book, obtain permission. Then quote and adequately attribute the researcher.

Digital Images

If you want the researcher to obtain digital images of documents or other evidence, explain the digital image size and resolution needed.

Where to Find a Professional Researcher

The Association of Professional Genealogists (www.apgen.org) has a database of genealogists for hire by location or specialty. They also have a good checklist for hiring a professional genealogist, (www.apgen.org/articles/hire.html). You will find the code of ethics members agree to abide by on their website.

Progenealogists (www.progenealogists.com) is Ancestry's official research firm. You can get an estimate online and talk with a researcher before agreeing to hire anyone. Genlighten (www.genlighten.com) lists researchers and their specialties.

You may find freelance research historians among the members of the American Society of State and Local History (www.aaslh.org) or the Society of American Archivists (www.statearchivists.org). Your local historical museum may also have suggestions.

The following private firms have employees who may take on freelance jobs:

- History Associates (www.historyassociates.com)
- History Factory (www.historyfactory.com)
- Historical Research Associates (hrassoc.com)

At the end of this round of research, you should have most of what you need to write the book. Writing and research are a cyclical process. There may be times when you will need to return to research momentarily in order to flesh out details of a story or two.

Hopefully, you have been organizing information and images as you have been researching so that you have all of the following:

- A full cast of characters
- Timelines for each of your events and locations
- Written notes about each piece of documentary evidence along with full citations
- Notes taken from your social history research
- Notes taken from your historical context research
- A list of images (physical and digital) in folders by person or subject
- A list of any remaining holes or outstanding items

෴

It is time to leave the comfort of research for a time, and start the process of writing. Do not worry. Like golf, you can take a few practice swings before you are expected to make it count. Just in case you are worried about staring down a blank page, the next chapter is full of tips to conquer writer's block.

Chapter 10

Writer's Block: Staring Down a Blank Page

Most writers experience a bit of anxiety when beginning a new project, and the prospect of having to stare down a blank page may seem daunting. Do not let it stop you. In this chapter, you will find exercises to stimulate the creative juices, and if you have been writing bits and pieces of stories as they came to mind, you already have some bits and pieces started. In other words, you conquered the blank page without even knowing you had.

Baby Steps

For novice writers, fear is often the biggest obstacle. Fear of making mistakes or of not finding the right words. Fear of getting started or fear of never finishing, are common complaints.

> The goal when you begin to write should be foremost to increase your confidence in yourself as a writer.
>
> **—Heather Sellers**
> *Page After Page*

The best way to gain confidence is to practice, practice, practice. Becoming a better writer is similar to becoming a better skier. You cannot merely imagine yourself skiing. You have to go to the mountain, ride to the top and come all the way back to the lodge, even if you fall a few times along the way. Writing is no different. Your first draft may not be perfect. In fact, it may not even be readable. Fear not! Put the stories down on paper. You can revise it all later.

Next Steps

One challenge every writer faces is portraying the people in a way that makes the reader want to know more.

> Without sympathy and imagination, the historian can copy figures from a tax roll forever—but he will never know or be able to portray the people who paid the taxes.
>
> **—Barbara Tuckman**
> *Practicing History*

How true. Your challenge is to remember enough about the people in your stories to demonstrate what kinds of people they were through their actions in the stories, or to give yourself enough research to place the people within the context of events that took place.

Les Edgerton in his book *Hooked*, gives a great example: "Instead of describing the mountains of West Virginia with such terms as 'purplish hills' and 'kudzu-covered mountainsides,' use descriptions such as 'flinty shale lying just beneath topsoil too thin to sustain any kind of decent crop,' to inform the protagonist's life as being hardscrabble. Any description should illuminate the character in particular ways." In other words, do not merely describe. Describe in a way that tells something about the people.

Giant Leaps

Stop and read a few of these cherished memoirs to see how each writer brought his or her memories to life.

- *Angela's Ashes* by Frank McCourt
- *Night* by Elie Wiesel
- *A Child Called "It"* by David Pelzer
- *Tuesdays with Morrie* by Mitch Albom
- *A Moveable Feast* by Ernest Hemingway
- *My Bondage and My Freedom* by Frederick Douglas

The rest of this chapter will give you a few issues to consider and story starters you can use to gain experience before you begin writing the complete book.

Before You Write

It is better to learn some lessons before you begin writing than after you finish a first draft. The following is a bit of collective wisdom from books, editors, and writing courses.

Give Yourself a Round of Applause

Not everyone is willing to undertake a project as big as writing a book, so congratulations. If you are still reading this book, then you have more tenacity than ninety percent of the people out there who will never get beyond the idea that they will write ... someday.

Discover What Motivates You

It is not enough to start a book project; you must complete it if anyone is to benefit from it. Focus instead on how much your family will appreciate reading it. Know that your family will be proud of the lengths you have gone to preserve your memories. Know that all of your precious work will not end up in the dumpster after you are gone, because there will be a book sitting on the shelves of your family members and libraries across the country.

Analyze What Makes You Doubt

If you are an inexperienced writer, you are not alone. There are few relatively writers who have written more than one or two books, so you are in the same place as most others were when they began. What is the worst that could happen? Nobody dies from a badly written book. There are no lives on the line. If you finish your manuscript and are unhappy with it, there is always an opportunity to fix it. That version can be a practice run. The next version will be better.

Set a Schedule

To finish your book project, you must write. The most common advice in the writing community is: "butt in chair." That pretty much says it all. You must *choose* to write and be there to do so. If you write one page a day, at the end of the year, you will have a 365-page book. You do not have to write in marathon sessions. You can write for fifteen minutes a day or one hour a week.

One caution, however. If you leave too much time between when you write, you may spend most of your time trying to remember what you wrote and what you had planned to write next. Schedule your dedicated writing time close together to get more actual writing done. Continuity is important, both to the substance of the book and to your ability to keep the project moving forward.

Just Say No

For many writers, a cloud passing over is excuse enough to abandon writing for some other task or activity. You may have to tell the people in your life that when you are writing, they are responsible for entertaining, or cooking, or cleaning, or driving—themselves. The withdrawal symptoms (for you and your family) will subside eventually.

Do Not Wait for Inspiration

You cannot wait for the right inspiration or perfect conditions if you expect to complete your book. There will always be laundry to fold, kids to pick up, and additional research that may be interesting. If you wait for perfect conditions, you may as well wait for perfect weather—72 degrees and sunny with a slight breeze blowing gently from the east, but not enough to rustle your papers or muss your hair. You cannot wait for a miracle either—nor a flash of genius—nor divine intervention.

Be Careful Who You Ask for Advice

Think twice about showing your manuscript to friends, family members and particularly to other people writing their own memoirs. I wish it were the case that everyone was not only *capable* of offering beneficial advice, but also *willing* to offer constructive criticism. Jack Bickham hits the nail on the head in his book, *The 38 Most Common Fiction Writing Mistakes (And How to Avoid Them)*, when he explains, "There are know-it-alls and know-nothings. If your work is good, many of them will be jealous. If your work is bad, few, if any, of them will know how to point out your mistakes in a constructive manner." If you need an editor, hire a professional. Exchange manuscripts with another person writing creative non-fiction, or join a writer's group where you can get constructive feedback from other people who write.

Consider ...

> Consider the possibility that you may be an excellent writer who simply needs to sit down and write.
>
> **—Mary Embree**
> *The Author's Toolkit: A Step-by-Step Guide to*
> *Writing and Publishing Your Work*

Enough said.

Choose Your Words

The following advice is universal. It applies to fiction, non-fiction, family histories and memoirs.

Write for Your Reader

You have identified your target market. You may be writing for your children, parents or siblings, the next generation, future generations, genealogical researchers or other people who have had similar experiences. If you keep your target audience in mind as you write, you are much more likely to write the kind of book that your readers will thoroughly enjoy. If you try to write for an audience of everyone, you are writing for no one in particular, and the book will suffer for it.

Too Clever by Half

It is better to be understood than not, so familiar words are better than more erudite-sounding words. If you are unfamiliar with the meaning of a word, consult a dictionary. Lose the shorthand used in email or text messages. Clarity is the key to communication. Do not try to reinvent English grammar, either. It is enough trouble to follow the rules as they exist. Write so the reader will understand you.

Three Words You Can Stop Using Today

Forget using the words very, just or really. While common in conversation for emphasis, they are unnecessary clutter in a book. A global search through your manuscript will tell you if these words have become so much a habit that you do not notice when they slip into your writing.

Verbs, Nouns, Adjectives, and Adverbs

If you ask editors what makes them spot a novice writer, most will point to the overuse of adjectives and adverbs. If you use a strong verb, you may not need an adverb to modify it. For example, state that he sprinted, not that he ran quickly.

Use strong nouns as well. Do not use the word container, if you mean a wicker basket. State that she owned a tilt-top table made of mahogany, rather than a round-topped, spindly-legged, deep brown table. Strong verbs and precise nouns get the job done better.

Active Voice is Better

Use the active rather than the passive voice. In the active voice, the subject is doing the whatever the verb indicates. Marvin mailed the letter. In the passive voice, the object is being acted on. The letter was mailed by Marvin.

There are times when the passive voice fits the situation best, but those instances are far fewer than opportunities to use a strong verb that describes exactly what is happening in the narrative.

> The habitual use of the active voice ... makes for forcible writing. ... [W]hen a sentence is made stronger, it usually becomes shorter.
>
> **—William Strunk, Jr. and E.B. White**
> *The Elements of Style*

The following is the conjugation of the verb, to be. If you find these verbs in combination with other verbs, you are using the passive voice (e.g. the letter was mailed, the letter was being mailed, the letter had been mailed).

Indicative	Past	Future
I am	was	will be
You are	were	will be
He is	was	will be
We are	were	will be
You are	were	will be
They are	were	will be

Perfect	PluPerfect	Indicative
I have been	had been	am being
You have been	had been	are being
He has been	had been	is being
We have been	had been	are being
You have been	had been	are being
They have been	had been	are being

It is best to use the most active, direct and succinct way to describe the action.

Neither Hedge Nor Wheedle

If you have a point to make, make it. There is no sense running around a subject until the reader is exhausted or confused. Hedging around a subject or wheedling your way into one is most common when addressing sensitive subjects. Try direct first. Then adjust or soften the tone, if need be.

Pick and Choose

Be discerning about what you include. No one wants to read a minute-by-minute account of an average day where nothing out of the ordinary takes place. Readers only want the good stuff.

Do Not Get Graphic

Describing the reality of war wounds is one thing. If, in the back of your mind, you can see your mother squinching up her face and saying, "Ewwww." Leave it out. Everybody poops. There is no reason to describe it for your readers. That is not edgy. That is icky.

Writing Should Have Rhythm

You are not writing an expository essay for school. Each paragraph does not require a topic sentence followed by neatly regimented supporting evidence. Overly long paragraphs will slow the rhythm of the story. Keep the paragraphs short and the story moving.

Imitation is the Finest Form of Flattery

If you are going to emulate another writer's style, choose someone who is still alive and writing. What readers were used to in the 19th century is not what readers expect today. You are better off imitating the style of Frank McCourt or Mitch Albom than Charles Dickens or Maxim Gorky.

Perfect Is Not Possible

You do not have to squeeze your style or the authenticity out of the story to achieve perfect words or grammar. A conversational tone is fine for a memoir. It is easy on both the writer and the reader. There is no need to twist yourself into a knot over every word, as did Oscar Wilde, who once said about himself, "I have spent most of the day putting in a comma and the rest of the day taking it out."

Do Not Edit as You Write

Stopping to re-write a small section over and over again, is an easy excuse not to move on. Get it all down, and then worry about the re-writing. You are more likely to see structural flaws in the larger manuscript than you may in a small section.

Items to Have on Hand

The following are handy items if you get stuck.

A Good Dictionary

The best is probably the *Merriam-Webster's English Usage Dictionary*, available in print or online (merriam-webster.com). If you prefer something different, you will find this online dictionary helpful (www.onelook.com). And Google, of course, will give you a definition if you put a word or phrase into the search box.

Thesaurus or a Synonym Finder

The *Merriam-Webster Dictionary* (and website) includes a thesaurus. Another good thesaurus is Thesaurus.com (www.thesaurus.com). *The Synonym Finder* by J.I. Rodale has not been updated in years but is still useful. And, there is a synonym finder online at Synonym.com (synonym.com). This website also has antonyms and definitions.

Word Usage Guide

If you need to know the etymology of a word (how the use of a word developed), the best source is the *Morris Dictionary of Word and Phrase Origins*. If you would rather use an online guide, consult Richard Lederer's *Verbivore* (www.verbivore.com) or Evan Morris's *Word Detective* (www.word-detective.com).

Editing Advice

If you find yourself in need of editing advice, consult The Editorium (www.editorium.com). They also provide useful tips for writers using Microsoft Word. Bill Walsh, editor and humorist, runs an advice site for copyeditors (www.theslot.com) or consult the following subscription site for copyeditors (www.copyediting.com).

A Wee Bit of Levity

Personally, I like to read something funny, especially when I am stuck for what to write next. It is often the only inspiration I need to keep going. The following are my favorites:

- *Eats, Shoots & Leaves: The Zero Tolerance Approach to Punctuation* by Lynne Truss
- *Sin and Syntax: How to Craft Wickedly Effective Prose* by Constance Hale
- *Lapsing into a Comma: A Curmudgeon's Guide to the Many Things that Can Go Wrong in Print—And How to Avoid Them* by Bill Walsh

Food for Thought

Every book project involves decisions about what to include and what not to include. You have done much of this already when you took stock of what you already have on hand. The following are a few more questions to ask yourself before you begin writing.

What Do You Want Your Readers to Know?

By the time the reader finishes the book, what is it you want the reader to understand about you and your story? Is there an overarching theme or idea you want the reader to take away?

Is there Something You Want Readers to Do?

You may want family members or people with similar experiences to contact you, continue your research, or gather for an event. If there is something you want readers to do as a result of reading the book, how will you communicate that?

How Will You Handle Sensitive Topics?

Not every individual or family has a simple, straightforward past. How much of what you have discovered do you want to reveal? You have an obligation to accuracy, but not at the expense of the feelings of living people. What happened long ago is fair game, but revealing hurtful or potentially embarrassing, private details about living people may be troublesome.

How Will You Handle Hearsay?

Most families have legends or stories that have been passed down, and if those stories play a role in your own memories, you may want to include them. Some of what you have been told may be the "God's honest truth," so to speak. Other stories may have been altered and changed over time and have little resemblance to what actually happened. Still others are wishful thinking. You may let your reader know what you have been told, and what you have been able to find to confirm it (or not). Dispelling a popular legend may cause disappointment among some family members. Are you prepared to handle their disappointment?

How Will You Deal with Speculation?

If there are relationships you cannot prove, or if your family's involvement in events is uncertain, how will you let the reader know that you are speculating? It is acceptable to let the reader ponder the possibilities. It is not acceptable to imply a connection without proof.

Let Your Subconscious Help You

If you stop to think about your book project every night before you go to bed for even five minutes, your subconscious will help you see the bigger picture or tackle the material when you sit down to write next. Many writers swear by this simple technique.

Story Starters

Story starters help get the juices flowing. Think of these exercises as the last practice swing before you have to face the pitcher. Tackle one exercise or all, or skip them entirely if you are ready to write.

Create a Good Habit

The best way to establish a habit is to commit to doing something each and every day for one month. At the end of that month, the activity will have become a habit. Write about something for just ten minutes a day for thirty days.

The following is a simple exercise to help you establish a habit for writing: pick a photograph and write what memories spring from the photograph. It does not matter whether you pick a photograph from your photo album or if you use a search engine to find an image of your hometown, first school or the car you drove in high school.

Help the Reader Feel the Experience

The best storytellers are those who use details to help the reader believe that they are experiencing what is happening in the story. Use your web browser to search for the following expressions as images, not news:

- And they're off. Kentucky Derby.
- Tornado. Joplin, Missouri.
- Pow Wow. Native American dancing.
- Teen Carries Younger Brother 40 Miles.
- Ferry sinks. 300 feared dead.

Now write a few paragraphs that make the reader feel as if they are experiencing the scene for themselves.

Personal Memory Joggers

The following is another way to stimulate memories. List your friends chronologically. Describe them how you remember them—their looks, their personality traits, the things they enjoyed doing, the foods they hated—whatever you can remember about them.

Do the same thing for the:

- Schools you attended
- Teams you played on
- Jobs you had
- Bands you followed
- Houses you lived in
- Associations you joined
- Cars you owned ... and so on

The following are books and a game full of memory joggers:

- *Mom [Dad], Share Your Life With Me* by Kathleen Lashier
- *Grandma [Grandpa], Tell Me Your Stories* by Kathleen Lashier
- *To the Best of My Recollection* by Kathleen Lashier
- *The Book of Myself: A Do-it-Yourself Autobiography in 201 Questions* by Carl and David Marshall
- *Q&A a Day: 5-Year Journal*
- *Reminiscing: 21st Century Master Edition*

Creative Writing Techniques

The following are exercises to inspire you to put words down on paper. The writing does not have to mean anything, and you do not have to use full sentences, although for some exercises it may be easier if you do. You do not have to limit yourself to only those things found in each suggestion. If you have a better idea, write about it.

Set the Table. Imagine yourself at the dinner table when you were young. Describe who was there, how the table was set, what was served and the conversation that took place.

Introductions. Think of two people well known to you but not known to each other and introduce them. How would you describe them to each other?

Make an Excuse. Make an excuse to your mom, to a teacher, to a police officer, to a friend—about anything.

Lost and Found. Describe how you got lost, and then the steps you took to find your way.

Folk Remedies. Make up a remedy for snoring, sneezing, chin stubble, tardiness, or stinky sneakers—imagine how it could work. Who knows? It may.

Oh No! Describe things you would do with a friend or sibling you would never do with a spouse or parent.

What Would You See? Describe the events you would witness if you lived across the street from a mortuary, police station, schoolhouse, livery stable, biker bar, or a newspaper office.

Land of Make Believe. If you could make up a place, what would it be like to live there? Or travel there?

Each of these exercises allows you to practice descriptive writing. You do not have to show these snippets to anyone else. These exercises will help you write about people and places.

ॐॐ

The only way to cure writer's block is to write. That does not mean you must tackle the intended project while you are feeling blocked, but it does mean you must write about something. If you will write every day, you will develop a habit of writing. Starting your book project will be easier, and once you begin, the words will come more naturally. When needed, step away from your book and write about something nonsensical, write about your activities the day before, or write down a set of instructions. When you are back in the swing of things, begin again with your memoir.

Chapter 11

Drafting a Preliminary Outline

If you read writer's guides or attend writer's workshops you will hear terms such as vision, focus, and structure. All of these terms imply "the bigger picture." Once you can see the big picture, you can draft a preliminary outline.

Vision

At this point, you should have narrowed your vision from what is possible to what is practical based upon the idea you have for the book so far, and any research you have done. You should be able to state your vision for the book in a short paragraph. For example: "The book covers my thirty-eight years in the military, from the West Point class of 1940 to retirement as a Major General in 1978."

Focus

Focus should describe the main events that shaped your life and story. For example: "As a new graduate of West Point, my military career was just beginning when Pearl Harbor was attacked. I served as a combat lieutenant during WWII in Europe seeing action in the Battle of the Bulge and the Ardennes. I served in Korea as a military tactician. By Vietnam, I was serving in the NATO command and by retirement, I advised the President from the Pentagon."

Structure

The structure is more concrete and describes the organization of the book—what happens and when. The structure, at this point, is still in rough terms because there is more than one way to combine a set of facts into a comprehensive story.

Consider the following ways to organize:

Chronologically

Organizing a book chronologically is the most common way to organize. If you organize chronologically, time is the unifying factor, but it need not be uniform. Some stretches of time will have a lot more action than others. For a farmer, the march of time could be season by season. For a teacher, time flows back and forth between summer break and the school year. For a career military person, time may flow from one conflict to the next without a lot of story in between.

Edward Rutherfurd's historical novels draw time out. His novel *London*, for example, begins in the Roman period and ends in the 20th century. He uses character traits that follow family lines to hold the stories together through the passage of time.

Bruce Catton in his non-fiction book, *A Stillness at Appomattox*, compresses time. The book deals only with the last days of the Civil War. The television show *24* did much the same showing a progression of events each hour during a 24-hour period.

Most memoirs have some type of ebb and flow in them. There is not usually enough material to tell stories about each and every month or even year of a person's entire history.

Convergent

Using a convergent structure allows you to tell stories running side by side that would be impossible to tell together. This style allows you to tell different parts of your story separately, and then bring them together (converge) by the end to answer any remaining questions.

David Laskin's book *The Family* uses a convergent structure. Events split his family into three groups—a branch that immigrates to New York, a branch that immigrates to Palestine (later Israel), and a branch that remains in Ukraine through WWII. He shifts back and forth to tell the stories of the three branches concurrently, and then brings the book to a close after the war.

Convergent structure is unusual in a memoir, but if, for example, there were events that shaped your life happening elsewhere, you could tell those stories alongside what you were doing at the time, converging them to show the impact of other events on the course of your life.

Functional

A functional structure is more typical for a how-to book than a memoir. In a how-to book, the author uses a functional structure to build new skills with each new lesson culminating in a final set of skills or a final product (i.e. a craft). Functional structure is a bit harder to describe in terms of a memoir, but in this case it means what series of events came together to bring about a result.

Mosaic

A mosaic structure puts the pieces of a puzzle together using different characters to tell their versions of an event. Mosaic structure is a common journalistic technique for assembling the parts of a catastrophic event that cannot be witnessed by a single individual, but together the re-telling gives the reader an idea of everything that took place. In the mosaic structure, more than one main character is telling his or her story. The stories together encompass the experience.

Mosaic structure is also unusual for a memoir, but there may be some events in your life where telling your siblings version of events alongside yours, for example, may generate a clearer picture than your version alone.

Memoir

A memoir structure does not follow any strict structure. Vignettes make up the book. Naturally, this is the most common way to organize a memoir because it is how most people recall events—in snippets. If you need an example, Bailey White's book, *Mama Makes Up Her Mind: And Other Dangers of Southern Living*, is written in this style.

Create an Outline

For many writers, creating an outline is a beginning point because it will help you keep track of a lot of information. By this point, you should have all (or most) of the following:

- A timeline of events
- A cast of characters who appear in each event
- Written summaries of some, if not all, stories intended for the book
- Social history research notes (with citations)
- Historical context research notes (with citations)
- A list of images by person or subject

Use these items together to form a detailed outline of your intended book. It does not have to become a road map set in stone as you write, merely a map to help guide your way.

❧⁕☙

In the next section, you will use your detailed outline to flesh out the broader story arcs, determine individual scenes within the story arcs, and establish where the natural chapter and section breaks should go.

SECTION 3

The goal in this section on writing is for you to learn how to become a good storyteller, write a first draft, and then edit and polish the manuscript.

Everyone should:

- Create a style guide. Style guides are big time savers.
- Edit. Every manuscript deserves editing.

Baby Steps

There is no getting around it—you have to tackle the first draft. If, however, learning the mechanics of storytelling seems overwhelming, skip it and start writing.

Once you have a draft, fact check it, make sure the captions on images are correct, and edit for typos. Every manuscript needs at least one good read through to catch mistakes.

Next Steps

If you take nothing else from this section, learn how to develop your characters. The people are why readers will turn the page rather than put the book down.

Once you have a draft, content edit, fact check, edit the captions and look for typos. The content editing is an additional step, but your manuscript will be better for it.

Giant Leaps

The story mechanics are there for a reason. Good storytelling requires sympathetic, believable characters involved in stories where the tension increases to a climax, then relaxes before the next story arc begins. Constant movement within the story arcs is what will make the reader want to know what happens next.

Once you have a draft, conduct a full edit. Your hard work deserves nothing less.

Chapter 12

Becoming a Storyteller

Writing your own story will involve writing about other people—the people who participated in the events you describe and the people who influenced your own stories. You may have relatively little difficulty telling stories about the people you know well—your siblings, parents, even grandparents—because you have heard them speak and have seen how they interact with other people. But how about those people whose memories have faded with time? Your challenge is to remember enough or gather enough research to get a sense of who those people were, so that you can describe their roles in your stories.

Creative Nonfiction

Before discussing the mechanics of telling good stories, I want to introduce you to a relatively new genre called creative non-fiction. Before we go any further—creative non-fiction is *not* fiction. You should build your memoir upon the facts, but the way the story is told can benefit from the techniques journalists use to tell stories in a vivid way.

Non-fiction, traditionally, solves problems, gives advice or illustrates techniques. Memoir, by contrast, is about people—real people—who lived in a time and place that may be unfamiliar to much of your audience.

Fiction has the advantage of being able to create larger-than-life characters with enormous obstacles to overcome, who emerge from a death-defying scrape, and just as the audience gives a sigh of relief, are plunged into another, even more dangerous situation. High-drama action keeps the reader turning the pages, to be sure. To make yourself or a character in one of your stories larger-than-life, however, could be perceived as narcissism or hero-worship, rather than an authentic recounting of a real person's life.

Your life may seem sedate by comparison to swashbucklers, suffragettes, and war heroes. Do not be too critical of your own story. An accurate recounting will be more interesting to read, ultimately, than a heavily embellished version. Creative non-fiction threads the needle between fiction and non-fiction so that you can tell your stories in a way that informs and entertains. The techniques later in this chapter come from creative non-fiction.

Learn from the Best

Reading is, by far, the best tool to teach writing. The more well-written family histories you read, the more likely you are to pick up the author's techniques without having to dissect each chapter to study how it was written. Not that you should imitate a favorite author's style *exactly*. Reading a talented author's work will help you discover how a good writer combines elements of a story in the most effective way.

I turn to the following when I need help with techniques:

Memoir
- Mary Karr, *The Liar's Club*
- Ernest Hemingway, *A Moveable Feast*
- David Pelzer, *A Child Called "It"*
- Frank McCourt, *Angela's Ashes*
- Elie Wiesel, *Night*

The following are examples of well-written family histories and biographies. Each of these authors employs creative non-fiction techniques in a way that makes their stories engaging.

Personal Narratives
- Ian Frazier, *Family*
- Daniel Mendelsohn, *The Lost*
- David Laskin, *The Family*
- Buzzy Jackson, *Shaking the Family Tree*
- Edward Ball, *Slaves in the Family*

Third-Person Narratives
- Boynton Merrill, Jr., *Jefferson's Nephews: A Frontier Tragedy*
- John Philip Colletta, *Only a Few Bones: A True Account of the Rolling Fork Tragedy and Its Aftermath*

Humorous Biography
- Bailey White, *Mama Makes Up Her Mind: And Other Dangers of Southern Living*

Dramatic Biography
- William P. Wood, *The Bone Garden**

(*This work is not a pure dramatic biography. It has some fictionalized elements.)

Each of the accounts above is based upon actual people and events. The personal narratives tell the writer's story along with their ancestors' stories. The third-person narratives do not. They tell only the ancestors' stories.

The humorous biography is as much memoir as it is a biography. Bailey White tells stories about her mother in a funny and endearing way.

The dramatic biography is the true story of a female serial killer. Though some may classify it as a police procedural, I call it a dramatic biography because it is based upon actual events. However, it has an asterisk next to it because it contains fictionalized elements. William Wood writes as if he knows what the characters are thinking, when he cannot. He can only surmise. Assuming what other people knew or thought is a potential pitfall for memoir writers, as well. I included it as a good example of compelling, page-turning, cannot-put-it-down reading, and a caution flag for places memoirs should not go.

Fictionalized Family History

- Oliver Pötzsch, *A Hangman's Daughter*
- Oliver Pötzsch, *The Dark Monk*
- Oliver Pötzsch, *The Beggar King*
- Oliver Pötzsch, *The Poisoned Pilgrim*

I added the Oliver Pötzsch series beginning with *A Hangman's Daughter* for comparison. These books are based upon his family history; however, the accounts are fictionalized, and he is clear about that.

I encourage you to pick up a few of these books, read them and keep them handy as you write, to refer to in case you have questions.

The Big Picture

Before I break down storytelling into its finer elements and techniques, first let us look at the bigger picture. Most authors, before they do anything else, must decide who is telling the story. In other words, from whose point of view? In a memoir, you will be telling a story from your point of view. The only reason I included this section on Point of View for you, is to make you aware of the possible points of view so that you do not inadvertently slip into another point of view while telling your own stories.

Point of View

Unfortunately, many inexperienced writers never consider the point of view before writing, and the result is a muddled manuscript where the reader remains unsure of who is telling the story at any given point. The easiest way to visualize point of view is to imagine a camera on a tripod looking out over a vast landscape. The point of view is not the landscape, nor the camera, but the person looking through the lens.

If *you* are looking through the lens, then you will be describing your experiences in the first person: "I saw her name for the first time on a gravestone."

If the *reader* is looking through the lens, then you are describing their role in the story (a bit tricky, I admit) in the second person: "You, my dear granddaughter, are descended from Kings."

If one or more *characters* take a turn looking through the lens, you are describing their experiences in the third person: "He surveyed the battlefield for any signs that his brother had survived."

The last possibility is that you, the *author*, are looking through the lens, but you are not describing your experience, rather those of the entire cast of characters: "He knew when they met, he would marry her some day. And so did she."

First Person Point of View

When writing in the first person, you are telling your story, from your point of view. The major personal pronoun used is "I."

In fictional first-person accounts, the main character generally tells the story from his or her point of view, but not always. In *The Great Gatsby*, Nick Carraway is telling his story about Jay Gatsby, the main character. Likewise, in the Sherlock Holmes novels, Dr. Watson tells the story from his point of view, in the first person.

The following is the opening scene of Sir Arthur Conan Doyle's *The Hound of the Baskervilles*, narrated by Dr. Watson:

> Mr. Sherlock Holmes, who was usually very late in the mornings, save upon those not infrequent occasions when he was up all night, was seated at the breakfast table. I stood upon the hearth-rug and picked up the stick which our visitor had left behind him the night before.

In a memoir, you will naturally be telling your story from your point of view.

Second Person Point of View

When writing from the second person point of view, the reader is the central character, so the major personal pronoun used is "you." You address the reader directly, which is common in how-to books. I have done so throughout this book because it is an easy, conversational way to relay information. Creating a more formal distance between us by referring to myself as "this author" and to you as an abstraction (i.e. author, publisher, or memoirist) sounds stilted and awkward.

One of the few examples I could find of any work written in the second person comes from fiction. The opening scene of *Bright Lights, Big City* by Jay McInerney, includes this passage:

> How did you get here? It was your friend, Tad Allagash, who powered you here, and he has disappeared. Tad is the kind of guy who would be at a place like this at this time of the morning. He is either your best self or your worst self, you're not sure which. Earlier in the evening it seemed clear that he was your best self. You started on the Upper East Side with champagne and unlimited prospects, strictly observing the Allagash rule of perpetual motion: one drink per stop. Tad's mission in life is to have more fun than anyone else in the New York City, and this likelihood that where you aren't is more fun than where you are.

I recently heard genealogist and author John Colletta state that he had read a family history written in the second person because it was created for a family reunion, and the author wished to show the grandchildren their place in the family. Writing directly to the next generation is an interesting idea for a memoir, but one I have not adequately explored—yet.

Third Person Point of View

Family histories, biographies, and local histories are most often written in the third person. The major personal pronouns used are "he," "she" or "they." There is more than one way to tell a story from the third person point of view, however.

Major Character's Viewpoint. You can tell the story from a major character's viewpoint only, so that the reader can only know what the major character knows when he or she knows it.

The following example is taken from Hilary Mantel's novel *Wolf Hall*. The novel is written from Thomas Cromwell's point of view:

> It knocks the last breath out of him; he thinks it may be his last. His forehead returns to the ground; he lies waiting, for Walter to jump on him. The dog, Bella, is barking, shut away in an outhouse. I'll miss my dog, he thinks. The yard smells of beer and blood. Someone is shouting, down on the riverbank. Nothing hurts, or perhaps it's that everything hurts, because there is no separate pain that he can pick out. But the cold strikes him, just in one place: just through his cheekbone as it rests on the cobbles.

Multiple Character Viewpoints. In this case, more than one person will be telling his or her story, and you will be switching back and forth as the story unfolds. The easiest way to describe this is to use the example of a couple separated by war. The man is seeing what is happening on the battlefield, and the woman is seeing what is happening at home. They cannot see what the other sees because they are separated by distance.

The following example shows how Herman Wouk, in his novel *The Winds of War*, changes viewpoint from (father) Victor 'Pug' Henry to (son) Byron Henry in the opening paragraphs of chapters six and seven:

Chapter 6

Pamela drove Commander Henry and her father to Swinemünde.

The train would have been faster, but Henry wanted to see the countryside and the small towns, and the Englishman was more than agreeable. One could almost get to like Germans, he said, if one stayed out of the cities. Pug was appalled at the girl's driving. She chauffeured the rented Mercedes around Berlin in docile conformity to the lights and the speed laws, but once on the autobahn she rocketed the needle to one hundred fifty kilometers an hour. ... He now thought there might be no war. The British were dealing seriously at last with the Russians about a military alliance.

Chapter 7

The announcement of the pact shrieked at Byron and Natalie from the news placards in the Rome airport. They had set out from Siena before dawn in an old Renault, and while the whole world was chattering about the astounding news, they had innocently driven down alongside the Apennines in golden Italian sunlight, amid old mountain towns, wild airy gorges, the green valleys where peasants worked their fields. With Natalie Jastrow at his side for a three-week journey that was only starting, Byron was in the highest of spirits, until he saw the bulletins.

Multiple character viewpoints can be an effective way to tell a story. However, you may want to limit the number of viewpoints to avoid confusion. When you switch viewpoints, the reader should be able to tell by the start of the paragraph which character's story is being told. Starting a new chapter or using some other type of visual device (i.e. a printer's mark or three asterisks centered on the page) also lets the reader know when the viewpoint has changed.

Omniscient Viewpoint. If you, the author, are telling the story with perfect knowledge of every event that takes place, you are an omniscient narrator. You are viewing the events from a point above the action as you would view actors on a stage. One caution when writing from an omniscient viewpoint is to not get ahead of what the characters could possibly know at each point during the story. You cannot describe a character taking action based upon an event that is in the character's future, since he or she cannot possibly know what is to happen.

The following example is from the chapter entitled "A Merry Christmas," in the novel *Little Women*, by Louisa May Alcott:

> Jo was the first to wake in the gray dawn of Christmas morning. No stockings hung at the fireplace, and for a moment she felt as much disappointed as she did long ago, when her little sock fell down because it was crammed so full of goodies. Then she remembered her mother's promise and slipping her hand under her pillow, drew out a little crimson-covered book. She knew it very well, for it was that beautiful old story of the best life ever lived, and Jo felt that it was a true guidebook for any pilgrim going on a long journey. She woke Meg with a "Merry Christmas," and bade her see what was under her pillow. A green-covered book appeared, with the same picture inside, and a few words written by their mother, which made their one present very precious in their eyes. Presently Beth and Amy woke to rummage and find their little books also, one dove-colored, the other blue, and all sat looking at and talking about them, while the east grew rosy with the coming day.

Do not confuse a convergent structure with multiple character viewpoints, even though they may seem similar. David Laskin's book, *The Family*, is a good example. He has three distinct family units whose stories are told by alternating back and forth from Europe, to America, to Israel. The stories are told in a parallel way until they converge at the end. But the structure does not imply *who* is telling the story. In this case, David Laskin, the author, is telling the story using the omniscient point of view rather than using multiple character viewpoints.

For the most part, memoirs are told from the first-person point of view. You can certainly experiment with other points of view, just be consistent with whichever one you choose.

Tone

Establishing the tone of your book is about telling stories in a consistent way. Will you take a conversational tone? A comedic or ironic tone? Academic? Most writers develop a natural storytelling style or tone, although it may not make itself apparent until you are well into a first draft, especially if you have not written much previously. Tone is not a decision to be made with absolute certainty before

you begin writing. It is something to be aware of and to watch for when review-
ing your first draft. The book will read more naturally if the tone is consistent
throughout.

Voice

Voice is a little harder to describe. Voice depends upon whether you are writing
objectively (not allowing your opinions to influence the stories) or subjectively
(allowing your feelings about the subject to become known to the reader). Voice
should also be consistent.

A subjective voice is easiest to slip into when writing about subjects that are
emotional such as slavery or the Holocaust. It is natural to feel a range of strong
emotions when writing about emotional subjects. Whether you inject your emotion and opinion into the storytelling is up to you.

Whether to write with an objective or subjective voice is another decision that
can wait until the first draft is finished. Then, evaluate whether or not you have
been consistent in your approach.

Theme

A theme is the central idea or message of a book. Often, the theme is echoed
throughout the book without explicitly stating what it is. For example: "This is a
book about courage." Courage is, however, only a topic. What you *express* about
courage becomes the theme.

The following are common topics often used as overarching themes: freedom, survival, courage, integrity, loyalty, disaster, regret, alienation, love, passion, sorrow, persistence, curiosity, tradition, persecution, steadfast, or pride.

Herman Wouk described the theme of his novel *The Winds of War,* this way:

> The theme and aim of *The Winds of War* can be found in a few words
> by the French Jew, Julien Benda:

> Peace, if it ever exists, will not be based on the fear of war, but on
> the love of peace. It was not be the abstaining from an act, but the
> coming of a state of mind. In this sense, the most insignificant writer
> can serve peace, where the most powerful tribunals can do nothing.

If curiosity is the theme, one memoir could treat curiosity as having a negative impact, and another could treat it as a positive. For example, if curiosity
leads to a lifetime of risk-taking and loss (e.g. failed businesses and failed marriages and so on), then curiosity affected you in a negative way. If, on the other
hand, curiosity was what drove you to invent a new piece of technology and you
prospered as a result, then curiosity had a positive effect.

A theme may not become obvious until you write a bit. That is fine. You do not need to begin writing with a theme in mind. After you have a draft finished, you may find that there are ways to reinforce the theme by telling some stories a different way. The upcoming discussion on story structure will show you how.

Coherence

The final big picture item is coherence—telling each story logically—moving from event to event making sure the reader remains firmly grounded in the correct time and space. For example, even though you have a picture in your imagination of what going to a sock hop was like in 1950, your reader may not. In order for the reader to follow along, the story needs enough detail to demonstrate whether the action takes place going to the dance hall or high school gymnasium, while there, or returning home—and logically, in that order.

I know this is a lot to think about, but I wanted to make you aware of each of these big picture issues—point of view, tone, voice, theme and coherence—before you begin structuring your stories.

Story Structure

If you have ever heard someone tell a story that meanders, you understand why the best stories have structure.

Plot

Plot is a sequence of events that are tied together. If you are planning to tell your story chronologically, your detailed outline is essentially the plot for your book. If you will be telling vignettes, each story will have a plot of its own. In memoirs, you do not have the luxury of forging the plot by adding elements that did not take place, but you can pick and choose from the actual events to shape how the stories are told.

> Plotting is a way of looking at things. A way of deciding what's important and then showing it to be important through the way you construct and connect the major events of your story.
>
> **—Ansen Dibell**
> *Plot*

Within the plot, you may also have subplots—events that are not quite as important as main plot points, but add to the story by reinforcing the theme, showing what other family members, friends or colleagues are doing at the same time, giving background about the place or era, or demonstrating why life was as complicated or uncomplicated as it was.

PUBLISH A MEMOIR

The following plot diagram shows a simple chronological construction with subplots. The importance of each subplot is indicated by the size of its block.

A few cautions about subplots: they should not be more important, or told in a more compelling way than the main plot. They should be connected in some way to the main plot, not merely a way to disclose other, unrelated information. To prevent reader confusion, limit the number of subplots that occur simultaneously.

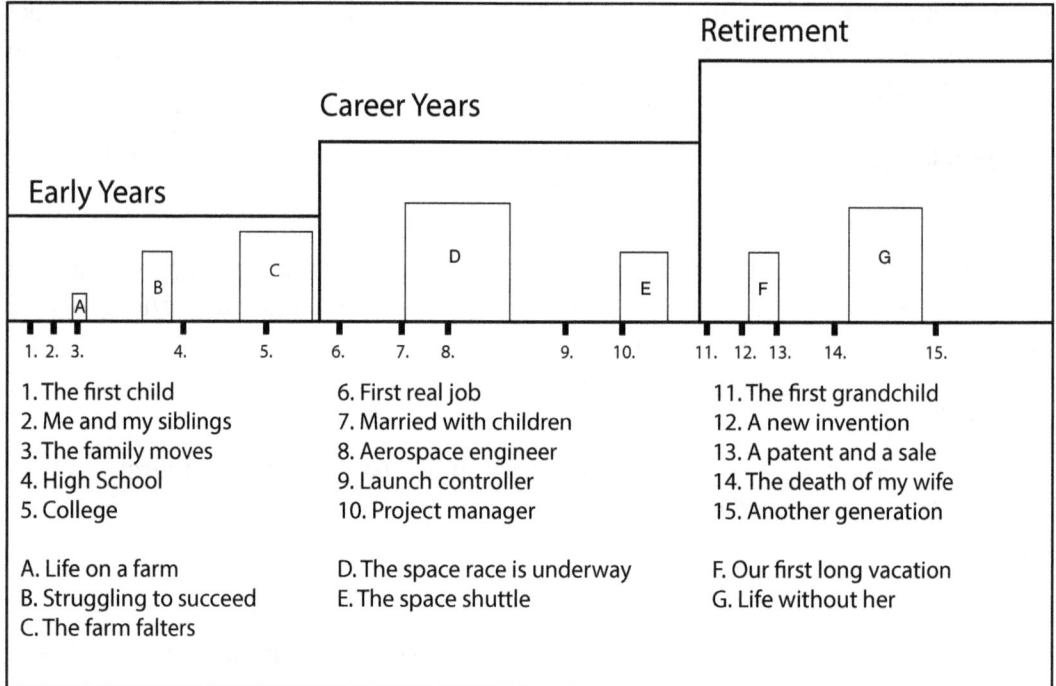

Plot diagram with subplots for a chronological story.

1. The first child
2. Me and my siblings
3. The family moves
4. High School
5. College

6. First real job
7. Married with children
8. Aerospace engineer
9. Launch controller
10. Project manager

11. The first grandchild
12. A new invention
13. A patent and a sale
14. The death of my wife
15. Another generation

A. Life on a farm
B. Struggling to succeed
C. The farm falters

D. The space race is underway
E. The space shuttle

F. Our first long vacation
G. Life without her

The Story Arc

The plot is made up of story arcs. A story arc is a series of scenes that begin with an inciting incident (something that sparks a change), action that rises to a climax (a turning point), then resolves (comes to a conclusion).

Episodic television makes good use of the story arc. A story arc can begin and end in a single episode. Oftentimes, however, a story arc will continue over multiple episodes with a cliffhanger at the climax to make you tune in to see what happens next.

Most television story arcs include subplots that begin and end within the story arc. Subplots run below the surface. In television, for example, subplots are a way to introduce forensic evidence in murder cases, to entangle characters in love stories, to provide back story information, to explain why characters act the way they do, and so on.

Story Arc
- Inciting Incident
- Action/tension rises
- Action climax
- Conclusion
- Arc 1

If you are using a chronological organization, typically, one story arc will come to a conclusion, and another one will begin although they can overlap. To connect the story arcs, plant the seeds of the next story arc within the current story arc. If you do not, the book will read like a series of short stories or vignettes. (Techniques for connecting story arcs follow in the Story Mechanics section.)

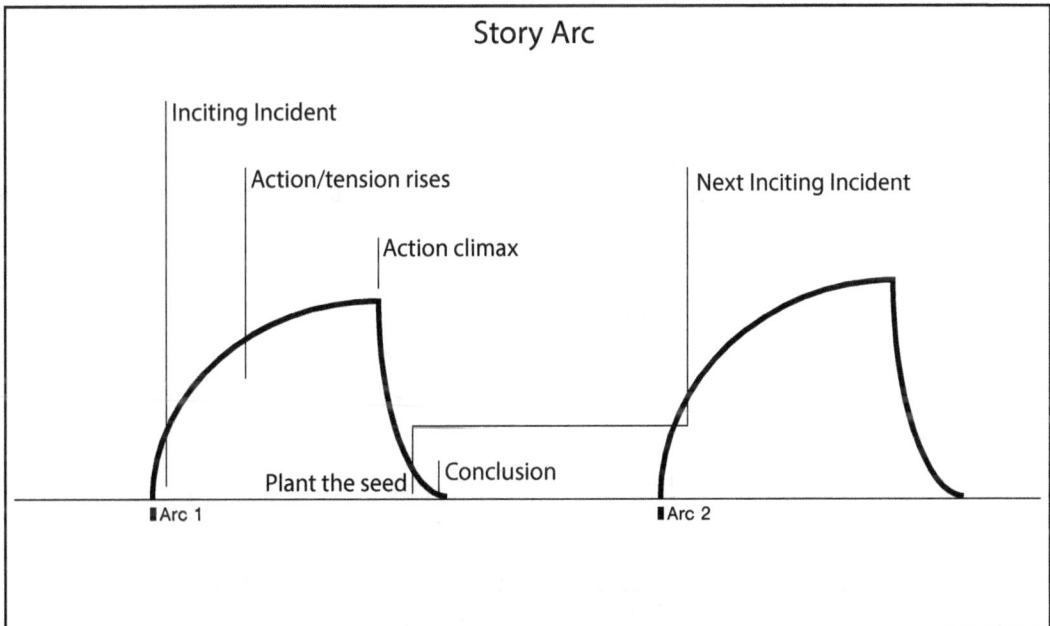

Story Arc
- Inciting Incident
- Action/tension rises
- Action climax
- Next Inciting Incident
- Plant the seed
- Conclusion
- Arc 1
- Arc 2

For a moment, look back to the different types of book structures covered in Chapter 11. The chronological and functional structures are linear. Chronological structures follow time, and functional structures build upon previous incidents or skills. Story arcs within these structures are also linear—one follows the other.

The convergent and mosaic structures are also linear, but because the story arcs follow different participants, the stories are told separately, and the timelines may overlap. You may tell one participant's story up to a certain point, and then turn to another participant for a few chapters, then back to the first participant. You will use each participant's part of the story to weave together the whole.

The memoir structure is not linear. It is a series of vignettes, so each vignette will have its own story arc, but may be completely unrelated to the others.

Your book may have many story arcs. When you look at your detailed timeline, look for the events that have the greatest dramatic potential—where you experienced turning points, successes, failures, new beginnings, reversals or disasters. From your entire inventory of events, begin with the events that can be told in the most vivid way.

If you are not writing in vignettes, you will then connect the story arcs by narrative summary—a way to fast-forward past the dull stuff.

Story Arc Ingredients

Satisfying story arcs follow this pattern—an inciting incident (an event that initiates change), rising tension (conflict that leads to action), climax (a turning

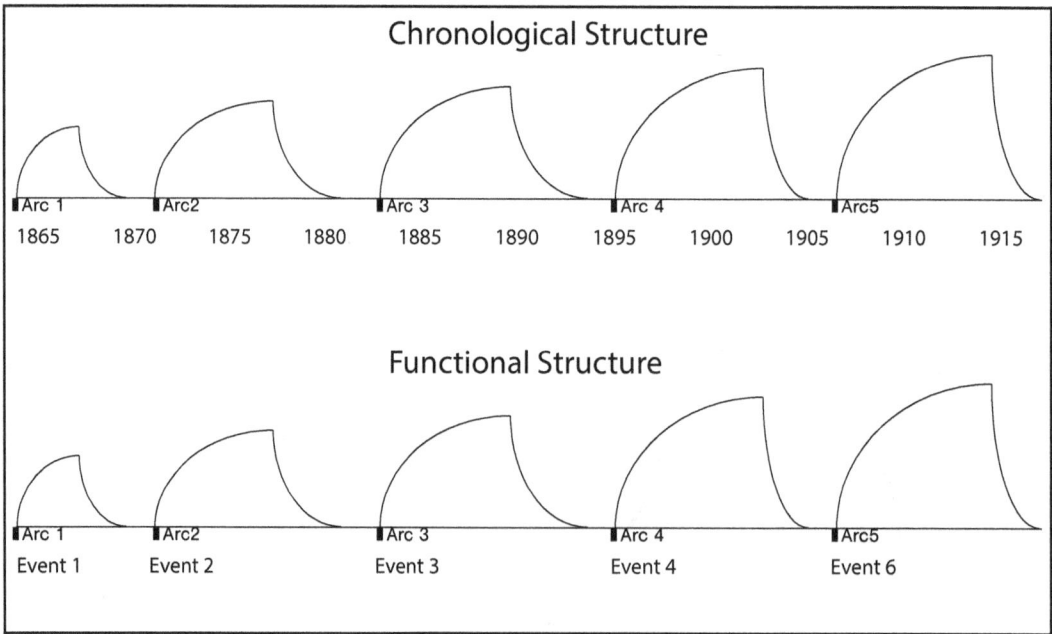

Chronological Structure

Arc 1	Arc2		Arc 3		Arc 4		Arc5	
1865	1870	1875	1880	1885	1890	1895	1900	1905	1910	1915

Functional Structure

Arc 1	Arc2	Arc 3	Arc 4	Arc5
Event 1	Event 2	Event 3	Event 4	Event 6

Plot diagram for the chronological and functional structures.

point), and resolution (conclusion). Story arcs may also include subplots, setting or back story. They also must have beginnings, middles, and ends.

Inciting Incident

An inciting incident is what upsets the day-to-day and causes a change. Not all inciting incidents are major events. A wedding certainly changes the status of that couple's day-to-day life, but it is not as dramatic as a business failure or a natural disaster. An inciting incident must cause a change.

Conflict

Conflict is the root of drama—the element that gives the reader an emotional attachment to the story and the people in it. Conflict is what builds tension up to a turning point.

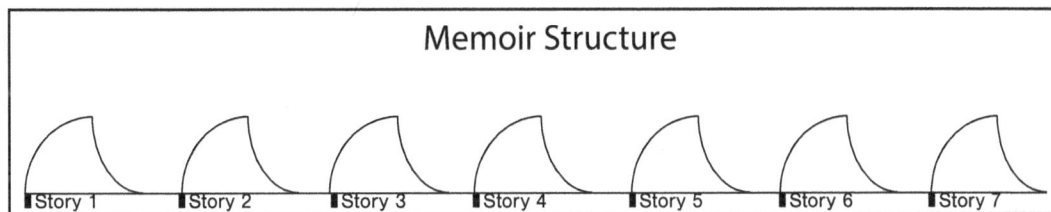

Plot diagram for the memoir structure.

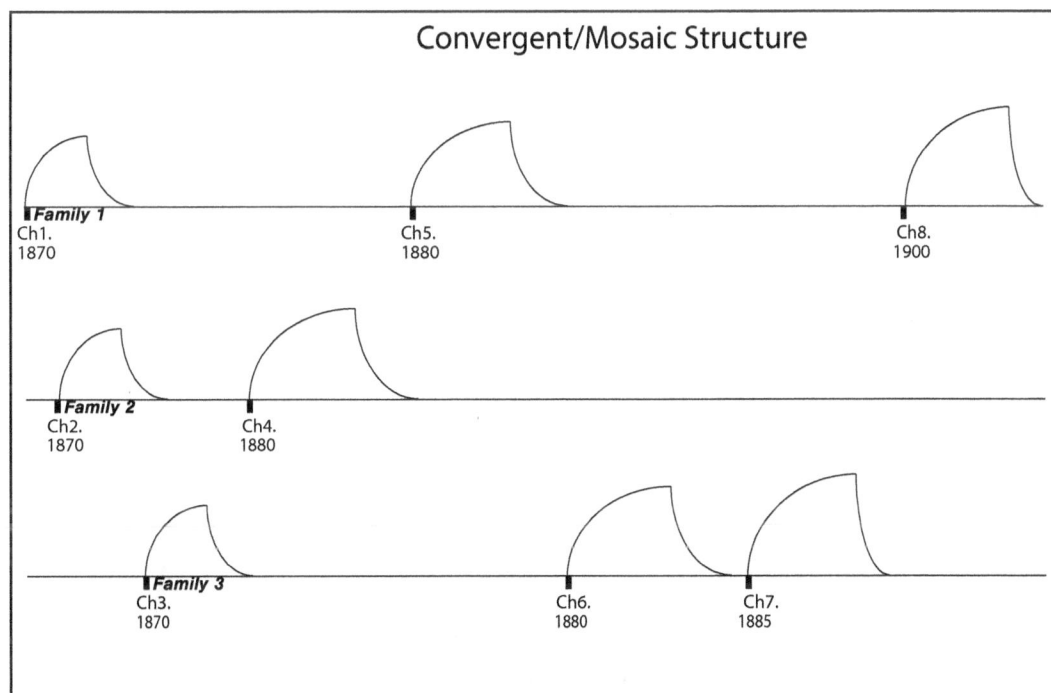

Plot diagram for the convergent and mosaic structures.

Conflict is an odd concept in memoir, however. Real people live with conflict and without it. Motivation, rather than conflict, may be a better way to describe why you did what you did.

Conflict can be categorized as:

Man against Man. Man against man may be a struggle between groups for dominance, such as workers against owners. It can be a struggle to gain position, such as working one's way up through the ranks. It may be an actual disagreement between people, such as a court case. Man against man can also be described in bigger terms, such as the effect of wars, regional economic collapse or the effects of sudden wealth.

Man against Society. There have always been people who have questioned societal norms, and they tend to struggle until their ideas gain acceptance. Today, gay couples seeking acceptance for same-sex marriages is an example. In this case the struggle is against ideas, ideals, or tradition.

Man against Nature. History is full of people who struggled against nature whether they were building the Erie Canal, clearing the wilderness, watching hail ruin the crops or crossing the oceans on stormy seas. Setting can play a role as important as the people.

Man against Himself. Man against himself describes an internal conflict or self-motivation—what motivated you to do the things you did, or what held you back, if the struggle proved insurmountable.

When choosing events to include in your story arcs, look for the places where conflict or motivation initiated a change.

Story Arc

Inciting Incident

Action/tension rises

Next Inciting Incident

Action climax

Plant the seed | Conclusion

Arc 1 | Summary | Arc 2

Action

Action is the life blood of good storytelling—where the reader gets to experience events as you experienced them. The action scenes are where you will engage the senses, use historically accurate details to make the scene true to life, and move the story arc toward the climax.

Climax

The climax is where events inspire a change. A climax can be dramatic. For example: "We left everything behind and ran for the forest when the Gestapo arrived in town." A climax can also be subtle. For example: "After the promotion, the men called me 'Sir,' but they were the same men I had been fighting and bleeding alongside for the past eleven months." Either way, a turning point occurs, and the tension of the story lessens as you work through the resolution.

Resolution

Resolution is necessary, not only to finish the story, but also to give the readers a break. Non-stop tension is exhausting. Even the biggest, baddest action movies stop the helicopters and explosions every now and again to let the audience take a breather.

Subplots

Subplots are one way to introduce other characters, give new information, reveal back story, or reinforce the overarching theme without interrupting the story arc directly. A subplot also may be a way to introduce the inciting incident for the next story arc.

Setting

Setting grounds the reader in specifics about where and when the story is taking place. The setting can play a role as important as a main character. You can establish the setting by describing its qualities: the closeness or enormity of the space, whether the atmosphere was tension-filled or relaxed, as well as the texture, peculiarities or uniqueness of the place.

Back Story

The back story is made up of events in the past that affect the story's present. For example, you could explain your struggle to succeed in college by your history with dyslexia as a child.

Scene

Plots are made up of story arcs, and story arcs are made up of scenes. Story arcs work the same way in your book as they do on television. They are the building blocks—where all of the storytelling takes place. You will use scenes to set the stage (time and place), to engage the senses, to show action and how the characters are moved or changed in some way. Scenes are also the cause and effect for the next scene.

You can give scenes different distances for different effects. A scene with a far-off view gives the reader the big picture—how vast the landscape is, or how crushingly close the crowds are in a major city. A scene with a middle-distance could make the reader feel the chaos that takes place backstage during a performance or the heat within a blacksmith shop. Closeup scenes are often personal and filled with emotion—cradling a dying child or struggling to unhook a seatbelt as the car fills with water.

Scenes are where you bring the story to life—where you make the reader believe that he or she is in the thick of the action along with you.

Beginnings

The book, as well as each story arc, must have a beginning, a middle, and an end. The beginning may determine whether or not the reader becomes engaged in the story and continues reading.

In 19th century literature, authors could leisurely set up the scene and slowly introduce characters and situations before anything dramatic took place. Today, readers are not as patient.

> What's not done today is the immediate helping of back story right after that (implied) "once upon a time." We don't fill readers in on the protagonist's life for the past ten years leading up to the story's actually beginning. We also don't spend a lot of time describing the village he lives in, the street he walks down each day to work, his waking habits, or the copious details of each room he enters. Or every bite of the breakfast he ingests or the primary colors of the songbird outside his window. No sir. No ma'am. Not anymore.
>
> —**Les Edgerton**
> *Hooked: Write Fiction That Grabs Readers at*
> *Page One and Never Lets Them Go*

Beginning in the middle of the action may seem as if you are starting the story arc off at the peak of the tension and conflict. It is not. The inciting incident is the situation that causes you to make a change from a known situation, even if it is a bad situation, to the unknown—where the outcome is uncertain. In the real world, the consequences of the change are what build tension and lead to the climax.

Along with the inciting incident, your beginning should include: enough set-up to let the reader understand the place and era; only enough back story to set the inciting incident in motion; a hint at the obstacles that result from the inciting incident (tension or conflict to come); a revelation of what kind of characters you and the other people in the story were by their reactions to the inciting incident; and to lead it all off, the best sentence in the entire story—no pressure there.

The following begins the first story arc in Ian Frazier's book, *Family*:

> The Twentieth Century began on a Tuesday. On that day, all my great-grandparents but one were living in Ohio or Indiana. Mr. and Mrs. Harry E. Frazier and their four children lived in Indianapolis, in a neighborhood of many vacant lots and telephone poles. Mr. and Mrs. Louis W. Wickham and their three children and a hired girl lived at 237 Benedict Avenue, Norwalk, Ohio. The Reverend John Backman and his wife and two daughters lived in New Knoxville, Ohio, where he was pastor of the First German Reformed Church. Mrs. Elizabeth C. Hursh and her three grown daughters and one son lived at 86 Greenfield Street, Tiffin, Ohio; her husband, Professor O.A.S. Hursh, lay in a nearby cemetery, beneath a $200 monument inscribed with a Latin quotation and the years, months and days of his life.

Immediately, Frazier lets us know who the main characters are and that the story will begin just after the turn of the Twentieth Century.

Oftentimes, it is easiest to tackle that first sentence last. Write the story arc first. Afterward, you may be better able to encapsulate the story arc in a riveting opening line.

Middles

The middle fulfills the promise you made in the beginning. The middle supports, develops and sustains the story. In the middle, you have more latitude to vary the pace, to introduce more back story, develop new characters or fill out the setting.

Ends

End the book and each story arc in a way that is satisfying. Hit the climax and wind it up. If you end abruptly, or with nagging questions unanswered, the reader will feel cheated.

Readers should be able to tell that the story arc has concluded. A common problem with endings is that they do not—that is—end. If you have more information you wish to include, look for a place in the middle to introduce it, do not wait until the end to throw in leftover pieces and parts.

Your last line, as your first, should give the reader something to ponder. Judy Garland's last line in *The Wizard of Oz*, "And oh, Auntie Em, there's no place like home," is satisfying because her troubles are over, and she got what she wanted.

Paul Newman ends the film *Butch Cassidy and the Sundance Kid* with irony when he says, "Oh good. For a moment there, I thought we were in trouble," as Butch and Sundance charge into a hail of gunfire.

You get the last word, make the most of it.

Character

People are the most important elements of any story. The best stories are not about what happens but to whom it happens. In a memoir, you may have to guard against pumping yourself up or pulling yourself down too much. And, you do not have the luxury of forming the other characters the way you want them to be either. You can, however, characterize people—make them seem more real than words on a page, by what you reveal about them.

It is relatively easy to characterize people you have known. For example: "Grandma was fastidious in her appearance, and always wore her thick, salt and pepper hair swept up in the style she adopted as a young schoolteacher before the war." It is a little more difficult to accurately characterize yourself.

Your challenge is to describe yourself and the other people in the story in a way that makes the reader feel something for you and for them and want to know more, while revealing yourself and the others in a way that is accurate.

Note: When referring to a "character," I am always referring to a real person and not to a fictionalized character.

Characterization Techniques

One mistake inexperienced writers often make is to start off describing every detail about a person. While you do gain a sense of a person when you see them for the first time, you do not learn everything about them all at once. You get to know people over time. Sprinkle in character traits and descriptions as they fit naturally into the story.

Another way to work in character traits and descriptions is to alter the distance from which you view the character. A closeup view will yield more intimate details—a chipped tooth, a quirky laugh, or the smell of her favorite perfume. A middle-distance view will show things you could observe from across a room, such as his gait, her beautifully tailored suit, or the way he fiddles with his glasses. Elements from a long-distance view may come more from documentary evidence and from a bit of the reader's imagination—she worked in a 50s beauty shop or he was a gambler and Las Vegas Elvis lookalike.

There are three ways to characterize people: directly, indirectly or by creating a general impression.

Create a General Impression

Create a general impression by using what the reader already knows about places, landscapes, professions, cities, neighborhoods and so on. The following example creates an impression based upon the description of the character's job: "He worked a hardscrabble farm of eighty acres in a place where rain was a ghost and the blowing wind a constant companion."

The following is a distinctly different impression based also upon a job: "He was a dentist, by trade, at a time when any local barber would offer to pull teeth."

Avoid stereotyping while creating a general impression. Not all New Englanders were Puritans, and not all Westerners were cowboys. Using specific words and phrases will help. The phrase "a hardscrabble farm of eighty acres" paints a more vivid picture than "he worked the land."

Direct Characterization

One way to reveal character traits is by doing so directly—to describe his or her personality. A direct description, of course, is your opinion.

There are multitudes of character-trait lists online. The following is a short list to get you started:

Able	Expert	Melancholy	Selfish
Adventurous	Faithful	Mischievous	Shy
Bossy	Generous	Organized	Stubborn
Brave	Helpful	Prim	Tireless

The story mechanics section below has more information about the concept of "show, don't tell." For now, direct characterization (telling) is to make a blanket statement about the person. For example: "He was organized." However, indirect characterization (showing) is often a more vivid way to describe the character. For example: "His office was so neat, there was never a book off the shelf or a paper out of place."

Indirect Characterization

Indirect characterization will reveal an individual's personality through their appearance, attributes, mannerisms, thoughts, or effect on other people.

Physical Appearance

It is natural to be curious about what people looked like. Physical description could include: race or ethnic group, height, weight, body type, age, physical condition, eye color, hair color, hair style, facial hair, distinguishing features or physical imperfections. Personal appearance goes along with physical description including clothing, clothing styles, grooming (neat or unkempt), and so on.

One caution about introducing physical characteristics is to avoid making the person sound as if he or she is on a wanted poster. "The suspect is 5'9", with brown hair, brown eyes, wears a shoddy pea coat, and is known to frequent the downtown bars." You get the idea.

A better way to introduce a physical description is to combine it with action. For example: "He was a lumberjack. His 6' 2" frame must have been honed like steel after a lifetime swinging an ax to cut notches on the area's ninety foot tall trees. Trees with trunks so thick it took crews on a sixteen foot long, two-man saw to bring them down." It is easier to envision the size and strength of a man who is swinging an ax than giving his height alone.

Mannerisms

Mannerisms are habits. The things people do or say without thinking. Mannerisms can describe behavior—how people act in different situations. Did she warmly embrace people or was she cool towards them? Was his gait was more a march or a stroll? Was he more likely to pet a dog or be annoyed by it?

Describing the effect of a mannerism paints a more vivid picture than making a statement about a mannerism. For example: "He rarely relaxed without a dog in his lap," is more revealing than "He loved dogs."

Mannerisms can describe speech or speech patterns. Did she sign each letter "fondly yours" or "love you always"? Did he start his stories the same way? Did he use colloquialisms? Were they common to the area or from another place or time? Were words from another language thrown in occasionally? Did she use jargon from her profession? Did she speak quickly? Was he soft-spoken, loud and boisterous, or colorful?

I often get the question, "Can you use dialog in a memoir?" The answer is yes, if you are relaying what you have heard, or if you are quoting from a court record, diary or letter. For example: "Grandma never called them 'the boys' the way we did. She always called them 'the fellas.'"

Giving the reader a bit of flavor using a person's accent or unique way of speaking is fine. A lengthy segment of "pahking cahs in Hahvad yahd," however, is difficult to read (and can be annoying).

Mannerisms can also describe gestures. Did he often push his glasses up on his nose? Did she twist her hair when she was nervous? Did he use his hands when he spoke? Mannerisms can include personality quirks, eccentricities, temperament, bad habits, vices, or sense of humor.

Including mannerisms, creates a sense of the person. Using too many mannerisms, however, is a pitfall. It can make the person seem unnatural, unreal or unbelievable.

Attributes

Some attributes are harder to categorize but may influence the way a person is characterized. The following are some attributes to consider: religion, years of schooling, family background, status, income, occupation, skills, abilities, talents, military service, hobbies, interests, sports, or pastimes. Any of these attributes could also affect mannerisms, thoughts or his or her effect on others.

Thoughts

Another way to characterize someone indirectly is by their thoughts or an expression of their opinion (attitudes). One thing you *cannot* do, is to get inside a person's head and tell the story as if you know what he or she was thinking. For example, "He drove our crew hard because he *knew* the rocket had to be perfect before it was rolled to the launch pad."

Rather than telling what a character thinks to explain his action, it is better to let the reader experience the story dramatically at the same time the character experiences it. For example: "He drove our crew hard throughout 1967 and 1968. After the loss of Apollo earlier that year, crews examined every piece of hardware and every line of code. Work days stretched to fifteen hours or more, and it was not unusual for crews to spend their weekends taking one more look before Apollo 7 was rolled to the launch pad."

It is easy to assume what someone must have been thinking when events were taking place. If you have direct evidence, then quote it. If you do not, tell the story in a way that does not assume thoughts not in evidence (so to speak).

Other issues that fall into knowing someone's thoughts include prejudices, gripes, political opinions, goals, and fears.

Effect on Others

What effect does the person have on other people? How do others feel about him or react to her? Here again, you cannot get into the heads of your friends and associates either, but there may be evidence of relationships that you can write about. For example: "The newspaper ran a half-page article about his funeral. Every member of his Masonic lodge was in attendance. Even a few members who had left the area, returned to take part. The cemetery sexton said he had never seen so many people in the cemetery at a single gathering in the thirty years he had worked there."

Story Mechanics

Narrative writing takes five essential forms: narration, exposition, action, description, and summary. Most writers need all five to tell a complete story.

Narration

Use narration to reveal information about your characters. It is through narration that you will "show, not tell." Telling is left to exposition. To *tell* is to give information. To *show* is more often to withhold it—to create an impression rather than making a flat statement.

> *Telling*: He was a bully.
>
> *Showing*: The little ones were the best targets. Easiest to shove. The most likely to cry. And when they cried, he mocked them—mercilessly.

> *Telling*: She wanted his attention.
>
> *Showing*: She moved between her boyfriend and the television, and slowly dropped her robe.

> *Telling*: He was an artist.
>
> *Showing*: He was never without a sketch pad. He sketched people, animals, architecture—whatever caught his eye for a moment. But it was a small girl who made him famous. The look in her eye and the tear on her cheek, melts the hardest of hearts and stops museum-goers in their tracks.

Use narration to engage the reader's imagination. Put yourself and other characters in the thick of things with the action moving the story forward. How you or the character reacts to what is happening will reveal the type of people you are.

Exposition

Use exposition to give information—to get to the point. Exposition will not move the story forward; it will not contribute to the action, it will explain.

Sometimes, a quick explanation is all you need. For example: "He was a pharmacist." Other times, a subject is so unfamiliar to the reader that it requires explanation. For example, if your neighbor ran a television repair shop in the 1960s, the concept of replacing cathode ray tubes may be so unfamiliar to your readers, that you would want to explain it.

The right piece of exposition can explain, clarify or enhance the action. The wrong piece can stop a story in its tracks. Use exposition to help the reader become familiar with new information, old-fashioned expressions, foreign words, or how tasks were accomplished in the past.

Action

Action is where all of the drama is. It is where the story moves forward, one step after another. Enough action strung together, and you have narration.

Word choice is important in action, because the more precise and concise the words or expressions, the more vivid the action.

Rhythm or pacing can also influence the effect of action. Shorter sentences help create suspense. Longer sentences slow the action down. A combination of long and short sentences can create a sense of chaos or uncertainty in the action.

Action also has to be logical. There must be a stimulus before a response. Action on paper has to happen the way it would be experienced in real life.

Use action to advance the story, to build tension, to reach the climax, and resolve the event.

Description

Description should enhance the story—to inform or explain, set a mood, or give sensory details—not included for its own sake.

Description can inform, clarify, show how things work or give examples. An informative description may be what the reader needs to understand the action or its consequences. For example: "Trading in their old 12-pound, smooth bore Howitzer for a new Whitworth, allowed the men to remain across the river out of range of the enemy's guns, while firing deadly shots that landed within inches of their aim."

Description can be used to create a mood—to create a feeling of being at the scene. A suggestive description can evoke a feeling or suggest the atmosphere of the scene. For example: "The attacking force was estimated to have exceeded 15,000 men. Men, who in the moment before Longstreet signaled Pickett to charge, looked out over the unmarred slope of green, tall grass to a stand of trees on the crest of the ridge nearly a mile in the distance."

A dramatized description with good sensory details sprinkled into the narrative as the story unfolds can help readers feel the experience, not just be told about it. For example: "The snap of the flags covered the sound of nervous conversations as Major General George Pickett mounted his horse. As Pickett motioned his men forward, a massive Confederate artillery bombardment filled the air with acrid smoke and flying debris, but did little to quiet the Union artillery and rifles fired from the advantage of high ground."

Use description to help the reader experience events and feel the action. Accurate description also builds your authority as the author, and lends credibility to the story.

Publish a Memoir

Summary

Summaries are a way to fast forward past events that took place and should be acknowledged, but are not important enough to a story arc or scene to tell in full detail. Summaries can also serve to bridge story arcs together.

Summaries can be informative, giving the reader a sense of moving through time by a sequence of events. For example: "He joined up on his seventeenth birthday using his brother's identification. Six weeks later, the war ended. He spent the next three years in a peacetime Navy, swabbing decks and writing letters home complaining that he had missed all the action."

Summaries can also be descriptive giving the reader the quality of the events taking place while advancing the story in time. For example: "David's three years in the Navy were uneventful, unless you count the numerous shore leaves in exotic ports, and occasional stints in the brig. Mother chose not to acknowledge the jail time. In an odd sort of way, however, Dad seemed proud of it, given the boastful stories he told."

Use summary to skip the boring stuff, and to move your characters through time and space to where the next story arc or action begins.

Pitfalls

There are a few pitfalls common to writing memoirs—items or information that have vanished with time, anachronisms, and superfluous information from source material that begs to be included.

Qualifiers

There may be times when you would like to describe something that influenced how you or your family lived, but you do not have perfect recollection or evidence to point to *directly* for proof. For example, you may want to describe your parents' first house, but have no idea what that house looked like exactly. It is acceptable to describe what was typical for the area and time, as long as you use a qualifier letting the reader know that you are not describing the actual house, but one that is representative.

Anachronisms

An anachronism is an item appropriate to a period *other* than that in which it exists or is described. If you chose to conduct research, I am certain you looked for historically accurate details to help describe your day-to-day life. However, it is not enough, for example, to establish that the Easy-Bake Oven was invented in 1963. If you were an infant that year, you probably did not have one—at least not yet. Anachronisms can slip in that easily.

Words or expressions specific to a place (or an era) are another area where anachronisms can creep in. Not all Southerners describe the exterior place where their rocking chair resides, for example, as a "veranda." And not all Northerners call the spot near the front door a "stoop."

Fact check early and often. If you are at all unsure, check again before you add the description or use the expression in your story.

Techniques

The following techniques will help you write in a compelling way.

Hooks

Hooks are used in advertising to gain the reader's attention and make the reader want to know more. They are used the same way in narratives, often as beginnings of scenes or story arcs. Skip the slow, deliberate windup and jump right into the action of the story.

One of my favorite examples of a hook comes from the opening lines of the short story "The Bad Part of Town," by Les Edgerton: "He was so mean that wherever he was standing became the bad part of town." How could you not want to know more about that character?

Les Edgerton's book, *Hooked: Write Fiction that Grabs Readers at Page One and Never Lets Them Go*, is a primer on starting a story with a bang.

Foreshadowing

Foreshadowing alludes to action that will happen later in the book. It builds anticipation, dramatic tension or suspense.

In the Prologue of his book, *Only a Few Bones: A True Account of the Rolling Ford Tragedy and Its Aftermath*, John Colletta sets up the events that will take place in the book, but ends with a good example of foreshadowing:

> The packet Joe intended to board this morning to return to Vicksburg never showed. So he is spending one more night in the Ring & Co. store.
>
> His last.

Without the other setup, those three lines not only would have been foreshadowing, but a cliffhanger.

Flashbacks

Flashbacks are the most common way to introduce elements of the past that affect the story in the present. They can also be annoying if overused. A good flashback will move the reader seamlessly from the story's present using a catalyst to trigger a release of information about the past.

For example: "It was a miracle to see her standing on that stage accepting her diploma. She came so close to losing her life a decade earlier. Her bicycle was her freedom and giggly spirit all rolled into one. She used to ride at breakneck speed until the accident. Afterward, it was months before she said a word, nearly a year before she took another step. And now, thankfully, she strides with perfect confidence across the stage."

An inartful use of a flashback will leave readers wondering about what is happening when. Watch the tenses carefully. If you are already telling a story in the past, and you jump even further back for a flashback, returning to the story's present (in the actual past) can be problematic.

Transitions

Readers today are sophisticated media consumers, so transitions in your book can mimic those found in other entertainment.

The jump cut is the most common transition used in books today. Put a little white space on the paper to indicate that something has changed and go on to the next scene. Readers do not need the big "back at the ranch" sign to let them know the scene has changed.

On occasion, you may want to introduce a time change, such as "It had been two seasons since I had hit the ball out of the park with the bases loaded."

Another way to transition from one topic to the next is to use a phrase taken from the last paragraph to begin the next paragraph. For example:

"Ever was my frustration with his *slow and methodical* pace.

Slow and methodical, however, was what made his reputation. His craftsmanship was second to none."

Use transitions to lead the reader from one scene to the next while minimizing any confusion.

Pace

One of the most common mistakes is letting the story slow to a pace that the reader skips ahead to see what happens next. To quicken the pace, examine the manuscript for anything unnecessary—setup descriptions, empty scenes, overlong explanation, and so on. Shorter chapters and shorter sentences will quicken the pace.

To slow the pace down, use longer sentences and chapters, spend more time setting a mood, or give a more thorough explanation.

Anecdotes

Anecdotes are short stories. They are a way to reminisce, make readers laugh, give a caution against doing something unwise, to persuade or inspire.

The best anecdotes in a memoir are those that illustrate something about the character of the person in the story.

The following is an example of an anecdote from David Bruce's eBook, *Mark Twain Anecdotes and Quotes*: "When Samuel Langhorne Clemens was a schoolboy, he was very good at spelling, and usually won the Friday afternoon spelling bee in his class. However, one Friday, he deliberately misspelled a word so a young girl he liked would win."

Analogy

An analogy is a comparison used to explain an object or an idea giving readers a way to use something familiar to gain insight into something unfamiliar.

Analogies can be simple, such as, "There is a resemblance between the boy and his father." They can also be more complex, such as: "A doctor searching for a difficult diagnosis is like a detective searching for clues in an unsolved crime."

Similes and metaphors are specific methods used to create analogies.

A simile compares one object to another quite different from it. For example: "Standing before the class explaining his science project he was *as brave as a lion*," or "The robbery suspect was *squirming like a fish out of water*." Similes often employ the words "like" or "as" to make the comparison.

A metaphor makes a direct comparison between objects that are different from each other but share similar characteristics. For example: "After we sampled the pie, Mother was *boiling mad*," or "After we made it past the kitchen door, it was *clear sailing* ... at least until Mother caught up with us."

Analogies, similes, and metaphors can add color to a story. Be careful not to use them too often or to reach for an easy cliché because it is familiar.

Argumentation

A genealogical proof statement is a form of argumentation where you lay out the evidence in a logical way and follow a set of rules that lead to a logical conclusion. Within a memoir where the stories take the lead role, stopping to make a genealogical proof statement may create a clash of styles.

If you wish to posit a theory about who your ancestor was and use the methods of a genealogical proof statement to present your case, you certainly may. However, because the style of storytelling is so different than a proof statement, you may want to push that information into the preface to setup the basis for the storytelling rather than mixing the two together.

Persuasion

Persuasion has a completely different role than argumentation. Persuasion is not so much about seeking the truth (or proof), as it is in changing minds. Using your memoir to change readers' minds can be a trap if you tailor the facts to shape the reader's opinion.

Tense

It can be difficult to keep tenses straight. For the most part, it is best to write the stories in the past tense since they have already happened.

On occasion, moving a scene into the present tense—yours at the time or a character's present—will give the scene more immediacy helping the reader feel more involved. In that case, whether or not to move from the past tense to the present can be a matter of style. You may be just as able to convey the scene in an equally vivid way in the past tense.

When describing records, however, you must use the present tense because the records still exist. For example: "Dad *appears* in the Bourbon County court records as the Clerk of the District Court."

Effective, engaging storytelling will strengthen your stories and bind your reader's interest to the people the stories memorialize.

∂୨ৎఞ

If you find yourself in need of help writing your book, you could engage the services of a personal historian or a ghostwriter.

Working with a Personal Historian

What is the difference between hiring a professional genealogist or historian and a personal historian? Professional genealogists or historians are hired primarily to conduct research. Personal historians are skilled interviewers. If you need help recalling and recording your experiences, a personal historian can help. Personal historians can also help you create a family, community, organization or business history. If you are organizing a reunion, for example, you may want a personal historian there to record each member of the family.

Where to Find a Personal Historian

Check with the Association of Personal Historians (www.personalhistorians. org). Their website has a handy "Find a Personal Historian" section where you can select a skill set plus define the area where the interviews will take place. The Association of Personal Historians lists the following skills for their members: audio histories, books, video (DVDs), archives preservation, editing and writing, genealogical research, photo digitizing and restoration, websites and blogs, transcripts of audio or video recordings, talks or workshops on creating or writing family histories, project management as you create your own project, tributes, memorials, and specialty projects such as heritage cookbooks, planning reunions and special events.

Initial Consultation

The initial consultation lasting 30 to 60 minutes should be free. While you are interviewing the personal historian make certain, they have the same passion for your project as you do and that they understand the nature of what you are asking. If you have survived something difficult such as war, it may be different to interview you than someone who has less intense, emotional experiences. Your personality and comfort with conveying your story will play a role in how successful the personal historian will be, as well.

Expectations and Deadlines

Be clear about your expectations and deadlines, but realize that some interviews are more difficult than others. It may take a period of time to establish a relationship before much substantive interviewing can take place. After an initial interview, the personal historian should be able to give you an estimate of how many hours it may take to complete the project. Ask whether there are other projects on the schedule that could interfere with your project.

Equipment

Ask what equipment will be used to record the interview. Most personal historians have video equipment with good microphones so that the audio portion of the video is clear. Good interviewers will help you forget about the camera after a few minutes.

Fees

Fees vary greatly, so shop around. Ask what is included in the price, and if there are additional fees for travel or research beyond the interview. Make sure any editing of video or audio is included, along with any transcription or writing. Expect to make a down payment, a payment(s) as the work progresses and a final payment upon end product delivery. The schedule of payments, however, should be negotiable.

End Product

Be clear about what you expect as the final product—a written history, a multimedia presentation that can be viewed on television or a computer, a website—or some combination of these. The personal historian should give you suggestions for how still photographs or documents could be included in the project and have the skills to prep those images for the final product.

Copyrights

Be sure to obtain the copyrights to your own story. Although, it could be to your advantage to negotiate away the personal historian's fee if he or she wants to write a book or produce a film of his or her own based upon your story.

Portfolio

Many personal historians have a portfolio online. Also check them out online in the popular social media sites such as Facebook, LinkedIn or Twitter. Look for testimonials but also ask for references.

Services Included

It may be difficult to estimate the number of interviews needed to capture the stories you want. Most personal historians will include a certain number of interviews in the estimate, plus the final product(s) such as a book or multimedia project. Leave open the possibility that additional interviews may be needed. For people whose stories are difficult to tell, it may take awhile for the personal historian to establish the kind of trust and rapport needed to make the stories flow.

Write a Formal Proposal or Contract

Write a formal proposal or contract that includes a complete project description, all services and fees, deadlines, how you will communicate, and how the final product(s) will be delivered to you.

❧❧

Working with a Ghostwriter

Working with a ghostwriter is a little different than working with a personal historian. A ghostwriter will take your ideas and turn them into a book. An astounding fifty percent of books in the marketplace today are written by talented ghostwriters, mostly for people who have great ideas but neither the time nor the skills to produce a well-written book (article, speech, movie script or screenplay).

The typical process includes an interview with you to understand your ideas and the scope of your planned book. The ghostwriter will take a look at what you have written, and may conduct additional research, mostly to help him or her better understand the events and the time period. The ghostwriter will then produce the manuscript in the format you agree upon. In most cases, book manuscripts are delivered complete, fully edited, and ready for typesetting. Your name will appear as the author, the ghostwriter's name will not appear, even as a co-author. The ghostwriter will be paid a fee, and if the book is sold, the ghostwriter will expect no royalties or further compensation.

It is best, of course, to use a ghostwriter who specializes in memoirs. You will find an abundance of ghostwriters through the Association of Ghostwriters (associationofghostwriters.org) and their individual websites. When searching the Association's website, I found several who have obvious memoir writing credentials. If you cannot find someone with memoir writing experience specifically, look for a ghostwriter with creative non-fiction experience.

Portfolio

Ask to see books the ghostwriter has written. Public portfolios can be problematic for ghostwriters who work for people who would rather the world not know they used a ghostwriter. Most ghostwriters also write under their own names. Choosing a ghostwriter who is familiar with the publishing process because they have been through it, is a good idea.

Cost

Costs vary widely from one ghostwriter to the next. Most give an estimate based upon the scope of the project. If you have a limited budget, let the ghostwriter know before he or she gives you an estimate. Be prepared for how much a ghostwritten book may cost. Professional ghostwriters charge professional fees for professional work. Be wary of ghostwriters who cannot possibly make a living by what they are charging. You do not want to hire someone who is perpetually overbooked, or who subcontracts out the writing to a cheap site overseas.

Expectations

The interviews should give you a sense of whether you and the ghostwriters have the same expectations for the book. If expectations differ greatly, find a different ghostwriter. At the end of the initial set of interviews, the ghostwriter should understand how you want the book written, how you wish to be perceived, and who your audience is.

Communication

After an initial set of interviews to lay out the project, the ghostwriter may need to check in with you from time to time to get your opinion. Rarely will that exceed more than an hour a week since most ghostwriters are accomplished project managers who can keep a project moving forward on schedule.

Approvals

You may want to see chapters as completed to gain a sense of how the project is proceeding. Keep in mind that the chapters you will be seeing may still be in their rough form. You will not want to put a final stamp of approval on the work until after the manuscript has been fully edited.

A full-length book can take as long as six months, and completion deadlines will reflect this. Payment deadlines vary from ghostwriter to ghostwriter, but often include half down, a quarter at a determined point in the project, and the final quarter upon completion.

Services Included

Most ghostwriters include a certain number of revisions in the price of the project to allow for you to request changes. Professional editing is often included within the contract, as well. Most ghostwriters have editors they work with often, and will contract for that service on their own.

Write a Formal Proposal or Contract

Most ghostwriters have a contract format they regularly use. If he or she does not, write a formal proposal or contract that includes a complete project description, all services and fees, deadlines, how you will communicate, and how the final product will be delivered to you.

❧❧

Learning the mechanics of storytelling requires patience and practice. If you are willing to try out the techniques, they will take your story arcs from flatline to fantastic, your characters from uninteresting to fascinating, and help you write a memoir your relatives will actually read.

Chapter 13

Creating Your Own Style Guide

Styles vary from newspaper to newspaper, magazine to magazine, and publisher to publisher. There is no one, all-encompassing style guide. There are a few stylistic conventions you may want to conform to because they are what readers will expect, and, usually, because the style helps reading comprehension. The final decisions, however, are up to you.

The purpose of creating your own style guide is to save time while you are writing the first draft and later when you edit. Create a file or a hand-written list that you can keep handy as you write to record each style decision you make as you make it. That way, you can adhere to your style guide as the book progresses.

Industry Style Guides

The two most used style guides are William Strunk & E.B. White's, *The Elements of Style* (or William Strunk Jr.'s *The Elements of Style, 2014*) and *The Chicago Manual of Style, 16th Edition.* There are dozens of other style guides available, most of which are designed for students, business writing, technical writing or other specific purposes.

Evidence Explained by Elizabeth Shown Mills is a source citation guide not a style guide for the body of the manuscript. You may choose to use her style guide for your footnotes or endnotes, or not.

If you have no experience with formatting a manuscript, you may want to jump ahead and read the four chapters on typesetting to get an idea of what conventions to follow during the production stage before you create styles that conflict with what will make the book look its best and read easiest.

Abbreviations and Acronyms

Use abbreviations to avoid incessant repetition of long expressions. If you abbreviate, be consistent and provide the reader with a key to the abbreviations in the front matter.

Acronyms are common. NASA is a good example. Few people will misidentify NASA as something other than the National Aeronautic and Space Administration. For most acronyms there is no need for punctuation between the letters—so NASA, not N.A.S.A. As with abbreviations, if you create acronyms that are not familiar to the reader, use the full name in the text first, followed by the acronym in parentheses. In some cases, you may want to use the full name a few times so that the reader becomes familiar with the name before switching to an acronym. For example: Rocky Mountain & Overland Stagecoach Company (RM&OS Co.) Include the acronym in your list of abbreviations and acronyms in the front matter.

Genealogical Charts

For the most part, I consider genealogical charts as images rather than text, but I include them here because they can help readers become familiar with the relationships between people at a glance.

Genealogical charts do not have to be uniform throughout the book, but should be consistent enough in appearance and content that the reader can find roughly the same information in each. In other words, do not use a four-generation pedigree chart on one page, and a ten-generation linear chart on the next. If you want to show a large or complex chart, put it in an appendix and reference it rather than splicing it into the narrative.

Numbering Systems

Numbering systems are necessary for a genealogy to help readers understand relationships. In a memoir, numbering systems are not necessary because you will use the stories to establish relationships between people.

If you wish to include a descendants list or an ancestors list in an appendix, however, use the Ahnentafel numbering system to go backward in time (ancestors) and the register-style numbering system to come forward in time (descendants). The modified register-style used by the National Genealogical Society Quarterly is also acceptable.

Most genealogical software will generate descendants or ancestors lists for you. If you are not using genealogical software, consult *Genealogical Writing in the 21st Century: A Guide to Register Style and More* by Henry B. Hoff, or *Dollarhide Numbering for Genealogists—An Authorized Guide for the Serious User* by Brian R. Smith.

Place Names

Place names can be tricky in a memoir because they are not as easy to spell out in their entirety within the narrative. For clarity, however, include full details of each place in footnotes or endnotes, or in an appendix in the back matter. Include city (or township), county, state and country *as they existed* at the time you are describing in the narrative.

If all locations are within the same country, however, you may indicate that fact somewhere at the beginning of the appendix or place names list, so that you do not have to repeat United States (or other country names) in each listing.

Spell checking place names can be challenging, but necessary. If in doubt, keep a geographical atlas handy while you are writing or get the place name from a good online map site, such as Google Maps or Bing Maps.

Most publishers use the Anglicized names of non-U.S. places when books are written in English because Anglicized names may be more familiar to the reader. How you wish to handle place names, both in the narrative and a place names list, is up to you. However, if a place name would be difficult for an English-speaker to recognize in the native language, give reference to both the local version and the Anglicized version. There are some locations (many in Eastern Europe) that have changed hands and languages a number of times for which you may want to give the reader an idea of the time period a place held one name, and when the name changed.

Names

In a memoir, you will use names in the context of the story. In other words, you introduce characters as they appear, and call them whatever they would have been called at the time rather than by their full, formal names. If you include a list of characters, ancestors or descendants elsewhere in the book, decide how you will use names and be consistent.

Spellings

Surnames, in particular, have been known to change over time, or even within close families depending upon individual preference. Sometimes, a name change requires explanation either within the narrative or in a footnote or endnote. If you choose to use a common or single spelling, explain that somewhere.

Name Changes

When people changed their names entirely, more often than not, an explanation within the narrative will be necessary. A cross reference in the index and any other list of names would be helpful, as well.

Nicknames

It is fine to use a person's nickname in the narrative if a nickname was the only name that person ever used. And, it is fine to use a formal name as well as a nickname if friends used nicknames, but parents and other relatives used another, as long as you make it clear. Include the nickname in the index and other lists of names, as well.

Women's Names

In the narrative, a woman should be referred to by the name she would have used at the time she appears in the story. In the index and other lists of names, include both maiden and married names. If a maiden name is unknown, you may want to use a symbol such as "(—)" to inform the reader. The following are examples of ways to list women's names:

Mary Jane Robertson (nee Smith)
Mary Jane (Smith) Robertson
Mary Jane Smith Robertson

Prefixes or Titles

There may be occasions within the narrative when you want to use Mr., Mrs., or Miss; or a title such as Reverend (Rev.) or Doctor (Dr.) as a prefix to a person's name. Prefixes are helpful to the reader when gender is not obvious from the name. Miss Leslie Gore would have a clearer meaning than simply Leslie Gore without other context. Use titles only after the individual earned the title, thus a high-school aged Martin Luther King would not hold the title of Reverend.

If you abbreviate, be consistent. The abbreviations for mister and missus are well-enough known that they need not be included in your list of abbreviations. Reverend (Rev.) and Doctor (Dr.) are well understood, as are most military ranks. If you have any doubts, include the abbreviation in your list.

Suffixes

Suffixes within the narrative can help distinguish one person from the other. Common suffixes are Sr., Jr., a roman numeral (such as III or IV), Esq., MD or M.D. (doctor), PhD or Ph.D. and DDS or D.D.S. (dentist). Some style guides use punctuation in suffixes, others do not.

Business Names

Business names, in general, should be listed however the business uses its own name. So, if the firm of Blanding & Fell, Inc., uses the abbreviation for incorporation after its name, so should you. If, at some point, you choose to abbreviate an unfamiliar business name, use the full name enough times in the narrative for readers to become familiar with it. In academic writing, it is acceptable to use the name once followed by the abbreviation in parentheses and never use the formal name again throughout the work. Readers may be frustrated, however, at having to remember an unfamiliar business name by its abbreviation.

Dates

Keeping dates straight can be a challenge for readers if you do not mention dates often in the narrative. One way to help the reader is to make a change in years clear or to give a complete date often enough to let the reader know how much time has passed during the story.

The genealogical convention for dates is to use the day (expressed in numbers) followed by the month (spelled out or abbreviated) followed by a four-digit year, such as 24 March 1900 or 24 Mar 1900. The reason for this is clarity. There is no mistaking whether someone is using the American-style Month/Day/Year or the European-style Day/Month/Year. Looking at 9/3/26 leaves readers wondering whether that date is the 9th of March or the 3rd of September and in the 26th year, but of what century?

In narratives, the most common date style is month (spelled out or abbreviated), day (expressed in numbers), followed by a comma, and a four-digit year, such as March 24, 1900, or Mar 24, 1900. Written dates may read better if they are given the way they would be spoken, such as March 24th, 1900.

Numbers

There are long-established rules for numbers that do not occur within dates. These rules are not hard and fast, although most publishers stick to the rules. Spell out numbers one through ten. You may use roman numerals for numbers 11 and greater. Similarly, centuries earlier than the tenth are spelled out (e.g. eighth century), but after the tenth, you may choose between spelled out or numerals (e.g. nineteenth century or 19th century) as long as you are consistent.

If two numbers appear in the same sentence referring to the same subject, follow the same rule. For example: "The glacier advances approximately one and a half inches per month or eighteen inches per year." And not, "The glacier advances approximately one and a half inches per month, or 18 inches per year."

When numbers occur next to each other, use a style that makes them easiest to read. For example: "He hauled 106 fifteen-foot boards" rather than "He hauled 106 15' boards."

When numbers begin a sentence, either spell them out or re-word the sentence to place the number later in the sentence. This is especially true if the number is large. For example: "Twenty-thousand four hundred and fifty-one people voted in the territorial election," would read better as, "In the territorial election, 20,451 people voted."

Captions

Every image should carry a caption identifying who or what is in the image, who owns the image and any permissions granted to use the image. The exception to this is if all of the images come from a single collection. In that case, use the caption to identify the subject of the image, but only the first image in the book need include name of the collection and any permissions granted. Another option is to create a list of permissions or credits and place those in the back matter. The captions, however, should stay with the photograph.

In Quotes or Italics?

Conventional style guides put the titles of articles, short stories and poems in quotes, but the titles of books, plays, magazines, newspapers, films, television programs, major musical compositions, and epic poems in italics. Use italics for foreign words or phrases, and if unfamiliar to your readers, explain them in a glossary. Use italics for the names of ships, aircraft, and space vehicles, as well.

Footnotes or Endnotes

Make a decision about how you will handle the placement of source citations, in footnotes or endnotes, before you begin writing. Most word processing software makes it easy to create either. The important consideration is what you feel will be easiest for your readers.

A suggestion: although footnotes provide instant access to a citation or supplemental information, if your footnotes could squeeze the main text down to less than half the real estate on the page, use endnotes. Most readers are more interested in what happens next than background information or explanation, and will ignore the footnotes anyway.

❧❧

Style guides have evolved over time, but their purpose is to help readers understand the text. For the most part, following established style guides is in your book's best interest, although there is room for your personal preferences.

Chapter 14

Writing a First Draft

The process of writing a first draft is different for each writer. Some prefer to get the entire book down on paper before going back to edit. Others tackle one section at a time until it shapes up. Proceed in whatever way makes the most sense to you. However, avoid fiddling and fussing with a single section so much that the thought of finishing the book becomes overwhelming.

Set Up Your Manuscript Files

Before you do anything else, set up your book in chapters so that your entire manuscript is not in one enormous file. It will be easier to work with smaller files. If you want feedback from others, you can send a small file at a time, and when you get ready to lay the book out in its final form, you will have all of the parts assembled in a way that makes creating the book easy.

To set up my manuscript files, I use a file-naming convention that lets the computer organize the files for me. I divide the book into front matter (FM), parts (P), chapters (CH) and back matter (BM).

The numbers preceding the file names are split up into front matter, body, and back matter. The front matter files all begin with 00_. Because there are parts in addition to chapters, Part 1 and the chapters within that part are given a file starting number of 10_. Part 2 starts with 20_, and so on. The back matter files start with 60_ because there are only five parts preceding the back matter.

An abbreviated file names list for this book would look like:

001FM_Title Page/Copyrights
002FM_Dedication
...

101P01_Getting Started
102CH1_Who Needs This Book?

...

201P02_Before You Write
202CH6_Identifying Your Target Market

...

301P03_Writing
302CH12_Becoming a Storyteller

...

401P04_Production
402CH16_Creating a Page Layout

...

501P05_Marketing
502CH23_Creating a Marketing Plan

...

601BM_Conclusion
602BM_About the Author

...

Wait to Add Images

If you add images to the manuscript files, they can become quite large, especially if you are adding the images in the correct size and resolution for printing. To save time, wait to add images until you are finished editing. If you need to give yourself a reminder of what image goes where, put the image name in brackets next to the appropriate text (e.g. [grandpa_ca1903.jpg]).

Learn a Few Word Processing Features

A few features in word processing programs can make your writing life easier if you take the time to learn them. Most word processing software has customizable features. Use the help guide in your word processing software to determine how to enable the following functions.

Track Changes

Enabling the Track Changes feature will allow you to show your manuscript to an editor, who can type their suggested changes directly into the document. You then have the option of accepting the changes you want and ignoring the ones you do not without any re-typing.

Customize AutoCorrect

If you find it annoying to type the same information repeatedly, you can set up a command that will automatically fill in the blank as you start typing. For example, if you must repeat the expression, "Clifton Forge, Alleghany County, Virginia," you could set up an AutoCorrect command to replace "Clift" with the full name of the city, county and state.

Customize AutoText

Most word processing programs allow you to build a gallery of frequently typed text or frequently inserted images (such as a logo or an icon), so that a simple combination of a function key and a letter will automatically add the text or image to your document.

Build a Custom Dictionary

If you use foreign words or have names that incorrectly trigger AutoCorrect or the squiggly red line of Spell Check, add them to the dictionary as you use them to save time spell checking later. I have managed to teach Microsoft Word to respect the iTunes company name even when the little "i" begins a sentence.

Use the Synonym Finder

If you are searching for a word and cannot come up with the perfect expression to convey your meaning, type a word with a similar meaning, then right-click on the word to activate the synonym finder for suggestions.

Find/Replace

Inevitably, I find mistakes in my manuscripts that could use a good, global Find and Replace, such as double spaces where only one was needed, the persistent misspelling of a name, or an incorrect use of a font or a feature. Each of these can be found and replaced using the Find/Replace feature in your software. In fact, you can replace text with other text, an icon or an image by using the characters "^c" in the replace field. This function grabs whatever you copied into the clipboard and places it into the manuscript.

Preliminary Fact Checking

For most professional book projects, fact checking is a part of the editing. You can save yourself time and frustration, however, if you take a critical look over the timeline for each story before you create a detailed outline for the entire book (see below).

The most common mistakes that creep into memoirs are improbable events—women having children at age four or age seventy, people living more than 110 years, mistaking a young child with the same name as his father or her mother, and so on.

The best reason to fact check before you create a detailed outline is perspective. A detailed outline forces you to take a closeup look at events. To catch major errors —improbable events—look at the bigger, broader picture.

Once you begin writing, if you have doubts about any detail, stop and check before you continue. It is much easier to correct a few details in your outline, than it is to rewrite. Removing a key detail once woven into the narrative may unravel a whole scene.

Create a Detailed Outline

Most writers benefit from a detailed outline. It will help you remember details from your research and keep you from wandering off onto tangents that do not fit the book as a whole. Also, it will give you an easy way to skip ahead a bit if you get stuck.

If your preliminary outline has enough detail for you to begin writing, then great, get started. If not, add whatever you need to the outline to clearly see the story arcs along with the events, characters and social or historical context important to each.

The following is an example of a detailed outline for the for the wedding of Jacob Smith and Emeline Coulter, intended only to help you see how detailed an outline could be. Everything in the example is fictional. If you are writing from your own memories, you may not need anything this detailed. Write a story or two and see how it goes. If you find you need more detail, flesh out your outline, if you do not, forge ahead with the rest of the book.

> 24 June 1841—Jacob Smith marries Emeline Coulter
> *Sources*:
> Marriage Book B, 1830–1844. Rutherford Co., Tennessee, pg. 305.
> > Groom—Jacob R. Smith
> > Bride—Emeline Sarah Coulter
> > Minister—Rev. Mason P. Elliot
> > Witnesses—Levi M. Smith, William S. Coulter
> Image. Painting, Cannonsburgh home, 1840s
> > Two stories, three gabled windows
> > Upper and lower wrap-around porch/balcony
> > Chimneys at each end of the home
> > Green tin roof
> > Painted yellow with white trim
> Reference. Wedding Dresses Through the Ages, 1840s
> > Typical period wedding dress:
> > Silk with fur-tipped over-shoulders cape
> > Tiny floral brocade with beaded accents
> > Champagne colored with white lace trim
> > Fully lined, floor-length
> > Image, pg 105

Reference. Wedding Customs, Godey's Lady's Book, 1838
    Ladies Lunch menu, pg 40
    Wedding cake preparation, pg 38
    Reception menu, pg 44
Reference. St. John's Episcopal Church Centennial, 1832–1932
    Rev. Mason P. Elliot history, pg 12
    Wedding vows, pg 15

Put as much detail into your outline as you think you need to write the scene.

If You Get Stuck, Get Help

Undertaking a memoir is an incredible task, even for experienced or professional writers who have an abundance of people with similar experience to ask for help if the writing bogs down. For those with less experience, it may take a good coach marking up a chapter or two before you can see your own storytelling errors clearly. If you become stuck or frustrated, banish any thoughts of abandoning the project and get help.

Attend a Writing Class

Most communities have extension learning courses where adults can take classes. Many local governments, senior services, universities, colleges and community colleges offer extension classes. If you can find a class on writing memoirs or creative non-fiction, fantastic. More likely, you will find writing courses on specific topics such as travel or business writing. Creative writing may be good practice, although creative writing encourages you to write from your imagination, where memoir writing should stay closer to the events as they happened.

Hire a Writing Coach

While you are searching through the extension learning catalogs for your area, look at who are teaching the courses. You may be able to find a writing coach by contacting an instructor. Look at the faculty of your local schools, as well. You may find an excellent writing coach in the local high school English department.

Join a Writer's Group

You can learn good techniques from fiction as well as non-fiction, but be sure to explain to members of the group that there are some lines you cannot cross with a memoir and remain true to the facts.

Most writer's groups will allow prospective members to attend a few meetings without contributing any writing to observe how the group works. Do so. A meeting or two will give you a feel for how constructive the criticism is and whether the group will be able to give you good advice.

PUBLISH A MEMOIR

I have a Facebook group called Genealogical Writers and Publishers (www.facebook.com/groups/187826861370278/). Come on in. Ask your questions. Perhaps someone in the group will have a great idea for you.

I have mentioned previously that showing your work to friends or family has potential pitfalls, and I will reiterate that sentiment here. Friends and family members who are not writers tend to fall into two groups—those who do not want to hurt your feelings, and those who do. I must warn you that some people who attend writing classes, coach writers and join writer's groups fall into the same categories.

You need neither obsequious nor domineering critics. If you encounter them, find another way to get help. What you need are honest critics with good intentions, and enough humility to let the good critics guide your writing without diminishing your enthusiasm for the project. Frankly, if you can listen to good criticism of your work and boldly return to the computer the next day to make necessary changes, I have no doubt you will finish your book.

⚜

The only thing left to do is to start writing.

Chapter 15

Editing Your Manuscript

Professional editing benefits most books. Unfortunately, professional editing is expensive. If you are going to invest in editing—even if you trade editing projects with another memoir writer—edit the manuscript yourself first, to catch any obvious errors and to make the manuscript the best it can be before you turn it over.

Professional editing addresses a manuscript first from the big, broad strokes (the themes, context, and organization) before looking at the finer details (spelling, punctuation, fact checking and typographical errors). While you edit your own work, you should do the same.

Context Editing

When a professional editor takes on a manuscript for the first time, the initial read through should reveal whether the book feels like a single entity or whether there are loose ends that need to be clipped or re-worked.

Does the manuscript reflect your focus for the project? Have you maintained the scope you intended? Or have you strayed into tangents? Straying is easy, especially if the additional stories are delicious. Bringing the focus back to your original intent, however, may tighten up the book and make it feel more coherent overall.

Did you focus too narrowly? Did you intend to write about your home life and career, but ended up with a book only about your work life? If that is the case, your focus changed while writing. If the book feels complete as is, fine.

Examine your literary crutches. Have you overused any techniques? It is not uncommon for writers to develop a method of introducing elements into a story in a way that is easiest at first, but becomes a habit over time. When the technique serves the story well, it is fine. Giving a critical eye to your own habits is hard but will improve your storytelling and your book.

Is your meaning clear? Determining whether readers will understand what you wrote, is the part of context editing that may be difficult for you to address yourself. You have the benefit of much more knowledge of the events than the reader. Readers cannot know what you *meant* to write. They have only the words on the page to make sense of the story.

Is the book organized logically? Ask yourself whether there is anything about the way the stories are organized or told that will confuse readers? This is another area you may have difficulty judging. As you read, you can fill in holes with independent knowledge. It may not be as obvious to you that an element or an event is missing as it would be to a reader.

How authentic are the stories? Have you put yourself or other people on pedestals, or have you been too critical? Answering these questions often requires reflection. If you suspect that you have been either too soft or too hard on the reality of the story, put the manuscript aside and read it again later. Inconsistencies may become more apparent with a little distance.

When context editing, set the font to a size that is comfortable for you to read, and use margins of an inch or more so that you have room to write notes while you read. Take your manuscript file to the local copy shop and have it printed on both sides of each page, and spiral bound. Even though the book will not be formatted or bound as it will be for final production, it will give you a sense of how the book reads.

If the manuscript requires changes, make them before you move to the next stage of editing.

Content Editing

Content editing is about making certain you wrote what you meant. Author and editor William Zinsser describes it as, "stripping down every sentence to its cleanest components." I like to describe it as making sure every sentence conveys your meaning and sounds like you wrote it.

I do not think a memoir must be written with such strict adherence to literary and grammatical rules that it comes out sounding like Leo Tolstoy wrote it. However, deleting the clutter, making meaning clear, assuring subjects and verbs agree, keeping to the active not passive voice when appropriate, and using smooth transitions between story elements will make your book better.

The content editing stage is also where you evaluate whether you have given some subjects too much attention (overkill). If you find long explanations, either break them up or dramatize them by showing the impact of the situation on the people, rather than merely explaining them.

There are some situations that are so obvious they need no explanation. If you have explained what should be common knowledge or common sense, eliminate it. Admittedly, cutting good writing is difficult. Deleting words or phrases you have struggled to put down on the page can be painful. However, if a slimmer, sleeker version moves the story forward better, cut away.

If, on the other hand, you find scenes that should be exciting but feel flat or emotionless, re-write them to give them more impact. The goal, remember, is not just to write. It is to tell the stories in a way that makes readers turn the pages. "Rewriting isn't bitter medicine, it's professional awareness," writes Kathleen Krull in her book, *12 Keys to Writing Books that Sell*. While you may not be a professional writer, I am sure you want your book to be as well-written and eagerly read as possible.

Look for redundancies. Do you use the same word again and again in the same paragraph? Are there repetitious story elements? Did you tell a story in a flashback and again in the story's present? Have you explained the same issue more than once? It happens, and not infrequently over a long manuscript. Content editing is a chance to eliminate the excess.

Look for contradictions. In a memoir, it is not unusual to have contradictions surrounding some facts memory or recall is not perfect. Dates and places are the most common culprits. Watch for areas where you may have stated something definitively in one place (i.e. "He was born in Ashland, North Carolina") and speculatively in another (i.e. "He is believed to have been born in Ashland, North Carolina").

When you are ready to edit for content, print your manuscript. Errors and contradictions are more obvious on paper than on the computer screen. Double space your manuscript so that it will be easy to make corrections between the lines. Print it single-sided on three-hole-punch paper, so you can remove a small section at a time from a binder, to edit. Make any changes necessary before moving on to copy editing.

Copy Editing

I promised no death by grammar, but the copy editing stage is when you *should* closely examine your words.

Have you mixed your metaphors, or used the active voice when a passive construction would be clearer? Have you let commas or exclamation points run amok? Have you used parallel construction in compound sentences and bulleted lists? Have any malapropisms slipped in? Do subjects and verbs agree, and have you used pronouns properly without muddling the meaning?

Have you followed your style sheet? Do dates conform? Are names spelled the way you intended throughout the book? Are abbreviations and acronyms consistent? Are sources cited appropriately?

Copy editing is what author Guy Kawasaki, in his book *APE: Author, Publisher, Entrepreneur—How to Publish a Book,* describes as "turning an amateurish book into a polished, professional one."

One of my favorite resources is *The Copyeditor's Handbook: A Guide for Book Publishing and Corporate Communications* by Amy Einsohn. She gives easy-to-read explanations for the most common grammatical errors and problems. Before you begin copy editing, you may want to consult this book.

The following software will check grammar, word use and suggest changes:

- Grammerly (www.grammerly.com)
- Hemmingway App (www.hemingwayapp.com)
- StyleWriter (www.stylewriter-usa.com)

While context and content editing take time, for me, copy editing is a chore. In fact, my house is never cleaner than during the copy editing stage because even cleaning out the garage can look like a lark, by comparison.

Steel yourself. Print out the manuscript double spaced, single sided on three-hole-punched paper so you can pull out a small section at a time from a binder. Set up a comfortable chair and table on which to spread out your style guide, a good dictionary, and a copy editing reference, or your laptop if you prefer Internet-based guides. I give you permission to stay in your jammies, drink as much coffee as you require, and consume an entire box of chocolates if need be.

Fact Checking

If you misstate facts, someone will notice and take issue with it. Errors not only cast doubt on other facts within the book, they diminish your relationship with your readers. Not every reader will notice every error, mind you, but if you can catch the errors before readers have a chance to, why not?

Some writers will fact check while copy editing. I cannot. I prefer to have the language in tip top shape before I crawl through every date, place and event in the book for accuracy. I will correct errors as I catch them, however, in whatever stage of editing it happens.

The most common errors that sneak into memoirs are:

Wrong Dates

In particular, look for places where the date was mis-typed. A person cannot die in 1919 and be born in 1956. Not many people live past one hundred, let alone more than one hundred and ten. Watch for dates that make a lifespan highly improbable.

Wrong Places

Arkansas is not abbreviated as AK. Abbreviations tend to be misused much more often than actual place names. However, look for places where the same city is listed in different counties, or the same counties are listed in different states. A change of boundaries can lead to the circumstance above, but make sure there is an explanation so that the reader does not assume you made an error.

Improbable Events

Look for events that were unlikely to have happened. Here is where a little research on the family lore can come in handy. Even though you may have heard that your great-grandpa was a Civil War soldier, make sure that he was indeed before telling of his reported exploits. If, in fact, he was too young or too old to have served some reader somewhere will notice.

John Colletta tells the story of the letter he received from an ornithologist who read Colletta's book, *Only a Few Bones: A True Account of the Rolling Fork Tragedy and Its Aftermath*. The ornithologist took issue with the description of starlings in the book, explaining that starlings were not introduced into the area until later. An incorrect fact about something as easy to gloss over as the presence of a specific species of bird, damaged the credibility of the book for that reader.

Graphic Elements

I usually wait until I have a manuscript in its best shape before I add images. Some writers prefer to see the images with the text as they write, and I appreciate that. If you have done so, great. If you have not, whether you add them now before a final proofread or as a part of your final draft, is up to you.

During the discussion of scanning in Chapter 8: Scanning and Optical Character Recognition, I made a suggestion that you scan each image at a size and resolution big enough for print production. One thing that is hard to determine at this stage, however, is the exact size you will need based upon the layout you will choose for the final book. Chapter 16: Creating a Page Layout will cover this.

Another consideration is whether you will create an eBook version because the size and resolution, as well as where the images are placed within an eBook, are different than for a print edition.

The best time-saving advice I can give you is to leave the images out until the manuscript is as close to perfect as it is ever going to be. That way, you can make a copy of the manuscript to be used for an eBook version and another for the print edition because the images will be placed into the manuscript in different ways. In addition, I usually leave one copy of the completed manuscript alone as a backup, and work from copies to create final eBook and print editions.

Once images are added in their appropriate size, resolution and placement for as many editions are you are planning, you can proofread the captions, copyrights and permissions that go along with the images.

Proofreading

I am sure you must be thinking, "I have just edited a half a dozen times, and now I have to proofread?" Well, yes. Every time you make changes to the manuscript, you introduce the possibility that an error crept in.

While spell check and grammar editors are helpful tools, there is nothing like a fresh set of eyes to catch the errors that software-based tools cannot. Your word processor will not alert you if you typed lack, when you meant lake.

Proofreading is a task that you could hand over to a paid professional or someone who is well-read. Make your instructions clear, however that you are asking for proofreading, not editorial advice.

Many proofreaders read each page starting at the bottom so that they are looking at snippets of sentences rather than whole passages. Misspellings are easier to spot this way. The misuse of words is easier to spot, however when reading in context.

If you hand over a printed copy to proof, ask your proofreader to use a red pen, common proofreader's marks, and to place a small "x" in the margin wherever a change has been made. You will find a nice chart of proofreader's marks on the Merriam-Webster website (www.merriam-webster.com/mw/table/proof-rea.htm). A more efficient method, however, is to use the review features of your word processor (e.g. Track Changes in Word) so that your proofreader can type directly into a copy of the manuscript file, and so you can accept or reject any changes with the click of a mouse.

Typescript Editing

The next stage in the publishing process is production, where you will typeset (format) the manuscript. It is not unusual for errors to creep in during the typesetting process. Typescript editing is one final chance to make changes. It occurs after the manuscript has been typeset or laid out as an eBook, and is described more fully in Chapter 22: Preparing the Final Files.

Making changes to the typescript can be problematic. It is frustrating to have to re-work perfect-looking pages to correct a misused word or phrase, and if a professional typesets your manuscript, changes can be expensive.

❧❧

Every manuscript can use a good edit. There are many people who can catch typos for you, fewer who can fact check, and even fewer who can conduct a professional edit while giving constructive advice. Professional editors are good at what they do, and charge accordingly. If your book is likely to appeal to the general public and therefore generate thousands of sales, you may wish to invest in professional editing before you release the book.

Working with an Editor

Editors help authors express what they mean. Editors know when to stick to the rules and when to break them. They look for consistency and fix muddled meaning. Most books benefit from professional editing, but a good editor can be expensive. Editors offer a range of services similar to the styles of editing described above. The more comprehensive the edit, the greater the cost.

Cost

Most editors charge either by the page or by the hour. The more experienced the editor, the more the hourly rate makes sense. Ask for an estimate based upon the number of pages in the final manuscript on standard paper with normal margins, double-spaced. An editor usually will want to see the table of contents and at least a chapter or two prior to giving you an estimate.

Portfolio

Most editors will be able to point you to commercially available work they have edited, and will have chapters or article-length pieces ready to show you.

Expectations

It is important for both you and the editor to make expectations clear in the beginning. Ask for what the book needs. The job and the cost of proofreading are different than content or context editing. Some editors do not proofread. They specialize in the bigger picture and will leave the proofreading or fact checking to others.

If you are asking for a more comprehensive edit, most editors will offer to edit a chapter to give you an idea of the editor's style before you give the go-ahead.

Personal Style

Good editors will tell you what you *need* to hear rather than what you *want* to hear about your work. That part of the job is not easy. Your editor should offer criticism in a way that will inspire you to make changes for the good of the book. He or she will never belittle or undermine your confidence. If you run into an editor who consistently rubs you the wrong way, find another editor.

Professional Style

The most common conflict between authors and editors is stylistic. No editor and author will write exactly the same way. Editors do not have the final say in what stays or goes in your manuscript, you do. Most editors will not suggest changes that alter your writing style without good reason. A good editor, when confronting stylistic problems, will stop the editing process and consult you before proceeding. There may be instances where your style conflicts enough with the editor's that choosing a different editor is best. A good editor will recognize this and tell you.

Be open to suggestion, however. Editors edit. They are going to make changes. Read the changes with an open mind, and if need be, leave it alone for a few days, and come back for a fresh look. A good editor wants you to be successful. He or she is making suggestions in the best interest of the manuscript.

Give the editor your best work. Run the spelling and grammar check. Use proper capitalization and punctuation. Give the book a good once-over before you give it to your editor.

Communication

Communication is a two-way street. If you hear feedback that does not make sense or hurts your feelings, say so. Misunderstandings have ruined many an author-editor relationship. If you have a question, ask. If you do not like the direction things are going, say so. Keep frustration between you and your editor private. Leave it out of your Twitter feed and off of your Facebook page. Spouting off in public will not end well.

Follow the Instructions

Most editors have a process. Give the manuscript to your editor in the form they prefer and follow the instructions for accepting or rejecting changes. The goal is to get the manuscript back to you in the fewest number of complete edits to keep costs down. If you make changes during the initial edit, for example, each section you change must be re-edited as a part of the whole. Anything that slows down the process, raises the cost.

Deadlines

Both you and your editor have schedules and deadlines to meet. Be realistic when setting deadlines to make certain you can both meet them. Giving an editor a month with your manuscript is a starting point. And, your book may be competing with others for time in the editor's schedule.

Write a Formal Proposal or Contract

Once you have a cost estimate from the editor, write an additional proposal making your expectations clear about the work to be done as well as deadlines for submissions, returns, and payment. Expect to pay half down, and half upon completion. Include how you will send the manuscript, receive changes, and communicate with the editor. Include all charges and fees, as well as a do-not-exceed clause if you want the editor to stick within a defined budget.

A Less-Costly Alternative

Some authors crowdsource the editing. They put the manuscript up online, ask readers for feedback and require that no one distribute the book. I like this idea for a non-fiction or a how-to book, but it is probably not the best idea for a memoir. Crowdsourcing may work in the early stages of planning while you are still gathering ideas. Beware, also, the potential pitfalls. You may get stellar advice, or you may get drivel—and the drivel is often mean-spirited.

❧❧

I often feel triumphant when finishing a manuscript. Unfortunately, triumph fades when the shadow of editing looms. Be kind to yourself in the first round of editing. Read the book through and put it away for a few days. Post pictures of family nearby to remind you who your readers will be. Then, return to editing with a critical eye and a red pen to benefit the book.

SECTION 4

The goal in this section is for you to learn how to produce a book that looks as good and reads as easily as any book produced by a traditional publisher.

There is not enough space in this book to give instructions for formatting using each of the major word processing or page layout programs. The terminology used in this section, however, should give you what you need to use the help features in your software to accomplish each task.

Most of this Section is devoted to print production because most memoirs are printed. If you are interested in producing an electronic or online version of your book, there is information about those formats in Chapter 22: Preparing the Final Files, or a more comprehensive look at the process is available in *Set Yourself Up to Self-Publish: A Genealogist's Guide*.

Baby Steps

If you are not familiar with your software and you are not interested in learning how to lay out the interior of your book, there are templates you can download from the Internet, or you can engage the services of a typesetter or book packager (more on this in Chapter 17). These services will also help you ready your images for print at the right size and resolution.

Many of the print-on-demand printers offer templates or there are templates for sale at sites such as Joel Friedlander's Book Design Templates (www.bookdesigntemplates.com). Even if you employ a template, it is still up to you to make sure the final product looks as good as it should.

Next Steps

A template is not right for every book, and you may want more flexibility to make your book look just right. If you can master the page layout basics (Chapter 16), choose appropriate fonts, set up paragraphs correctly, and avoid widows and orphans (Chapter 17), you will be well on your way to a professional-looking book layout.

Giant Leaps

If you want your book to be the best it can be, to pass muster with even the pickiest of critics, then you must learn the remaining rules for page layouts and typesetting (Chapters 16–20). And if you have gone this far, you may as well learn how to create a stunning book cover (Chapter 21), and to prepare the final files for the printer (Chapter 22).

Note: In this section you will see examples that are filled with text beginning, "Lorem ipsum." Latin text is used as filler so that you can see how different layouts would look.

Chapter 16

Creating a Page Layout

The most important element in laying out a page for print is to make the page easy to read. A poorly or unusually designed book may make your readers skeptical of the quality of the information. Too much work goes into writing your story to have that effort spoiled by poor design, when good design is so easy to accomplish with a little knowledge of the rules.

The best way to create a good page layout design is to follow the long-established rules of readability. Desktop publishing offers many options for innovative ways to create columns, employ fonts, and place illustrations—too many perhaps. Leave the wild innovating to the graphic designers on magazine staffs. The tried and true rules for book design are still the best.

Page Size

How much real estate you have to work with depends upon the trim size of the page. The trim size is the finished size of the book. Choosing a trim size pits look against cost, and usability. A 12" x 12" coffee table book is fabulous to look at, but a 6" x 9" book is much easier to sit and read.

An offset printer can create books in just about any size, but you must order a minimum number of books to make the price per book worth it. If the cost of setup for a run of specially sized books is $500 and the print-per-book charge is $20, if you only order 10 books, the cost per book would be $70 ($50 + $20).

You will save money if you choose one of the common page sizes offered by print-on-demand printers. Most print-on-demand printers do not charge a fee for setup, they only charge to produce each book—and they can produce books one at a time. The most common page sizes for print-on-demand printers are (in inches) 6 x 9, 7 x 10 and 8.5 x 11.

No matter what page size you choose, the rules for good layout are essentially the same. The one small exception is that the larger the page, the larger proportionally the elements such as fonts, white space and images should be.

Page Count

Book interiors must be multiples of two (front and back of a single sheet). If you use an offset printer, they may require page counts in signatures (multiples) of 4, 8, 16, 32, 48, 64 or even 80. Offset printers print use paper on rolls many feet wide, and when the paper is folded and cut, it will form a signature of one of the multiples of four (4).

Signatures can be an issue if, for example, you have written a one hundred-page book, but the printer's signature requirement is eighty pages. In that case, you would have to reduce your book by twenty pages, or increase it by sixty pages in order to meet the signature requirement. Otherwise, you would have sixty blank pages at the end of your one hundred-page book.

Luckily, print-on-demand printers use simple two-page signatures—front and back.

Blank Pages

By publishing tradition, chapters and most front matter and back matter elements, should begin on a right-hand page. You may have blank pages if a chapter runs an odd number of pages because the last page will be blank so that the next element will begin on a right-hand page.

If you have blank pages, they should be completely blank—no headers and no page numbers.

White Space

The biggest misconception about laying out a book is that you must economize the space by cramming as much as you can onto a single page. Please do not. The reader needs a break from solid text either from the margins around the edges, the space between columns, paragraphs, words, and letters, or all of the above.

Altering the spacing between the letters (tracking) and the space between the lines of text (leading) can make the page look more or less dense. If you want to make the page look a little less dense or dark, use a book font such as Bookman because it is wider and more open, rather than a newspaper font such as Times which is thin and meant to be read in narrow newspaper columns. By increasing the space between the lines of text (leading) or between the paragraphs, the page will look less dense. In the example, the page on the left looks dense. The one on the right is much more open.

While giving the page white space, you must also follow the rules governing proximity. Proximity means that objects that belong together should be closer

6   Book Title

Lorem ipsum dolor sit amet, consectetur adipisicing elit, sed do eiusmod tempor incididunt ut labore et dolore magna aliqua. Ut enim ad minim veniam, quis nostrud exercitation ullamco laboris nisi ut aliquip ex ea commodo consequat. Duis aute irure dolor in reprehenderit in voluptate velit esse cillum dolore eu fugiat nulla pariatur. Excepteur sint occaecat cupidatat non proident, sunt in culpa qui officia deserunt mollit anim id est laborum.

Lorem ipsum dolor sit amet, consectetur adipisicing elit, sed do eiusmod tempor incididunt ut labore et dolore magna aliqua. Ut enim ad minim veniam, quis nostrud exercitation ullamco laboris nisi ut aliquip ex ea commodo consequat. Duis aute irure dolor in reprehenderit in voluptate velit esse cillum dolore eu fugiat nulla pariatur. Excepteur sint occaecat cupidatat non proident, sunt in culpa qui officia deserunt mollit anim id est laborum.

Lorem ipsum dolor sit amet, consectetur adipisicing elit, sed do eiusmod tempor incididunt ut labore et dolore magna aliqua. Ut enim ad minim veniam, quis nostrud exercitation ullamco laboris nisi ut aliquip ex ea commodo consequat. Duis aute irure dolor in reprehenderit in voluptate velit esse cillum dolore eu fugiat nulla pariatur. Excepteur sint occaecat cupidatat non proident, sunt in culpa qui officia deserunt mollit anim id est laborum.

Lorem ipsum dolor sit amet, consectetur adipisicing elit, sed do eiusmod tempor incididunt ut labore et dolore magna aliqua. Ut enim ad minim veniam, quis nostrud exercitation ullamco laboris nisi ut aliquip ex ea commodo consequat. Duis aute irure dolor in reprehenderit in voluptate velit esse cillum dolore eu fugiat nulla pariatur. Excepteur sint occaecat cupidatat non proident, sunt in culpa qui officia deserunt mollit anim id est laborum.

Lorem ipsum dolor sit amet, consectetur adipisicing elit, sed do eiusmod tempor incididunt ut labore et dolore magna aliqua. Ut

Chapter Title   7

Lorem ipsum dolor sit amet, consectetur adipisicing elit, sed do eiusmod tempor incididunt ut labore et dolore magna aliqua. Ut enim ad minim veniam, quis nostrud exercitation ullamco laboris nisi ut aliquip ex ea commodo consequat. Duis aute irure dolor in reprehenderit in voluptate velit esse cillum dolore eu fugiat nulla pariatur. Excepteur sint occaecat cupidatat non proident, sunt in culpa qui officia deserunt mollit anim id est laborum.

Lorem ipsum dolor sit amet, consectetur adipisicing elit, sed do eiusmod tempor incididunt ut labore et dolore magna aliqua. Ut enim ad minim veniam, quis nostrud exercitation ullamco laboris nisi ut aliquip ex ea commodo consequat. Duis aute irure dolor in reprehenderit in voluptate velit esse cillum dolore eu fugiat nulla pariatur. Excepteur sint occaecat cupidatat non proident, sunt in culpa qui officia deserunt mollit anim id est laborum.

Lorem ipsum dolor sit amet, consectetur adipisicing elit, sed do eiusmod tempor incididunt ut labore et dolore magna aliqua. Ut enim ad minim veniam, quis nostrud exercitation ullamco laboris nisi ut aliquip ex ea commodo consequat. Duis aute irure dolor in reprehenderit in voluptate velit esse cillum dolore eu fugiat nulla pariatur. Excepteur sint occaecat cupidatat non proident, sunt in culpa qui officia deserunt mollit anim id est laborum.

Lorem ipsum dolor sit amet, consectetur adipisicing elit, sed do eiusmod tempor incididunt ut labore et dolore magna aliqua. Ut enim ad minim veniam, quis nostrud exercitation ullamco laboris nisi ut aliquip ex ea commodo consequat. Duis aute irure dolor in reprehenderit in voluptate velit esse cillum dolore eu fugiat nulla

Dense page (left); Less dense (right).

to each other. A caption for a photograph, for example, should be closer to the bottom of the photograph than the next line of text.

Even spacing, between paragraphs or between subheads and paragraphs, is a red flag that the person who designed the layout has little experience. It is easiest in a word processing program to use double returns to separate paragraphs, or to put extra space between a paragraph and the next headline or subhead. Easiest, yes. Most attractive, no. Use styles to create additional space either above or below paragraphs, headlines or subheads without using an extra return. A headline or a subhead should be closer to the text below it than the paragraph above it. In the example on the next page, the type on the left has even spacing. The type on the right has correct spacing.

Page Spreads

Books are laid out in spreads (pages side by side), not individual pages. When a reader opens a book, they see page spreads as a single visual unit. Because of the binding in the center, right and left pages are laid out differently. The rules for what goes on each side of the page spread follows shortly.

Lorem ipsum dolor sit amet, consectetur adipisicing elit, sed do eiusmod tempor incididunt ut labore et dolore magna aliqua. Ut enim ad minim veniam, quis nostrud exercitation ullamco laboris nisi ut aliquip ex ea commodo consequat. Duis aute irure dolor in reprehenderit in voluptate velit esse cillum dolore eu fugiat nulla pariatur. Excepteur sint occaecat cupidatat non proident, sunt in culpa qui officia deserunt mollit anim id est laborum.

Headline Headline Headline

Lorem ipsum dolor sit amet, consectetur adipisicing elit, sed do eiusmod tempor incididunt ut labore et dolore magna aliqua. Ut enim ad minim veniam, quis nostrud exercitation ullamco laboris nisi ut aliquip ex ea commodo consequat. Duis aute irure dolor in reprehenderit in voluptate velit esse cillum dolore eu fugiat nulla pariatur. Excepteur sint occaecat cupidatat non proident, sunt in culpa qui officia deserunt mollit anim id est laborum.

Headline Headline Headline

Lorem ipsum dolor sit amet, consectetur adipisicing elit, sed do eiusmod tempor incididunt ut labore et dolore magna aliqua. Ut enim ad minim veniam, quis nostrud exercitation ullamco laboris nisi ut aliquip ex ea commodo consequat. Duis aute irure dolor in reprehenderit in voluptate velit esse cillum dolore eu fugiat nulla pariatur. Excepteur sint occaecat cupidatat non proident, sunt in culpa qui officia deserunt mollit anim id est laborum.

Lorem ipsum dolor sit amet, consectetur adipisicing elit, sed do eiusmod tempor incididunt ut labore et dolore magna aliqua. Ut enim ad minim veniam, quis nostrud exercitation ullamco laboris

Lorem ipsum dolor sit amet, consectetur adipisicing elit, sed do eiusmod tempor incididunt ut labore et dolore magna aliqua. Ut enim ad minim veniam, quis nostrud exercitation ullamco laboris nisi ut aliquip ex ea commodo consequat. Duis aute irure dolor in reprehenderit in voluptate velit esse cillum dolore eu fugiat nulla pariatur. Excepteur sint occaecat cupidatat non proident, sunt in culpa qui officia deserunt mollit anim id est laborum.

Headline Headline Headline

Lorem ipsum dolor sit amet, consectetur adipisicing elit, sed do eiusmod tempor incididunt ut labore et dolore magna aliqua. Ut enim ad minim veniam, quis nostrud exercitation ullamco laboris nisi ut aliquip ex ea commodo consequat. Duis aute irure dolor in reprehenderit in voluptate velit esse cillum dolore eu fugiat nulla pariatur. Excepteur sint occaecat cupidatat non proident, sunt in culpa qui officia deserunt mollit anim id est laborum.

Headline Headline Headline

Lorem ipsum dolor sit amet, consectetur adipisicing elit, sed do eiusmod tempor incididunt ut labore et dolore magna aliqua. Ut enim ad minim veniam, quis nostrud exercitation ullamco laboris nisi ut aliquip ex ea commodo consequat. Duis aute irure dolor in reprehenderit in voluptate velit esse cillum dolore eu fugiat nulla pariatur. Excepteur sint occaecat cupidatat non proident, sunt in culpa qui officia deserunt mollit anim id est laborum.

Lorem ipsum dolor sit amet, consectetur adipisicing elit, sed do eiusmod tempor incididunt ut labore et dolore magna aliqua. Ut enim ad minim veniam, quis nostrud exercitation ullamco laboris nisi ut aliquip ex ea commodo consequat. Duis aute irure dolor in reprehenderit in voluptate velit esse cillum dolore eu fugiat nulla

Even spacing (left); Correct proximity (right).

Grids

A basic grid pattern imposes order on the layout. Grids align objects and space them properly which is pleasing to the eye. Used throughout, grids employ repetition to help the reader move through the book easily.

Grids help with consistency. For the most part, columns should be the same width and used to help the text fit within the grid. Images should be sized to fit the grid and maintain uniform distance from the text. Grids are determined by margins, columns, and the size of the page. The smaller the page, the fewer columns you can use comfortably before they become too narrow. The larger the page, the more columns you need to keep line lengths short enough to read easily.

In the example, you can see a 3x4 grid on the left-hand page, and a 3x3 grid on the right. Another possibility for smaller pages is a 2x2 grid.

Text can flow across two grid columns as seen on the left-hand page in the example labeled "Filled-in grid," or, an image could fill two grid columns as seen on the right-hand page example. A grid should not limit flexibility, rather, it should bring predictability to the page.

Lines, also called rules or strokes, should be of the same weight whenever they are used, with rare exceptions for emphasis (see Pull Quotes below).

6   Book Title

Chapter Title   7

3x4 grid (left); 3x3 grid (right).

6   Book Title

Chapter Title   7

2x2 grid (left); 2x3 grid (right).

PUBLISH A MEMOIR

Lorem ipsum dolor sit amet, consectetur adipisicing elit, sed do eiusmod tempor incididunt ut labore et dolore magna aliqua. Ut enim ad minim veniam, quis nostrud exercitation ullamco laboris nisi ut aliquip ex ea commodo consequat. Duis aute irure dolor in reprehenderit in voluptate velit esse cillum dolore eu fugiat nulla pariatur. Excepteur sint occaecat cupidatat non proident, sunt in culpa qui officia deserunt mollit anim id est laborum.

Lorem ipsum dolor sit amet, consectetur adipisicing elit, sed do eiusmod tempor incididunt ut labore et dolore magna aliqua. Ut enim ad minim veniam, quis nostrud exercitation ullamco laboris nisi ut aliquip ex ea commodo consequat. Duis aute irure dolor in reprehenderit in voluptate velit esse cillum dolore eu fugiat nulla pariatur. Excepteur sint occaecat cupidatat non proident, sunt in culpa qui officia deserunt mollit anim id est laborum.

Lorem ipsum dolor sit amet, consectetur adipisicing elit, sed do eiusmod tempor incididunt ut labore et dolore magna aliqua. Ut enim ad minim veniam, quis nostrud exercitation ullamco laboris nisi ut aliquip ex ea commodo consequat. Duis aute irure dolor in reprehenderit in voluptate velit esse cillum dolore eu fugiat nulla pariatur. Excepteur sint occaecat cupidatat non proident, sunt in culpa qui officia

Lorem ipsum dolor sit amet, consectetur adipisicing elit, sed do eiusmod tempor incididunt ut labore et dolore magna aliqua. Ut enim ad minim veniam, quis nostrud exercitation ullamco laboris nisi ut aliquip ex ea commodo consequat. Duis aute irure dolor in reprehenderit in voluptate velit esse cillum

Lorem ipsum dolor sit amet, consectetur adipisicing elit, sed do eiusmod tempor incididunt ut labore et dolore magna aliqua. Ut enim ad minim veniam, quis nostrud

Lorem ipsum dolor sit amet, consectetur adipisicing elit, sed do eiusmod tempor incididunt ut labore et dolore magna aliqua. Ut enim ad minim veniam, quis nostrud exercitation ullamco laboris nisi ut aliquip ex ea commodo consequat. Duis aute irure dolor in reprehenderit in voluptate velit esse cillum dolore eu fugiat nulla pariatur. Excepteur sint occaecat cupidatat non proident, sunt in culpa qui officia deserunt mollit anim id est laborum.

Lorem ipsum dolor sit amet, consectetur adipisicing elit, sed do eiusmod tempor incididunt ut labore et dolore magna aliqua. Ut enim ad minim veniam, quis nostrud exercitation ullamco laboris nisi ut aliquip ex ea commodo consequat. Duis aute irure dolor in reprehenderit in voluptate velit esse cillum dolore eu fugiat nulla pariatur. Excepteur sint occaecat

cupidatat non proident, sunt in culpa qui officia deserunt mollit anim id est laborum.

Lorem ipsum dolor sit amet, consectetur adipisicing elit, sed do eiusmod tempor incididunt ut labore et dolore magna aliqua. Ut enim ad minim veniam, quis nostrud exercitation ullamco laboris nisi ut aliquip ex ea commodo consequat. Duis aute irure dolor in reprehenderit in voluptate velit esse cillum dolore eu fugiat nulla pariatur. Excepteur sint occaecat

exercitation ullamco laboris nisi ut aliquip ex ea commodo consequat. Duis aute irure dolor in reprehenderit in voluptate velit esse cillum dolore eu fugiat nulla pariatur. Excepteur sint occaecat cupidatat non proident, sunt in culpa qui officia deserunt mol-

Lorem ipsum dolor sit amet, consectetur adipisicing elit, sed do eiusmod tempor incididunt ut labore et dolore magna aliqua. Ut

Filled-in grid.

Four column grid in Word.

In a page layout program, you can set up margins and columns in master pages—different master pages for different uses, such as the first page in a chapter, main body pages, and a final blank page, if needed.

In a word processing program, you can establish the size of the grid squares and turn on the grid lines so that you can see them as you work. Word processing programs are not as flexible with layouts as page layout programs. You can design a good looking book using a word processing program, however, if you will learn the more advanced features of the software.

Margins

Set your margins to accommodate headers, footers, the text and images. In general, no element should violate the margins. All elements, headers, footers, page numbers, text and images must fit within the margins. Margins impose order and help create white space on the page.

When the Gutenberg bible was printed, margins were set so that facing pages were close together. That was the style of the times—to make a two-page spread look as if it were a single image.

With binding methods today, text set too close to the middle creates an optical illusion that the pages run together. Set a slightly larger margin toward the

Lorem ipsum dolor sit amet, consectetur adipisicing elit, sed do eiusmod tempor incididunt ut labore et dolore magna aliqua. Ut enim ad minim veniam, quis nostrud exercitation ullamco laboris nisi ut aliquip ex ea commodo consequat. Duis aute irure dolor in reprehenderit in voluptate velit esse cillum dolore eu fugiat nulla pariatur. Excepteur sint occaecat cupidatat non proident, sunt in culpa qui officia deserunt mollit anim id est laborum.

Lorem ipsum dolor sit amet, consectetur adipisicing elit, sed do eiusmod tempor incididunt ut labore et dolore magna aliqua. Ut enim ad minim veniam, quis nostrud exercitation ullamco laboris nisi ut aliquip ex ea commodo consequat. Duis aute irure dolor in reprehenderit in voluptate velit esse cillum dolore eu fugiat nulla pariatur. Excepteur sint occaecat cupidatat non proident, sunt in culpa qui officia deserunt mollit anim id est laborum.

Lorem ipsum dolor sit amet, consectetur adipisicing elit, sed do eiusmod tempor incididunt ut labore et dolore magna aliqua. Ut enim ad minim veniam, quis nostrud exercitation ullamco laboris nisi ut aliquip ex ea commodo consequat. Duis aute irure dolor in reprehenderit in voluptate velit esse cillum dolore eu fugiat nulla pariatur. Excepteur sint occaecat cupidatat non

aliquip ex ea commodo consequat. Duis aute irure dolor in reprehenderit in voluptate velit esse cillum dolore eu fugiat nulla pariatur. Excepteur sint occaecat cupidatat non proident, sunt in culpa qui officia deserunt mollit anim id est laborum.

Lorem ipsum dolor sit amet, consectetur adipisicing elit, sed do eiusmod tempor incididunt ut labore et dolore magna aliqua. Ut enim ad minim veniam, quis nostrud exercitation ullamco laboris nisi ut aliquip ex ea commodo consequat. Duis aute irure dolor in reprehenderit in voluptate velit esse cillum dolore eu fugiat nulla pariatur. Excepteur sint occaecat cupidatat non proident, sunt in culpa qui officia deserunt mollit anim id est laborum.

Lorem ipsum dolor sit amet, consectetur adipisicing elit, sed do eiusmod tempor incididunt ut labore et dolore magna aliqua. Ut enim ad minim veniam, quis nostrud exercitation ullamco laboris nisi ut aliquip ex ea commodo consequat. Duis aute irure dolor in reprehenderit in voluptate velit esse cillum dolore eu fugiat nulla pariatur. Excepteur sint occaecat cupidatat non proident, sunt in culpa qui officia deserunt mollit anim id est laborum.

Lorem ipsum dolor sit amet, consectetur adipisicing elit, sed do eiusmod tempor incididunt ut labore et

Margins in the Gutenberg bible.

Lorem ipsum dolor sit amet, consectetur adipisicing elit, sed do eiusmod tempor incididunt ut labore et dolore magna aliqua. Ut enim ad minim veniam, quis nostrud exercitation ullamco laboris nisi ut aliquip ex ea commodo consequat. Duis aute irure dolor in reprehenderit in voluptate velit esse cillum dolore eu fugiat nulla pariatur. Excepteur sint occaecat cupidatat non proident, sunt in culpa qui officia deserunt mollit anim id est laborum.

Lorem ipsum dolor sit amet, consectetur adipisicing elit, sed do eiusmod tempor incididunt ut labore et dolore magna aliqua. Ut enim ad minim veniam, quis nostrud exercitation ullamco laboris nisi ut aliquip ex ea commodo consequat. Duis aute irure dolor in reprehenderit in voluptate velit esse cillum dolore eu fugiat nulla pariatur. Excepteur sint occaecat cupidatat non proident, sunt in culpa qui officia deserunt mollit anim id est laborum.

Lorem ipsum dolor sit amet, consectetur adipisicing elit, sed do eiusmod tempor incididunt ut labore et dolore magna aliqua. Ut enim ad minim veniam, quis nostrud exercitation ullamco laboris nisi ut aliquip ex ea commodo consequat. Duis aute irure dolor in reprehenderit in voluptate velit esse cillum dolore eu fugiat nulla pariatur. Excepteur sint occaecat cupidatat non proident, sunt in culpa qui officia deserunt mollit anim id est laborum.

Lorem ipsum dolor sit amet, consectetur adipisicing elit, sed do eiusmod tempor incididunt ut labore et dolore magna aliqua. Ut enim ad minim veniam, quis nostrud exercitation ullamco laboris nisi ut aliquip ex ea commodo consequat. Duis aute irure dolor in reprehenderit in voluptate velit esse cillum dolore eu fugiat nulla pariatur. Excepteur sint occaecat cupidatat non proident, sunt in culpa qui officia

Lorem ipsum dolor sit amet, consectetur adipisicing elit, sed do eiusmod tempor incididunt ut labore et dolore magna aliqua. Ut enim ad minim veniam, quis nostrud exercitation ullamco laboris nisi ut aliquip ex ea commodo consequat. Duis aute irure dolor in reprehenderit in voluptate velit esse cillum dolore eu fugiat nulla pariatur. Excepteur sint occaecat cupidatat non proident, sunt in culpa qui officia deserunt mollit anim id est laborum.

Lorem ipsum dolor sit amet, consectetur adipisicing elit, sed do eiusmod tempor incididunt ut labore et dolore magna aliqua. Ut enim ad minim veniam, quis nostrud exercitation ullamco laboris nisi ut aliquip ex ea commodo consequat. Duis aute irure dolor in reprehenderit in voluptate velit esse cillum dolore eu fugiat nulla pariatur. Excepteur sint occaecat cupidatat non proident, sunt in culpa qui officia deserunt mollit anim id est laborum.

Lorem ipsum dolor sit amet, consectetur adipisicing elit, sed do eiusmod tempor incididunt ut labore et dolore magna aliqua. Ut enim ad minim veniam, quis nostrud exercitation ullamco laboris nisi ut aliquip ex ea commodo consequat. Duis aute irure dolor in reprehenderit in voluptate velit esse cillum dolore eu fugiat nulla pariatur. Excepteur sint occaecat cupidatat non proident, sunt in culpa qui officia deserunt mollit anim id est laborum.

Lorem ipsum dolor sit amet, consectetur adipisicing elit, sed do eiusmod tempor incididunt ut labore et dolore magna aliqua. Ut enim ad minim veniam, quis nostrud exercitation ullamco laboris nisi ut aliquip ex ea commodo consequat. Duis aute irure dolor in reprehenderit in voluptate velit esse cillum dolore eu fugiat nulla pariatur. Excepteur sint occaecat cupidatat non proident, sunt in culpa qui officia

Top margin allowing for the book title, chapter title and page number.

spine than on the outside. The smallest margin you should consider is a one-half inch (.5") margin, and the larger the page size, the larger the margins should be.

Typical margin settings for a 6" x 9" book are: top—1"; inside—.75"; outside—.625" and bottom—.625." On an 8.5" x 11" book, typical margins are: top—1.25" to 1.5"; inside—1"; outside—.75"; and bottom—.75." The most common error is creating margins that are too narrow and of equal size.

Most books have running headers with the book's title on the left-hand page, and the chapter title on the right-hand page. Headers may also include the page numbers. If the header includes the page number, do not repeat page numbers in the footer.

In a page layout program, set up your master pages so that the top margin allows the book title or chapter title to rest above the text. In a word processor, choose one of the pre-installed headers for left and right pages and enter the appropriate text.

Page Numbers

Place page numbers in either the header or footer. Typically they are placed at the outside edge or in the center of the page, but not at the spine edge. It is difficult to locate page numbers while flipping through the book if they are near the spine.

Page numbers in the front matter (title page, table of contents, and so on) are given in lowercase Roman numerals, so the first half-title page would be page

i. Page numbers beginning with the introduction are given in Arabic numerals, so the first page of the introduction would be page 1, although some publishers continue page numbering from the front matter.

Columns

Columns are the easiest way to control line length. Text stretching too far across the page is difficult for the reader to follow. Pages six inches wide or narrower can be set in a single column, but larger books need two or more columns.

Columns have two components—distance between (gutter) and width (line length). Try to keep line lengths from 60 to 70 characters. Columns do not have to be equal in width, but most often they look best when they are. In both page layout programs and word processors, you can adjust the number of columns, the line length, and the distance between the columns. A distance of one-quarter of an inch (.25") is a good starting place. Too much distance between columns looks awkward, and too little distance between columns makes the text difficult to read, as you can see in the example.

Images

Adding images to a page can present layout challenges, especially if the image does not fit neatly into the grid. Your book will look best if they do, however, so you may need to re-scan at a larger size or crop images down to fit.

Columns incorrectly spaced; too far (left); too close (right).

6   Book Title

Lorem ipsum dolor sit amet, consectetur adipisicing elit, sed do eiusmod tempor incididunt ut labore et dolore magna aliqua. Ut enim ad minim veniam, quis nostrud exercitation ullamco laboris nisi ut aliquip ex ea commodo consequat. Duis aute irure dolor in reprehenderit in voluptate velit esse cillum dolore eu fugiat nulla pariatur. Excepteur sint occaecat cupidatat non proident, sunt in culpa qui officia deserunt mollit anim id est laborum.

Lorem ipsum dolor sit amet, consectetur adipisicing elit, sed do eiusmod tempor incididunt ut labore et dolore magna aliqua. Ut enim ad minim veniam, quis nostrud exercitation ullamco laboris nisi ut aliquip ex ea commodo consequat. Duis aute irure dolor in reprehenderit in voluptate velit esse cillum dolore eu fugiat nulla pariatur. Excepteur sint occaecat cupidatat non proident, sunt in culpa qui officia deserunt mollit anim id est laborum.

Lorem ipsum dolor sit amet, consectetur adipisicing elit, sed do eiusmod tempor incididunt ut labore et dolore magna aliqua. Ut enim ad minim veniam,

Chapter Title   7

Lorem ipsum dolor sit amet, consectetur adipisicing elit, sed do eiusmod tempor incididunt ut labore et dolore magna aliqua. Ut enim ad minim veniam, quis nostrud exercitation ullamco laboris nisi ut aliquip ex ea commodo consequat. Duis aute irure dolor in reprehenderit in voluptate velit esse cillum dolore eu fugiat nulla pariatur. Excepteur sint occaecat cupidatat non proident, sunt in culpa qui officia deserunt mollit anim id est laborum.

Lorem ipsum dolor sit amet, consectetur adipisicing elit, sed do eiusmod tempor incididunt ut labore et dolore magna aliqua. Ut enim ad minim veniam, quis nostrud exercitation ullamco laboris nisi ut aliquip ex ea commodo consequat. Duis aute irure dolor in reprehenderit in voluptate velit esse cillum dolore eu fugiat nulla pariatur. Excepteur sint occaecat

cupidatat non proident, sunt in culpa qui officia deserunt mollit anim id est laborum.

Lorem ipsum dolor sit amet, consectetur adipisicing elit, sed do eiusmod tempor incididunt ut labore et dolore magna aliqua. Ut enim ad minim veniam, quis nostrud exercitation ullamco laboris

officia deserunt mollit anim id est laborum.

Lorem ipsum dolor sit amet, consectetur adipisicing elit, sed do eiusmod tempor incididunt ut labore et dolore magna aliqua. Ut enim ad minim veniam, quis nostrud exercitation ullamco laboris nisi ut

Lorem ipsum dolor sit amet, consectetur adipisicing elit, sed do eiusmod tempor incididunt ut labore et dolore magna aliqua. Ut

Grid filled incorrectly.

6   Book Title

Lorem ipsum dolor sit amet, consectetur adipisicing elit, sed do eiusmod tempor incididunt ut labore et dolore magna aliqua. Ut enim ad minim veniam, quis nostrud exercitation ullamco laboris nisi ut aliquip ex ea commodo consequat. Duis aute irure dolor in reprehenderit in voluptate velit esse cillum dolore eu fugiat nulla pariatur. Excepteur sint occaecat cupidatat non proident, sunt in culpa qui officia deserunt mollit anim id est laborum.

Lorem ipsum dolor sit amet, consectetur adipisicing elit, sed do eiusmod tempor incididunt ut labore et dolore magna aliqua. Ut enim ad minim veniam, quis nostrud exercitation ullamco laboris nisi ut aliquip ex ea commodo consequat. Duis aute irure dolor in reprehenderit in voluptate velit esse cillum dolore eu fugiat nulla pariatur. Excepteur sint occaecat cupidatat non proident, sunt in culpa qui officia

Lorem ipsum dolor sit amet, consectetur adipisicing elit, sed do eiusmod tempor incididunt ut labore et dolore magna aliqua. Ut enim ad minim veniam, quis nostrud exercitation ullamco laboris nisi ut aliquip ex ea commodo consequat. Duis aute irure dolor in reprehenderit in voluptate velit esse cillum

Lorem ipsum dolor sit amet, consectetur adipisicing elit, sed do eiusmod tempor incididunt ut labore et dolore magna aliqua. Ut enim ad minim veniam, quis nostrud

Chapter Title   7

Lorem ipsum dolor sit amet, consectetur adipisicing elit, sed do eiusmod tempor incididunt ut labore et dolore magna aliqua. Ut enim ad minim veniam, quis nostrud exercitation ullamco laboris nisi ut aliquip ex ea commodo consequat. Duis aute irure dolor in reprehenderit in voluptate velit esse cillum dolore eu fugiat nulla pariatur. Excepteur sint occaecat cupidatat non proident, sunt in culpa qui officia deserunt mollit anim id est laborum.

Lorem ipsum dolor sit amet, consectetur adipisicing elit, sed do eiusmod tempor incididunt ut labore et dolore magna aliqua. Ut enim ad minim veniam, quis nostrud

cupidatat non proident, sunt in culpa qui officia deserunt mollit anim id est laborum.

Lorem ipsum dolor sit amet, consectetur adipisicing elit, sed do eiusmod tempor incididunt ut labore et dolore magna aliqua. Ut enim ad minim veniam, quis nostrud exercitation ullamco laboris nisi ut aliquip ex ea commodo consequat. Duis aute irure dolor in reprehenderit in voluptate velit esse cillum dolore eu fugiat nulla pariatur. Excepteur sint occaecat

exercitation ullamco laboris nisi ut aliquip ex ea commodo consequat. Duis aute irure dolor in reprehenderit in voluptate velit esse cillum dolore eu fugiat nulla pariatur. Excepteur sint occaecat cupidatat non proident, sunt in culpa qui officia deserunt mol-

Grid filled correctly.

210

Avoid placing images so that their edges end in the middle of grid squares causing narrow columns of text to form beside the image. Neither should images and text fill grid columns incompletely leaving awkward white space as seen on the right-hand page in the example (previous page).

Most images can stand a bit of cropping. In fact, many images are stronger after they are cropped because the subject of the image takes center stage.

Size indicates relative importance. Try to keep this in mind when choosing images. The bigger the image, the more important the reader will think it is to the story.

Images need space around them. In most cases, the space between the columns serves as a good rule for the space to leave around your images. If the space between your columns is one-quarter of one inch (.25"), use the text wrap feature to give the image space on every side except the side where you want to place a caption. Captions, because they belong to the photo, should be closer (see below).

Note: Captions and credits are not the same. Captions explain who or what is in the image. Credits acknowledge who owns or has possession of the image. Captions should accompany the image on the page, aligned left beginning at the left edge of the photograph, not centered underneath. Centering captions creates visual obstacles for the reader. Credits can be given on the page with the image just after the caption, or in a list of credits at the end of the book or each chapter.

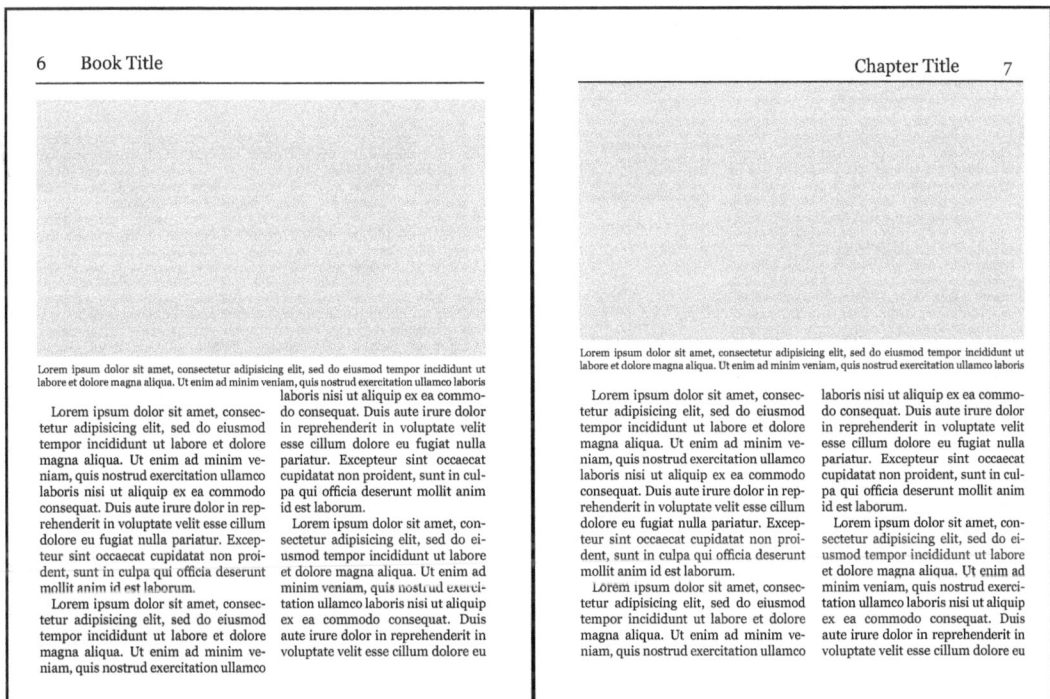

Images with captions.

PUBLISH A MEMOIR

Lorem ipsum dolor sit amet, consectetur adipisicing elit, sed do eiusmod tempor incididunt ut labore et dolore magna aliqua. Ut enim ad minim veniam, quis nostrud exercitation ullamco laboris nisi ut aliquip ex ea commodo consequat. Duis aute irure dolor in reprehenderit in voluptate velit esse cillum dolore eu fugiat nulla pariatur. Excepteur sint occaecat cupidatat non proident, sunt in culpa qui officia deserunt mollit anim id est laborum.

Lorem ipsum dolor sit amet

Lorem ipsum dolor sit amet, consectetur adipisicing elit, sed do eiusmod tempor incididunt ut labore et dolore magna aliqua. Ut enim ad minim veniam, quis nostrud exercitation ullamco laboris nisi ut aliquip ex ea commodo consequat. Duis aute irure dolor in reprehenderit in voluptate velit esse cillum dolore eu fugiat nulla pariatur. Excepteur sint occaecat cupidatat non proident, sunt in culpa qui officia deserunt mollit anim id est laborum.

Lorem ipsum dolor sit amet, consectetur adipisicing elit, sed do eiusmod tempor incididunt ut labore et dolore magna aliqua. Ut enim ad minim veniam, quis nostrud exercitation ullamco laboris nisi ut aliquip ex ea commodo consequat. Duis aute irure dolor in reprehenderit in voluptate velit esse cillum dolore eu fugiat nulla pariatur. Excepteur sint occaecat cupidatat non proident, sunt in culpa qui officia deserunt mollit anim id est laborum. Ut

Lorem ipsum dolor sit amet, consectetur adipisicing elit, sed do eiusmod tempor incididunt ut labore et dolore magna aliqua. Ut enim ad minim veniam, quis nostrud exercitation ullamco laboris nisi ut aliquip ex ea commodo consequat. Duis aute irure dolor in reprehenderit in voluptate velit esse cillum dolore eu fugiat nulla pariatur. Excepteur sint occaecat cupidatat non proident, sunt in culpa qui officia deserunt mollit anim id est laborum.

Lorem ipsum dolor sit amet

teur sint occaecat cupidatat non proident, sunt in culpa qui officia deserunt mollit anim id est laborum.

Lorem ipsum dolor sit amet, consectetur adipisicing elit, sed do eiusmod tempor incididunt ut labore et dolore magna aliqua. Ut enim ad minim ve

Pull-quotes across columns (left); Pull-quotes within a column (right).

Lorem ipsum dolor sit amet, consectetur adipisicing elit, sed do eiusmod tempor incididunt ut labore et dolore magna aliqua. Ut enim ad minim veniam, quis nostrud exercitation ullamco laboris nisi ut aliquip ex ea commodo consequat. Duis aute irure dolor in reprehenderit in voluptate velit esse cillum dolore eu fugiat nulla pariatur. Excepteur sint occaecat cupidatat non proident, sunt in culpa qui officia deserunt mollit anim id est laborum.

- Lorem ipsum dolor sit amet
- Consectetur adipisicing elit
- Sed do eiusmod tempor
- Incididunt ut labore
- Magna aliqua
- Ut enim ad minim veniam
- Quis nostrud exercitation

Lorem ipsum dolor sit amet, consectetur adipisicing elit, sed do eiusmod tempor incididunt ut labore et dolore magna aliqua. Ut enim ad minim veniam, quis nostrud exercitation ullamco laboris nisi ut aliquip ex ea commodo consequat. Duis aute irure dolor in reprehenderit in voluptate velit esse cillum dolore eu fugiat nulla pariatur. Excepteur sint occaecat cupidatat non proident, sunt in culpa qui officia deserunt mollit anim id est laborum. Ut

Text spread across two columns with a side bar (left); Three columns (right).

If you want to add fancy photo corners or edge effects to your images, do so in your image editing software after you have re-sized the image for its spot within the grid. Pick one or two fancy effects, and stick with them for consistency.

Advanced Page Layouts

What follows are advanced layout options often found in non-fiction books. Use them for visual interest, but only if they benefit the reader in some way.

Pull Quotes

Pull quotes are used by magazines to entice readers to stop flipping pages and start reading. They are an opportunity for a little creativity on the page. In a book, they can be used effectively, although they should be used sparingly.

Side Bars

Sidebars are another way to use your grid to add information that you may not want to include within the narrative. It may be information about a photograph that is too long for a simple caption, or something you want the reader to know alongside the narrative (see the example opposite).

❧❧

If you take the time to create a basic page layout that is easy to flow text and place images into, your book will look better than most. Look through your personal library and find a simple layout that you like. Look at books of the same physical size—it can be hard to match layouts if you do not.

Now that you have a feel for the general layout of the page, the next chapter will explore the fundamentals of typesetting.

Chapter 17

Typesetting—The Basics

Typesetting conventions have developed over the last 400 years to make books both beautiful and easy to read. If you mess with the rules of readability, reading comprehension drops dramatically.

The rest of this chapter will help you avoid leaving little clues that the book is "self-published."

The Basics

Before you can start typesetting the different parts of your book, you need a good understanding of what affects reading comprehension.

The Rules of Readability

In addition to hundreds of years of publishing tradition, modern studies have determined what affects our ability to read and comprehend type. The rules that follow are based upon the results of tradition, observation and studies.

Use serif fonts, also called typefaces. Twice as many readers are able to understand words printed in serif typefaces. Serif fonts have small extenders between letters. Sans serif typefaces are easier to read on the screen, so these fonts are fine for websites and electronic communications, but stick to serif fonts for printed books.

High contrast is best. Black type on a white page is optimal. Even dark blues and browns are more difficult to read than black. Avoid placing type on a colored background unless the background is very light. Avoid reverse outs. It is difficult for readers to digest white type on a black background for more than a one- or two-word headline.

Avoid all capitals (all caps). Not only do readers feel as if you are shouting at them, they recognize words based upon the top half of the letters. Letters in all caps lack the characteristic upper extenders and rounded forms readers use to recognize whole words at a time, so text in all caps slows reading to a crawl.

Give the letters room to breathe. Squeezing type together makes text uncomfortable, if not impossible, to read.

Use bold sparingly. Headlines and subheads in bold help the reader skim through the material, but large blocks of type in bold looks dense and is difficult to read.

> A brilliant piece of graphic design which goes unread is a waste of paper, ink, money and effort, and perhaps above all, a lost opportunity to communicate something of value.
>
> **—Colin Wheildon and Mal Warwick**
> *Type & Layout: How Typography and Design*
> *Can Get Your Message Across or Get In the Way*

Fonts

Typography does not have to be sophisticated to look good and read easily. Typefaces often come in families that include Roman (plain), italics, bold and bold italics. A few font families will also have black (heavy) or light (narrow).

Choose a serif typeface for the main body of the book. These are common serif typefaces used in books: Adobe Caslon, Adobe Garamond, Baskerville Old Face, Bookman Old Style, Goudy Old Style, Palatino, and Utopia.

Common Body Text Fonts	Common Headline Fonts		
Adobe Caslon	Franklin Gothic Book	**Gill Sans** Adobe Caslon	**Franklin Gothic Book** Goudy Old Style
Adobe Garamond	Gill Sans		
Baskerville Old Face	Hypatia Sans Pro	**Myriad Pro** Baskerville	**Tahoma** Palatino
Bookman Old Style	Myriad Pro		
Goudy Oldstyle	Tahoma	**Hypatia Sans** Bookman	
Palatino			

Common body and headline fonts (left); Font pairs (right).

You can keep the same font for headlines and subheads, but make them bolder and bigger, or you can use a sans serif typeface. If you prefer a sans serif font, choose one that creates a good contrast with your body text font. Weak contrasts do not look as good as strong contrasts.

These are common sans serif headline fonts: Franklin Gothic Book, Gill Sans, Hypathia Sans Pro, Myriad Pro, Nimbus Sans, Segoe and Tahoma.

Fonts to avoid: Times New Roman and Helvetica (both are newspaper fonts meant for narrow columns), Arial (overused), Copperplate (all caps), Courier (unless you want to look like you have used a typewriter), Papyrus (so overused it has become a cliché), Brush Script, Comic Sans, Curlz, anything that implies handwriting, and fonts supposed to make one think of the Dark Ages, the Middle Ages, the Renaissance, or the Book of Kells.

Avoid script fonts, even for something personal such as a transcription of a letter or a page from a diary. Loosely set script fonts may be fine for chapter titles but are difficult to read for more than a few words. Italics in one of the basic book fonts will distinguish itself enough to make a transcription stand out.

There are three major font file types: Open Type, TrueType and Postscript. Apple opened the world of scalable type design with its TrueType fonts. Adobe got into the game a bit later with its Type1 (Postscript) fonts. OpenType has been a collaboration of Microsoft and Adobe and looks to be winning over publishers and printers.

Some fonts require purchase in order to use them; others come pre-installed in your word processing or page layout programs already licensed for you to use. Avoid free fonts available on the Internet (mostly TrueType). Some have serious technical issues that you will not want to discover after your book is printed.

Avoid any font that will not embed into a PDF (Portable Document Format—the file type most commonly requested by printers). If you do not have a license for your fonts, they will not save correctly into a PDF. If you are unsure, type a few words in each of your chosen fonts and convert that test file into a PDF. Most word processors will save files to PDFs using a simple "save as" command. If no error messages appear, the fonts are most probably all right.

There is no need to go wild with fonts. It is rare to use more than two to three fonts in a book's interior. Stick to the commonly used book fonts. You can be a little more creative with the font on the cover.

Type Size

For the main body of the book, make the font size big enough to read easily, and appropriate to the column width. Narrower columns can handle smaller fonts.

For adults, most fonts are readable between point sizes 10 and 12. Smaller font sizes are difficult to read. Smaller type is fine for captions or footnotes, down to 7 or 8 points, depending upon the font. Larger font sizes, 14 points or larger, should be reserved for large print books made for people with impaired vision. Larger font sizes are acceptable for headlines and subheads.

Leading

The term leading comes from a time when type was set by hand and thin strips of lead divided lines horizontally to create a space above and below each line.

Standard leading is two points greater than the type height for standard text and proportionally larger with larger sized text. Your body text may be 12 points tall with 14 point leading, whereas your cover font could be 48 points tall with 58 point leading—an amount proportional to the size of the large letters.

One way to decrease the density on the page (or lengthen a manuscript) is to increase the leading. Increasing the leading too much, however, will look like double spacing which is not attractive.

Emphasis

It is always better to make the reader feel emphasis with your words rather than using typesetting tricks. Italics is the most common way to show emphasis. Italics is also used to highlight foreign words, indicate book or movie titles, and the thoughts of a character—a rare occurrence in non-fiction.

Use bold, if you must, but only for short phrases. Paragraph after paragraph of bold text looks dense and uninviting.

Keep the exclamation points under control. If everything is important, nothing is—relatively. Avoid all capitals in running text unless you want the reader to feel that you are shouting your message.

There is no need to put everyday expressions in quotes, except to indicate irony. When air quotes became a popular hand gesture, they also proliferated in printed works. Try not to litter your book with unnecessary quotes. Save them for the places where you are actually quoting another author.

Avoid underlining, except as hyperlinks. Underlining had a place when typewriters offered little else, but underlining is not used for emphasis today.

Case

In English, when to use upper case and when to use lower case is fairly straight forward. Sentence case is used in paragraphs where capital letters begin sentences. Title case is used for headlines and subheads only. In title case, most words are capitalized except prepositions (by, to, from, of, on, with, at), articles (a, an, the), and coordinating conjunctions (and, but, or, for, and nor).

Capitals are used for proper nouns, such as the names of people (George Washington), businesses (General Motors), specific places (Savannah, America, the Mississippi Delta), nationalities (German), languages (French) and religions (Methodist).

Job or honorary titles are capitalized, but only when it refers to a specific person and precedes their name. So, there are presidents elected in the United States, but President Lincoln gets a capital in his title.

Capitals, like commas, can run amok. In book publishing, fewer capitals are preferred. If in doubt, use the lowercase letter.

Letter Spacing and Kerning

Letter spacing and kerning affect the distance between letters. Letter spacing (tracking) affects the spacing between all letters. Adjusting the letter spacing can open up the look of a page and make some fonts easier to read. In most cases, however, your software will correctly determine letter spacing. On occasion, altering letter spacing can help avoid orphans (more on this shortly).

Kerning adjusts the spacing between two, side-by-side letters to make them look more natural sitting next to each other. The auto-kerning feature in most software is fine for most body text. Kerning individual pairs of letters may be important, however, to make the large letters on your cover look their best.

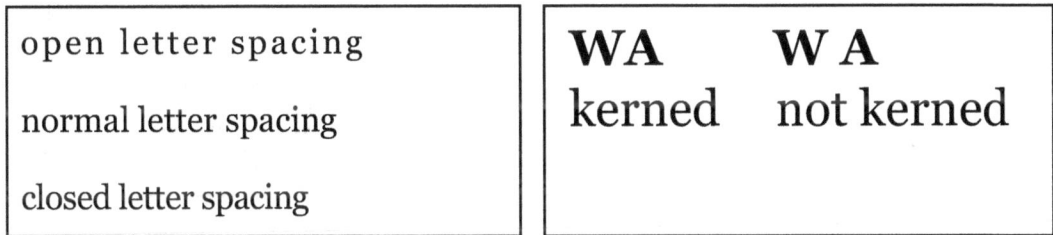

open letter spacing	**WA** **W A**
normal letter spacing	kerned not kerned
closed letter spacing	

Letter spacing (left); Kerning (right).

Titles, Headlines, and Subheads

Titles, headlines and subheads are about hierarchy—clues to what is the most important. At the top of the hierarchy (and also in the largest font size and strength) are the chapter titles. Next are the headlines that should be bigger and bolder than subheads. If needed, create sub-subheads down to a second or third level.

The lowest level could be a run-in subhead where the subhead does not sit above the paragraph, but begins the paragraph and ends in a period (see below).

For most books, headlines and subheads should be aligned flush left. Centered or right-aligned headlines and subheads can work (albeit a challenge), but only over fully justified paragraphs. Whichever style you choose, be consistent.

Keep headlines and subheads short and sweet. Avoid having them run onto a second line, if possible. Headlines and subheads do not end in punctuation, except if you are using a run-in subhead, such as:

Tuesday. On the first sunny morning in a month, ...
Wednesday. We began to harvest ...

Aesthetically, headlines and subheads are never stacked one on top of another. There is always a paragraph in between them.

Lorem ipsum dolor sit amet, consectetur adipisicing elit, sed do eiusmod tempor incididunt ut labore et dolore magna aliqua. Ut enim ad minim veniam, quis nostrud exercitation ullamco laboris nisi ut aliquip ex ea commodo consequat. Duis aute irure dolor in reprehenderit in voluptate velit esse cillum dolore eu fugiat nulla pariatur. Excepteur sint occaecat cupidatat non proident, sunt in culpa qui officia deserunt mollit anim id est laborum.

Headline Headline Headline

Lorem ipsum dolor sit amet, consectetur adipisicing elit, sed do eiusmod tempor incididunt ut labore et dolore magna aliqua. Ut enim ad minim veniam, quis nostrud exercitation ullamco laboris nisi ut aliquip ex ea commodo consequat. Duis aute irure dolor in reprehenderit in voluptate velit esse cillum dolore eu fugiat nulla pariatur. Excepteur sint occaecat cupidatat non proident, sunt in culpa qui officia deserunt mollit anim id est laborum.

Subhead Subhead Subhead Subhead

Lorem ipsum dolor sit amet, consectetur adipisicing elit, sed do eiusmod tempor incididunt ut labore et dolore magna aliqua. Ut enim ad minim veniam, quis nostrud exercitation ullamco laboris nisi ut aliquip ex ea commodo consequat. Duis aute irure dolor in reprehenderit in voluptate velit esse cillum dolore eu fugiat nulla pariatur. Excepteur sint occaecat cupidatat non proident, sunt in culpa qui officia deserunt mollit anim id est laborum.

Sub-Subhead Sub-Subhead Sub-Subhead Subhead

Lorem ipsum dolor sit amet, consectetur adipisicing elit, sed do eiusmod tempor incididunt ut labore et dolore magna aliqua. Ut enim ad minim veniam, quis nostrud exercitation ullamco laboris nisi ut aliquip ex ea commodo consequat. Duis aute irure dolor in

Lorem ipsum dolor sit amet, consectetur adipisicing elit, sed do eiusmod tempor incididunt ut labore et dolore magna aliqua. Ut enim ad minim veniam, quis nostrud exercitation ullamco laboris nisi ut aliquip ex ea commodo consequat. Duis aute irure dolor in reprehenderit in voluptate velit esse cillum dolore eu fugiat nulla pariatur. Excepteur sint occaecat cupidatat non proident, sunt in culpa qui officia deserunt mollit anim id est laborum.

Headline Headline Headline

Lorem ipsum dolor sit amet, consectetur adipisicing elit, sed do eiusmod tempor incididunt ut labore et dolore magna aliqua. Ut enim ad minim veniam, quis nostrud exercitation ullamco laboris nisi ut aliquip ex ea commodo consequat. Duis aute irure dolor in reprehenderit in voluptate velit esse cillum dolore eu fugiat nulla pariatur. Excepteur sint occaecat cupidatat non proident, sunt in culpa qui officia deserunt mollit anim id est laborum.

Subhead Subhead Subhead Subhead

Lorem ipsum dolor sit amet, consectetur adipisicing elit, sed do eiusmod tempor incididunt ut labore et dolore magna aliqua. Ut enim ad minim veniam, quis nostrud exercitation ullamco laboris nisi ut aliquip ex ea commodo consequat. Duis aute irure dolor in reprehenderit in voluptate velit esse cillum dolore eu fugiat nulla pariatur. Excepteur sint occaecat cupidatat non proident, sunt in culpa qui officia deserunt mollit anim id est laborum.

Sub-Subhead Sub-Subhead Sub-Subhead Subhead

Lorem ipsum dolor sit amet, consectetur adipisicing elit, sed do eiusmod tempor incididunt ut labore et dolore magna aliqua. Ut enim ad minim veniam, quis nostrud exercitation ullamco laboris nisi ut aliquip ex ea commodo consequat. Duis aute irure dolor in

Headlines and subheads.

Lorem ipsum dolor sit amet, consectetur adipisicing elit, sed do eiusmod tempor incididunt ut labore et dolore magna aliqua. Ut enim ad minim veniam, quis nostrud exercitation ullamco laboris nisi ut aliquip ex ea commodo consequat. Duis aute irure dolor in reprehenderit in voluptate velit esse cillum dolore eu fugiat nulla pariatur. Excepteur sint occaecat cupidatat non proident, sunt in culpa qui officia deserunt mollit anim id est laborum.

Lorem ipsum dolor sit amet, consectetur adipisicing elit, sed do eiusmod tempor incididunt ut labore et dolore magna aliqua. Ut enim ad minim veniam, quis nostrud exercitation ullamco laboris nisi ut aliquip ex ea commodo consequat. Duis aute irure dolor in reprehenderit in voluptate velit esse cillum dolore eu fugiat nulla pariatur. Ex-

cepteur sint occaecat cupidatat non proident, sunt in culpa qui officia deserunt mollit anim id est laborum.

Lorem ipsum dolor sit amet, consectetur adipisicing elit, sed do eiusmod tempor incididunt ut labore et dolore magna aliqua. Ut enim ad minim veniam, quis nostrud exercitation ullamco laboris nisi ut aliquip ex ea commodo consequat. Duis aute irure dolor in reprehenderit in voluptate velit esse cillum dolore eu fugiat nulla pariatur. Excepteur sint occaecat cupidatat non proident, sunt in culpa qui officia deserunt mollit anim id est laborum.

Lorem ipsum dolor sit amet, consectetur adipisicing elit, sed do eiusmod tempor incididunt ut labore et dolore magna aliqua. Ut enim ad minim ve-niam, quis nostrud exercitation

---

1. Lorem ipsum dolor sit amet, consectetur adipisicing elit, sed do eiusmod tempor incididunt ut labore et dolore magna aliqua. Ut enim ad minim veniam, quis nostrud exercitation ullamco laboris nisi ut aliquip ex ea commodo consequat. Duis aute irure dolor in reprehenderit in voluptate velit

---

Lorem ipsum dolor sit amet, consectetur adipisicing elit, sed do eiusmod tempor incididunt ut labore et dolore magna aliqua. Ut enim ad minim veniam, quis nostrud exercitation ullamco laboris nisi ut aliquip ex ea commodo consequat. Duis aute irure dolor in reprehenderit in voluptate velit esse cillum dolore eu fugiat nulla pariatur. Excepteur sint occaecat cupidatat non proident, sunt in culpa qui officia deserunt mollit anim id est laborum.

Lorem ipsum dolor sit amet, consectetur adipisicing elit, sed do eiusmod tempor incididunt ut labore et dolore magna aliqua. Ut enim ad minim veniam, quis nostrud exercitation ullamco laboris nisi ut aliquip ex ea commodo consequat. Duis aute irure dolor in reprehenderit in voluptate velit esse cillum dolore eu fugiat nulla pariatur. Ex-

cepteur sint occaecat cupidatat non proident, sunt in culpa qui officia deserunt mollit anim id est laborum.

Lorem ipsum dolor sit amet, consectetur adipisicing elit, sed do eiusmod tempor incididunt ut labore et dolore magna aliqua. Ut enim ad minim veniam, quis nostrud exercitation ullamco laboris nisi ut aliquip ex ea commodo consequat. Duis aute irure dolor in reprehenderit in voluptate velit esse cillum dolore eu fugiat nulla pariatur. Excepteur sint occaecat cupidatat non proident, sunt in culpa qui officia deserunt mollit anim id est laborum.

Lorem ipsum dolor sit amet, consectetur adipisicing elit, sed do eiusmod tempor incididunt ut labore et dolore magna aliqua. Ut enim ad minim ve-niam, quis nostrud exercitation

---

2. Lorem ipsum dolor sit amet, consectetur adipisicing elit, sed do eiusmod tempor incididunt ut labore et dolore magna aliqua. Ut enim ad minim veniam, quis nostrud exercitation ullamco laboris nisi ut aliquip ex ea commodo consequat. Duis aute irure dolor in reprehenderit in voluptate velit

Correct paragraph spacing.

It may not seem natural in memoirs to use many headlines and subheads, but your reader will appreciate the visual break if you do.

Paragraphs

Paragraphs are the basic building block of your book, so make paragraphs look their best.

The first paragraph in a chapter or after a headline or subhead should not have an indent—all other paragraphs should.

Indents should not be created by using a tab or by spacing over. Create a style with a first-line indent instead. If you turn your manuscript over to a typesetter full of extra spaces or tabs, he or she will have to remove them which will cost them time and you money.

Set your indent to one-quarter of an inch (.25") and not larger unless you are using big type for the visually impaired. Unfortunately, many word processing programs have the default set to an ungainly half inch (.5").

Never use a double return to create space between paragraphs. Most of the time, you will not need extra space between paragraphs, the indent will give the reader enough of a visual break. If you want more white space on the page, create a paragraph style with slightly more space above each paragraph.

Quotes

If you transcribe a document or quote another author directly, the entire paragraph(s) should be indented from both sides to form a narrower block of text. Create a bit more space above and below quoted paragraphs, as well. Quoted paragraphs should be fully justified (explanation below).

Justified Text

In books, paragraphs should be fully justified not justified ragged right. That is, they should look like a square block of text. In the era of typewriters, ragged right was unavoidable. The type along the right-hand edge of the page was uneven (ragged). Modern software creates much better looking fully justified text blocks.

One potential problem with full justification is the text on the last line of each paragraph. If there are only a couple of words, full justification will spread the words out to the right-hand edge leaving unnaturally large spaces between the words. Most word processing programs give you a way to keep the last line of each fully justified paragraph together on the left.

Use centering and ragged right justification sparingly; in fact, almost never. Poetry with short lines can be centered, but a full paragraph that is centered is difficult to read.

Justified Ragged Right	Justified Ragged Left
Lorem ipsum dolor sit amet, consectetur adipisicing elit, sed do eiusmod tempor incididunt ut labore et dolore magna aliqua. Ut enim ad minim veniam, quis nostrud exercitation ullamco laboris nisi ut aliquip ex ea commodo consequat. Duis aute irure dolor	Lorem ipsum dolor sit amet, consectetur adipisicing elit, sed do eiusmod tempor incididunt ut labore et dolore magna aliqua. Ut enim ad minim veniam, quis nostrud exercitation ullamco laboris nisi ut aliquip ex ea commodo consequat. Duis

Ragged right.   Ragged left.

Fully Justified Correctly	Fully Justified Incorrectly
Lorem ipsum dolor sit amet, consectetur adipisicing elit, sed do eiusmod tempor incididunt ut labore et dolore magna aliqua. Ut enim ad minim veniam, quis nostrud exercitation ullamco laboris nisi ut aliquip ex ea commodo consequat.	Lorem ipsum dolor sit amet, consectetur adipisicing elit, sed do eiusmod tempor incididunt ut labore et dolore magna aliqua. Ut enim ad minim veniam, quis nostrud exercitation ullamco laboris nisi ut aliquip ex ea commodo consequat.

Fully justified correctly (left); Fully justified incorrectly (forced outward spacing) (right).

Hyphenation

Most of the time, automatic hyphenation is fine because it avoids creating rivers of white down the page which disturbs the reader's ability to move smoothly from left to right, word to word. On occasion, automatic hyphenation will result in lines of hyphens stacked on top of each other (see above left). If this happens, you can artificially hyphenate a few words to make the paragraph look better.

Watch for odd hyphenation breaks. You would not want menswear to become men-swear, or therapist to become the-rapist.

Widows and Orphans

Widows and orphans are bits of text that do not fit neatly into the column grid.

Widows are created when: the last line of a paragraph appears on the following page or at the top of the next column; a headline or subhead is in one column (page) but the paragraph that follows it is in another column (page); or the last bullet in a list is in another column (page).

Page layout programs have much better tools to control widows and orphans than do word processors, including ways to control white space and hyphenation, commands to keep lines together, and the ability to alter the length of a column to force a line into the next column.

6　Book Title

Lorem ipsum dolor sit amet, consectetur adipisicing elit, sed do eiusmod tempor incididunt ut labore et dolore magna aliqua. Ut enim ad minim veniam, quis nostrud exercitation ullamco laboris nisi ut aliquip ex ea commodo consequat. Duis aute irure dolor in reprehenderit in voluptate velit esse cillum dolore eu fugiat nulla pariatur. Excepteur sint occaecat cupidatat non proident, sunt in culpa qui officia deserunt mollit anim id laborum.

Lorem ipsum dolor sit amet, consectetur adipisicing elit, sed do eiusmod tempor incididunt ut labore et dolore magna aliqua. Ut enim ad minim veniam, quis nostrud exercitation ullamco laboris nisi ut aliquip ex ea commodo consequat. Duis aute irure dolor in reprehenderit in voluptate velit esse cillum dolore eu fugiat nulla pariatur. Excepteur sint occaecat cupidatat non proident, sunt in culpa qui officia deserunt mollit anim id est laborum.

Lorem ipsum dolor sit amet, consectetur adipisicing elit, sed do eiusmod tempor incididunt ut labore et dolore magna aliqua. Ut enim ad minim veniam, quis nostrud exercitation ullamco laboris nisi ut aliquip ex ea commodo consequat. Duis aute irure dolor in reprehenderit in voluptate velit esse cillum dolore eu fugiat nulla pariatur. Excepteur sint occaecat cupidatat non proident, sunt in culpa qui officia deserunt mollit anim id est laborum.

Lorem ipsum dolor sit amet, consectetur adipisicing elit, sed do eiusmod tempor incididunt ut labore et dolore magna aliqua. Ut enim ad minim veniam, quis nostrud exercitation ullamco laboris nisi ut aliquip ex ea commodo consequat. Duis aute irure dolor in reprehenderit in voluptate velit esse cillum dolore eu fugiat nulla pariatur.

Headline headline

Excepteur sint occaecat cupi-

Chapter Title　7

datat non proident, sunt in.

Lorem ipsum dolor sit amet, consectetur adipisicing elit, sed do eiusmod tempor incididunt ut labore et dolore magna aliqua. Ut enim ad minim veniam, quis nostrud exercitation ullamco laboris nisi ut aliquip ex ea commodo consequat. Duis aute irure dolor in reprehenderit in voluptate velit esse cillum dolore eu fugiat nulla pariatur. Excepteur sint occaecat cupidatat non proident, sunt in culpa qui officia deserunt mollit anim id est laborum. UtLorem ipsum dolor sit amet, consectetur adipisicing elit, sed do eiusmod tempor incididunt ut labore magna aliqua. Ut enim ad minim veniam, quis nostrud exercitation ullamco laboris nisi ut aliquip ex ea commodo consequat. Duis aute irure dolor in reprehenderit in voluptate velit esse cillum dolore eu fugiat nulla pariatur. Excepteur sint occaecat cupidatat non proident.

• sunt in culpa qui officia
• deserunt mollit anim id
• est officia laborum.

Lorem ipsum dolor sit amet, consectetur adipisicing elit, sed do eiusmod tempor incididunt ut labore et dolore magna aliqua. Ut enim ad minim veniam, quis nostrud exercitation ullamco laboris nisi ut aliquip ex ea commodo consequat. Duis aute irure dolor in reprehenderit in voluptate velit esse cillum dolore eu fugiat nulla pariatur. Excepteur sint occaecat cupidatat non proi-

Lorem ipsum dolor sit amet, consectetur adipisicing elit, sed do eiusmod tempor incididunt ut labore et dolore magna aliqua. Ut enim ad minim veniam, quis nostrud exercitation ullamco laboris nisi ut aliquip ex ea commodo consequat. Duis aute irure dolor in reprehenderit in voluptate velit esse cillum dolore eu fugiat nulla pariatur. Excepteur sint occaecat cupidatat non proi-

Widows and orphans.

If you are using a word processor, one way to control widows is to add a hard return before a widowed headline to force it into the next column or onto the next page. If you have a widowed bullet or a widowed line, see if you can cut the text above without changing the meaning to allow enough space for the line or bullet to remain with the paragraph or list.

Orphans are created when: the first line of a paragraph appears in one column (page) but the rest of the paragraph appears in the next column (page); the last word of a paragraph is left on a line by itself.

One way to control orphans is to turn on or off automatic hyphenation for the paragraph. This may shift another word onto the last line of the paragraph. Another option is to alter the text without altering the meaning, so there are fewer words to fit in the paragraph.

Initials and Acronyms

How you handle initials and acronyms is a matter of preference as long as you are consistent throughout.

How you handle people known only by their initials is a matter of style. Typically, there are no spaces between initials, so D.S. Yates rather than D. S. Yates.

Acronyms typically do not have periods between the letters, so NASA rather than N.A.S.A.

Some acronyms, such as AM and PM, are typically set in small caps (AM and PM) rather than in full caps, although some style guides use a.m. and p.m. (or am and pm) instead. Small caps are a function of the font, although not all fonts have a small caps option.

Web and Email Addresses

Because we are in the Internet age, your book may include website URLs (website addresses), or email addresses. In electronic books (eBooks), these addresses can be made into hyperlinks so that the reader can click on the link to be taken to the website, or to launch an email program. In printed books, it is up to you whether or not you leave the color and underlining that word processing programs add when addresses are hyperlinked. Most word processors use a bright blue for hyperlinks, which may not be readable in print. Changing them to black will help. Increasing the letter spacing in website addresses also makes them easier to read.

Punctuation

Punctuation can make or break meaning. If you have not already read Lynne Truss's book, *Eats, Shoots & Leaves: A Zero Tolerance Approach to Punctuation*, you should. Single-handedly, she is conducting a rather hilarious war on the proliferation of commas.

Dashes and Hyphens

Hyphens are used to create compound adjectives, such as state-of-the-art computer. Hyphens are used for compound numbers (forty-four books), double last names (Sir Watkin Williams-Wynn), and spelled-out fractions (two-thirds). Hyphens once were used to distinguish all pre-fixes (pre-arranged), but less so today. If eliminating the hyphen would cause confusion with another word (recovered a lost wallet versus re-covered a sofa), then use the hyphen.

Dashes are not hyphens, nor double hyphens. Fortunately, most word processors will turn double hyphens into an em dash. Unfortunately, most word processors do not know the difference between the em dash and the en dash.

An en dash, a dash approximately the width of the letter n, is used to indicate duration, so October–December (October through December), or 10–12 (ten to twelve).

An em dash, a dash approximately the width of the letter m, is used when you want the reader to pause a bit longer than they would for a comma, but not as long as they would for a period. Em dashes are a matter of preference. Many authors will use parentheses to set off a change in thought, others prefer em dashes.

En and em dashes do not have spaces—before or after them.

Ellipses

Ellipses, a series of three periods (...) with a bit of extra space in between, are used to indicate a long pause in thought, or that material was left out of a quote. Fortunately, if you put three periods in a row without adding a space in between, most word processors will display them correctly.

If you end a sentence with an ellipsis, you still need a period to end the sentence, so there will be four dots.

Ellipses require a full space before and a full space after.

Special Characters

Special characters include bullets, copyright symbols, and accent marks on foreign language words. These special characters are found in glyph or symbols menus. Fortunately, many word processors and page layout programs automatically insert correct accents on common words such as cliché.

Serial Commas

Although Lynne Truss is waging an admirable war on the proliferation of commas, sometimes the serial comma is needed when listing items. For example, you could eliminate the last comma from a list such as bananas, oranges, and apples. If however, you eliminated the last comma from, "To my siblings, Mom, and Grandma," you would be implying that your mother and grandmother were your siblings (i.e. "To my siblings, Mom and Grandma").

It is up to you how you handle serial commas, as long as meaning is clear.

Quotation Marks

Quotation marks are not apostrophes. Quotation marks are the curly-cue-looking marks that face one way at the beginning of a quote, and the other way at the end. Make this simple on yourself by turning on the "smart quotes," in your word processing or page layout program and avoid fonts that do not have true, left and right quotation marks.

Quotation marks should not be used for emphasis. Use italics if you want to get the reader's attention. Use quotation marks for direct quotations, to alert readers that a term is being used in a non-standard way such as for irony or sarcasm, or to replace the words "so-called."

Place commas and periods inside quotation marks. Colons and semi-colons belong outside quotation marks. Place question marks or exclamation points inside if they belong to quoted material, otherwise outside.

Semi-Colons

Semi-colons are used to link two independent clauses together. Most of the time, however, you can use a period and start a new sentence with the same effect.

You can also use a semi-colon to link items in a list together where a comma could cause confusion. For example, "some people choose to go places by motorized vehicles, cars, motorcycles or buses; but others, for different reasons, choose to walk, bicycle or roller skate."

Apostrophes

Apostrophes are used to indicate possession (e.g. John's book), to create contractions (e.g. don't) and to indicate the omission of letters, so Rock and Roll becomes Rock 'n' Roll because both the "a" and the "d" in "and" are replaced with an apostrophe.

A single, straight apostrophe indicates feet (e.g. 125'). A double, straight apostrophe indicates inches (e.g. 3").

In the 80s, means the temperature is in the 80s. In the '80s, means the decade of the 1980s (or 1880s). There is no apostrophe when referring to a decade (1850s) unless you are indicating possession (1850's clothing styles).

Lines, Rules, and Strokes

The terms lines, rules and strokes all mean a line. Most often lines are used in the header to separate the book title or chapter title from the body text.

If you use lines, choose a numbered point size for the thickness of your lines. Avoid the hairline setting, because "hairline" is interpreted differently by each printer's machinery, so the results may be unexpected.

Color

If the interior of your book is color throughout, you can use color for headlines and subheads to make them stand out. Black text is still the easiest to read, so if you use a color for headlines or subheads, choose one that is dark enough to be read easily, and use the same color throughout the book for consistency. Any dark color can work, although people with red-green color blindness will appreciate it if you avoid those two colors.

Cross-References

You may need to include cross-references to chapters, numbered sections, illustrations or pages. The only way to create cross-references without creating a lot of extra work for yourself, is to leave a visual indicator in the text (e.g. [XXXXX]), and wait until the final page proofs are available before adding the appropriate reference.

Most memoirs do not need cross-references except in the index. You can accomplish much of the same with good explanations in foot- or endnotes.

Clean Up Your Manuscript Files

Before you begin typesetting, clean up your manuscript files.

One common habit of people who learned to type on typewriters is to put two spaces before the beginning of a new sentence. Modern word processors use proportional spacing at the end of sentences so they do not need the extra space. Use the Find/Replace command to search for two spaces and replace them with a single space. Repeat this task until the software indicates that no more replacements have been made. This will eliminate the extra spaces created by the old typewriter trick of spacing over instead of using tabs, as well.

Remove extra tabs. Paragraphs should not be created by tabbing over. They should be given a style with a first-line indent instead (see Creating Styles below).

Eliminate double returns using Find/Replace. Double returns should not separate paragraphs. The first-line indent in the next paragraph will be enough to distinguish when one paragraph ends and the next begins.

Extra space is used to indicate the start of a new section or a change in topic where a new chapter or headline is not necessary. Double returns are not used to create this extra space. Instead, create a paragraph style to govern this situation, with even more space above the paragraph than that above a subhead, but less than a double return.

Look for odd line breaks, out of place page breaks, and missing punctuation.

Once your manuscript is clean, you can begin creating styles to govern how the text will look.

Create Styles

Most word processing and page layout programs allow you to create styles for different types of text (paragraphs, headlines and so on), and then apply the style when appropriate.

The easiest way to start formatting an entire chapter is to create a style for the majority of the body copy and apply it to the entire chapter. Then you can create new styles for first paragraphs that do not have indents, headlines that could be in bigger or bolder text than the body, and image captions that should be somewhat smaller than the body text.

In most software, each time you encounter a need for a new style, you can manually format the text, and then select that text to create a new style—the software will copy each of the attributes of the new text into the new style. After you create the new style, simply highlight text and apply the new style when needed.

If you do not believe you can typeset the book yourself, you could hire a book packager to help you.

Working with a Book Packager

Book packagers (designers) offer layout and design services, including book design, typesetting, image preparation, cover design and in some cases indexing. Most book packagers will offer these services together or individually, depending upon your needs.

Interior Design

Provide your manuscript along with a few examples of layouts you like to the book packager so they can understand the type of book you have written, as well as your style preferences. Acquiring good examples may necessitate a trip to a library with a good memoir collection or to a bookstore that wells a wide variety of non-fiction works.

Fiction tends to be formatted in a different way than non-fiction, although you will find good family histories formatted as fiction, such as *The Family* by David Laskin. Non-fiction formatting tends to be content specific, so choosing a nice-looking computer manual may not do you much good either. Using a good memoir as your guide is probably best. A book designer who has worked with memoirs before may have suggestions for you.

Most book designers will offer two to three designs plus two rounds of revisions before you pay more than the initial quote. The better you can explain or demonstrate what you want at the outset, the more likely the designer is to create what you are looking for in the first round of designs.

Typesetting

Most of the time, if you have a professional design your book, you will also have them typeset the book because you may not use the same software they use, so there would be no way to hand over the master layout to you. Before you submit your manuscript for typesetting, clean up any overlooked double spaces, tabs and section breaks. Then proofread carefully so you are not paying the typesetter to do that for you.

Print it out. A printout is a way to be sure that nothing is missing or misplaced in the manuscript files. Check it over carefully first. If you find errors and make corrections to the manuscript, print a clean copy for the typesetter.

Image Preparation

You cannot prepare your images for the correct display size at the correct resolution until you have a layout in order to know how big or small each image must be in order to fit into the grid. If you have scanned the images at sizes larger than what will be needed, much of the hard work should already be done. Your book packager can then help you to correctly size the image for the book's layout.

Indexing

Not all book designers offer indexing services, although some do. Using a book packager or a professional indexer can be costly because he or she must read the manuscript in order to determine what should or should not be indexed, and that takes time.

Often called a poor man's index, you can make the job of indexing easy for a book packager by printing a copy of the final layout, and highlighting the items to be indexed. The highlighted copy along with a style sheet of how you want names, places and subjects indexed should be enough for your book packager to take care of the indexing for you.

Another option is to mark the index entries for yourself in your word processor. Index tags from Word import into InDesign, for example, and most book designers accept Word documents. Before you spend the time to index this way, make certain that the book packager can import your index tags.

Cover Design

Every book should have a cover worthy of the work it took to write the book. Book packagers offer cover design services, or you may want to use a cover designer—a graphic artist who only designs covers. Either way, he or she will need to know whether the book will be available for sale. Commercial books have different requirements than books solely for your family's enjoyment. The elements of a book cover meant for commercial sale are described in Chapter 21: Designing the Cover.

The cover will be the last part of your project finalized because spine width is dependent upon the final page count and the paper used, which may be different from printer to printer. In most cases, you will receive a template from your printer after you have a final page count, so that the dimensions and spine width are correct in the template. The designer can assemble the elements ahead of time and make final adjustments to the file when the page count is known.

File Formats

Most book packagers can work with any type of file format generated by one of the common word processors (.doc, .docx, .wpd) as well as plain text files (.txt) or rich text files (.rtf). Most word processors will also convert their native file formats to something more common such as a Microsoft Word file, if that is what the designer prefers.

Ask before converting anything. Converting to a plain text file will eliminate all of your formatting. Converting to a PDF is not helpful either, since PDFs are not easily re-formatted.

Portfolio

Before you ask about cost, look at the designer's work. You want to make sure that he or she has experience preparing books for a printer. Many book packagers have an online portfolio or can send you examples.

Another option is to hire someone who is looking to create a portfolio piece and is willing to do whatever it takes to finish the job to your satisfaction—at a lower price. Students and people who are learning the craft are often willing to work for much less than established book designers.

Cost

Book packagers charge for some services by the piece (image preparation), other services by the page (typesetting), and a few services by the hour (indexing). If you would rather have the designer give you a bid for the whole project, they will need to know the approximate page count and number of illustrations. They will set limits on the number of designs and revisions they will give you on the interior and cover. If you reject the initial round of designs all together, you may have to pay an additional fee to see more designs.

Write a Formal Proposal or Contract

Once you have a cost estimate from the designer, write an additional proposal making your expectations clear about what work will be taken care of by the designer, and what you are responsible for providing to him or her. Include firm deadlines and a do-not-exceed price—the price beyond which you cannot go. Most designers will give you an estimate with a price range since it is difficult to know exactly what you will or will not like until the work is started. You may want to make more changes than what the original agreement calls for, which may necessitate a new estimate. The designer should take care of any errors that are their fault, but be prepared to pay extra if you edit once the typesetting is done.

❧❧

Typesetting is all about making your manuscript easy to read. Choosing appropriate fonts and type sizes, spacing between letters and lines, and justifying body text are the heart and soul of the typesetting rules. If you can also avoid common punctuation errors, and eliminate any widows and orphans, your book's interior will look like it was typeset by a professional.

Chapter 18

Typesetting the Front Matter

This chapter will take you through the front matter in the order the front matter should appear in your book, from the first item (the endsheets) to the last item (the introduction). How many of these front matter pieces are appropriate for your book is project specific. A memoir solely for the enjoyment of family may not need much beyond the title page.

Almost every front matter element should begin on a right-hand (recto) page which means that there may be blank pages within your front matter. Beginning each new section on a right-hand page is a publishing convention—a tradition, but in the interest of saving space, many publishers today are running each successive part on the next available page.

There are not many examples in this chapter because you will find working examples in the front matter of this book.

Endsheets

In hardcover books, endsheets are used to reinforce the attachment from the cloth cover to the sewn-together pages of the interior, so you will find an endsheet in the front and the back of the book. If you are using an offset printer, you may be able to choose the illustration or design for your endsheets. Other printers have stock designs for you to choose from, although many use a common endsheet.

Endsheets are not necessary to hold the covers onto softbound (paperback) books, therefore, are not used. With some printers, it is possible to print an illustration on the inside cover of a paperback book, but it is almost always an extra charge. Most print-on-demand printers do not offer this option.

Frontispiece

A frontispiece is an illustration on the left-hand (verso) side facing the title page. These are common, mostly in high-end coffee table books.

Although an illustration could go on the reverse side of the endsheet, a frontispiece is usually a separate page using the same paper as the interior, rather than the heavier endsheet paper.

Endorsements or Blurbs

Endorsements are also called blurbs. It is common for publishers with commercially available books to solicit short blurbs from well-known authors or experts. The best blurbs belong on the cover or dust jacket flaps. Any others go on pages before the half-title page, and these pages are not numbered.

It is uncommon for memoirs to include blurbs, except in the case where a well-known person is writing his or her memoir. If you are going to solicit them, five or six will do. Keep them short and sweet. If you are soliciting a well-known author, expert, or member of your family, offer a blurb already written for his or her approval or to edit as he or she sees fit.

Blurbs are typically set in the main body font, in quotes. The name of the blurb's author follows on a separate line either centered or flush right, followed by a line containing any titles, awards or books he or she has written, also centered or flush right. Use italics for book titles.

Half-Title Page

A half-title page was used more than a century ago to identify an unsold book. In those days, books were printed, but not bound until sold, so that the new owner could choose the binding. Today, half title pages are not necessary but if you include one, the reverse side should be blank.

The half-title page should be typeset in whatever font you have chosen for your chapter headers, but big enough to make a statement, placed about one-third of the way down the page.

Ad Card

One option for the reverse side of the title page is to include an ad card—a list of other books you have written. Look at the ad card in this book. It begins with: "Other books by the author" and lists the titles. You could begin with: "Author of ..." or "Also by ..."

The ad card is typeset in the main body font, flush left, but justified ragged right. If you are only listing titles, full justification may stretch the words apart unnaturally.

Title Page

Typeset the title in the same font and size as the half-title page, and place it about one-third of the way down the page. The title should be followed by the subtitle in the same font but smaller. The author's name should be placed about two-thirds of the way down the page, followed by the publishing company, and the city where the book was published (the city of the publishing company not the printer) at the bottom. If you have a logo for your publishing company, it can go on this page, as well.

The reverse side of the title page is the copyrights page.

Copyrights Page

The copyrights page belongs on the back of the title page and should include:

- The title and subtitle
- The author's name
- The publisher's name and physical address
- A copyright notice (the symbol and year)
- The name of the copyright owner
- The expression "all rights reserved" to give you the maximum protection in case of copyright infringement
- A disclaimer, if needed. Most books today include one even if not needed.
- Publishing history (edition or print run if there has been more than one)
- Printed in the United States of America (or wherever the book was printed)

If you plan to sell your book commercially or to libraries, also consider:

Library of Congress (LOC) Cataloging-in-Publication Data [LCC CIP]. The CIP data is bibliographic data prepared by the Library of Congress to help libraries and book dealers correctly catalog the book.

Before the book is published, apply for the CIP Program online (www.loc. gov/publish/cip/).

You can also create your own CIP data, called the Publisher's CIP data, if you do not want to wait months for the Library of Congress to do this for you.

Library of Congress Catalog Number (LCCN or PCN—Preassigned Control Number). A Library of Congress catalog control number (or preassigned number) is a unique identification number given by the LOC, that is included in their national database available to libraries, book stores and other commercial suppliers. Before your book is published, apply for a Library of Congress PCN (www.loc.gov/publish/pcn/).

International Standard Book Number (ISBN). An ISBN is like the Social Security number for you book. It is a unique number assigned by the U.S. ISBN Agency run by the Bowker Company (www.isbn.org). From the website, you can purchase a single ISBN, a block of ten, a block of 100, and so on. A single ISBN costs $125.00. A block of ten costs $295.00.

If you are planning to publish through a print-on-demand printer, many offer ISBNs free of charge. The only drawback to using one of your printer's ISBNs is that the printer becomes the publisher of record, and not you or your publishing company. For many memoir authors, however, using the printer's free ISBN is the simplest way to go.

The copyrights page should be typeset in the main body font, but the majority of the text will be set at a point size small enough to fit all of the above information onto one page. Use the copyrights page of this book as a guide.

Dedication

Many authors use the dedication page to thank whoever has been the greatest influence while writing the book. Most dedications are short. Longer tributes belong in the acknowledgments section.

The dedication page should be typeset in the main body font, in Roman (plain) text or italics.

Dedication pages are optional. If used, they should occupy a right-hand page, and the back should be blank.

Acknowledgments

Acknowledgments are your opportunity to thank anyone who helped you research or write the book. Acknowledgments are optional.

If used, be rigorous when checking the spelling of each person's name, and if they have a title, use the correct, most recently earned title.

Acknowledgments begin on a right-hand page, and can be placed after the dedication, after the preface, within the preface, or in the back matter. If your acknowledgments run an odd number of pages, the last page should be blank.

Acknowledgments should be typeset in the main body font, and if there are many paragraphs, should follow the rules for the rest of the book. If there is a single paragraph, it can be set in italics about one-third of the way down the page.

Epigraph

An epigraph is a pertinent quote that sets the tone for the book, and is optional. Epigraphs are sometimes used on the first page of each chapter.

If the epigraph is typeset on a right-hand page, the back of the page should be blank. Epigraphs can also go on the left-hand page facing the table of contents, if that page is blank.

Epigraphs should be in quotes, in the main body font, in Roman (plain) text or italics. The author's name (or anonymous, if not known) should be placed on a line beneath the quote, followed by the source of the quote on another line. If the source is a book title, it should be typeset in italics.

Table of Contents

The table of contents (TOC) begins on a right-hand page. If there is only one page, the reverse side should be left blank. If the contents run more than one page, they are called contents *only* and can be set *either* on a left-right, two-page spread (pages ii and iii, for example), or beginning on a right-hand page with the remainder on the next left-hand page (pages iii and iv, in this case).

The table of contents can be set in either the main body font or the font you have chosen for your headlines and subheads. The page numbers should be typeset with a right-aligned tab to keep the right-hand edges of the page numbers even down the page.

The table of contents should show the number of the first page of each part of the front matter, the parts (or sections), each chapter, the back matter and the index. How much else you include beyond the chapter number, is up to you. You could include the chapter title (if there are chapter titles), and a running list of subtitles to give the reader an idea of what to expect in each chapter. The example (below) from Buzzy Jackson's book *Shaking the Family Tree* uses a running narrative to give readers an idea of what is included in each chapter.

Table of Contents.

Illustrations

If your book has many illustrations, include a list of illustrations (also called a list of figures). If the illustrations correspond closely with the text, the list is probably not necessary because the information will be provided in the captions, descriptive text or footnotes.

A list of illustrations should include the name (or a description) of the illustration, plus the page number where it occurs. The page numbers should be typeset with a right-aligned tab to keep the right-hand edges of the page numbers even down the page. The back side of a list of illustrations should be blank.

Tables

Lists of tables are common in scientific literature and occasionally in military histories but are uncommon in family histories. If you need one, the back of the page should be left blank. A list of tables should be typeset in the same way as a list of illustrations.

Foreword

A foreword is statement about the book written by someone other than the author. Forewords are common in biographies of famous people, but not common in memoirs.

If you include one, a foreword longer than two to three pages should have a title of its own with the author's name at the beginning, rather than at the end, which is typical for short forewords.

The foreword should be typeset in the main body text and follow the same rules as the body as far as paragraphs, headlines and subheads. If your foreword runs an odd number of pages, the next page should be left blank so that the next section will begin on a right-hand page.

Typeset the following using the same rules as the foreword:

Front Matter	Body	Back Matter
Preface	Epilogue	Postscript
Methods	Afterword	About the Author
Contributors		Glossary
Chronology		Colophon
Characters		
Permissions		
Prologue		

Preface

A preface is optional. It is a way for you to address the reader directly. A preface is one place to explain the reasons you undertook this project, or what you have include or have left out. Many authors include their acknowledgments in the preface. If you do, there is no need for other acknowledgments elsewhere.

Methods

A methods section (also called editorial method) is used in scholarly works where the author's analysis needs explanation. In a memoir, you may want to alert readers to certain information, if the explanation is important before they begin reading. Some of this could be included in footnotes or endnotes rather than in the front matter.

Contributors

A list of contributors is optional. If someone provided expertise that calls for more than a simple acknowledgment, a list of contributors is the place to give credit along with a short explanation describing how each person or group helped you with this project.

Chronology

A chronology can be helpful if the order of events is not clear, as may happen in a collection of letters, or in a diary with missing entries.

Use a chronology to provide a broader historical context if your personal recollections do not. For example, a list of events preceding U.S. involvement in Vietnam and the battles that took place thereafter may be helpful because younger readers may not be well acquainted with the Vietnam War.

A chronology should begin on a right-hand page, unless it would be simpler for the reader to use a left-right spread.

Characters

Occasionally, in fiction you may find a list of characters. You could include a list of people who appear frequently in your book.

Alphabetize by last name followed by a comma and the first name along with a short, descriptive paragraph about each person. Typeset the names in bold or italics either as subheads or run-in subheads.

Permissions

If you have only a few places where you need to acknowledge permissions given to use material for the book, they could be placed in a footnote, an endnote, an image credit or a sidebar. A list may be easier if you have many permissions to acknowledge.

A list of permissions can be placed in either the front or the back matter and should begin on a right-hand page. You can organize the list of permissions in order as the items occur, or alphabetically by repository to avoid repeating information if many items came from one repository. When describing sources, give the location in the book by chapter and (or) page, then use the same style as endnotes or footnotes, typically using either *Evidence Explained* or *The Chicago Manual of Style*.

Prologue

A prologue is used in fiction to set the scene for the story and is told in the voice of one of the characters rather than by the author. If you want to set the scene for your readers this way using another person's point of view, go ahead.

Second Half-Title Page

If the front matter is long, you can use a second half-title page to give readers a visual clue where the body of the book begins. The second half-title page should look exactly like the first half-title page.

Introduction

Use an introduction to set the stage. Explain your purpose or goals in writing the book. Give the reader historical context or to make clear the organization and scope of the book.

The introduction, although technically a part of the front matter, is the beginning of the book. The introduction should follow the typesetting rules for the body, with one exception. Although the page numbers in the preceding front matter sections are set in lowercase Roman numerals, switch to Arabic numerals when you begin the introduction.

Some publishers will continue the page numbers from the front matter, so if the last page of the front matter was page viii, then the first page of the introduction would be page 9. Others will restart the numbering with page 1 on the first page of the introduction. The first style is more traditional, although the latter style is becoming more common.

෩෨

Much of what can be included in the front matter is optional. The sections that *are* necessary are the title page, the copyrights page, and the table of contents. Beyond that, it is up to you as the publisher to decide what else to include.

Chapter 19

Typesetting the Body

Most of the typesetting for the body of the book is about the paragraphs, headlines and subheads covered in the previous section. The remainder is how to create first pages different enough to give the reader a visual clue that a new section or chapter is beginning.

Parts or Sections—First Pages

If you have divided the manuscript into parts or sections, you will need an opening page for each. These pages should act as dividers and should be right-hand pages with the reverse side left blank unless you wish to use an epigraph or illustration there.

Typeset the part or section title in large letters about one-third of the way down the page using the same font as your title and subtitle. You can use the part or section title alone, or include a mini-table of contents for the section.

Neither the front nor the back of this page should have a running header or a page number, but these pages contribute to the page count. So even though they should not have page numbers on them, count the pages following a part or section divider as if they did.

Chapters—First Pages

The first page of each chapter should be easy to find while thumbing through a book. Traditionally, chapters begin on a new page on the right-hand side. If you end up with many blank pages because chapters have an uneven number of pages, you can ignore the convention to minimize the number of blank pages—with two exceptions: chapters *must* begin on a *new* page (whether left or right) and Chapter One *must* begin on a *right-hand* page.

Chapter titles are optional, but numbers are not. If you use titles, they should be consistent in tone from one chapter to the next. In other words, do not use a whimsical title for one, and a serious statement for the next.

Chapter numbers start at one and are consecutive no matter what section they are in, so that chapter numbers are never repeated.

The first page of a chapter should not have a page number or a running header. The chapter number and (or) title should begin at least two inches from the top of the page, but could be as low as one-third of the way down the page with the body text beginning about half-way down the page.

Footnotes or Endnotes

Whether you put any source citations in footnotes or endnotes is up to you. Opinions are divided about whether readers would rather refer to an endnotes page or read footnotes as they occur in the text.

If you use footnotes, leave enough room between the text and the footnote to make it obvious, or use a rule (line) in between. Most word processing and page layout programs create footnotes for you, so they are not technically footers because the amount of space they occupy will change from page to page depending upon how many notes there are on each page.

If you use endnotes, place them either at the end of the chapter, or together in the back matter.

<table>
<tr>
<td>

**Section
II**

Springfield

1939-1950

</td>
<td>

Section 2

Springfield 1939-1950

Chapter 8: First Day of School
Chapter 9: My First Job
Chapter 10: Summer Travels
Chapter 11: Baseball
Chapter 13: Best Friends
Chapter 14: High School

</td>
</tr>
</table>

Section divider with number and title (left); Section divider with mini-table of contents (right).

Typical formatting for footnotes or endnotes is as follows:

1. Author (first then last), *Title in Italics* (City of publication: Publisher, date), p. number.

Epilogue

An epilogue is a final note from you, the author, or as a continuation of the main narrative to bring closure to the book.

Afterword

An afterword, is a way for you, the author, to give your final thoughts. Set the book into a larger context within the family, let readers know about additional research you are doing, tell a funny story that wraps up the book, or give the reader an enticing preview of your next book.

Conclusion

If you did not do so in the epilogue, use the conclusion to provide a brief summary of the main points.

Chapter 4

Lorem ipsum dolor sit amet, consectetur adipisicing elit, sed do eiusmod tempor incididunt ut labore et dolore magna aliqua. Ut enim ad minim veniam, quis nostrud exercitation ullamco laboris nisi ut aliquip ex ea commodo consequat. Duis aute irure dolor in reprehenderit in voluptate velit esse cillum dolore eu fugiat nulla pariatur. Excepteur sint occaecat cupidatat non proident, sunt in culpa qui officia deserunt mollit anim id est laborum.

Lorem ipsum dolor sit amet, consectetur adipisicing elit, sed do eiusmod tempor incididunt ut labore et dolore magna aliqua. Ut enim ad minim veniam, quis nostrud exercitation ullamco laboris nisi ut aliquip ex ea commodo consequat. Duis aute irure dolor in reprehenderit in voluptate velit esse cillum dolore eu fugiat nulla pariatur. Excepteur sint occaecat cupidatat non proident, sunt in culpa qui officia deserunt mollit anim id est laborum.

Lorem ipsum dolor sit amet, consectetur adipisicing elit, sed do eiusmod tempor incididunt ut labore et dolore magna aliqua. Ut enim ad minim veniam, quis nostrud exercitation

Chapter 4

School Years

Lorem ipsum dolor sit amet, consectetur adipisicing elit, sed do eiusmod tempor incididunt ut labore et dolore magna aliqua. Ut enim ad minim veniam, quis nostrud exercitation ullamco laboris nisi ut aliquip ex ea commodo consequat. Duis aute irure dolor in reprehenderit in voluptate velit esse cillum dolore eu fugiat nulla pariatur. Excepteur sint occaecat cupidatat non proident, sunt in culpa qui officia deserunt mollit anim id est laborum.

Lorem ipsum dolor sit amet, consectetur adipisicing elit, sed do eiusmod tempor incididunt ut labore et dolore magna aliqua. Ut enim ad minim veniam, quis nostrud exercitation ullamco laboris nisi ut aliquip ex ea commodo consequat. Duis aute irure dolor in reprehenderit in voluptate velit esse cillum dolore eu fugiat nulla pariatur. Excepteur sint occaecat cupidatat non proident, sunt in culpa qui officia deserunt mollit anim id est laborum.

Lorem ipsum dolor sit amet, consectetur adipisicing elit, sed do eiusmod tempor incididunt ut labore et dolore magna aliqua. Ut enim ad minim veniam, quis nostrud exercitation ullamco laboris nisi ut aliquip ex ea commodo consequat. Duis aute irure dolor in reprehenderit in voluptate velit esse cillum dolore eu fugiat

Chapter with number (left); Chapter with number and title (right).

❧✦❧

Because most of the typesetting for the book concerns paragraphs, headlines, subheads and running headers, what is left is to create visual breaks for parts (sections) and the first page of each chapter, and to decide where to place the source citations—in footnotes or endnotes.

Chapter 20

Typesetting the Back Matter

The back matter begins when the stories cease and you have had your last word as the author—well, almost. There is the possibility of a postscript. Back matter typically includes appendices, endnotes, a bibliography and an index. Your back matter could also include a postscript, an about the author section, a glossary, errata, a colophon, an excerpt from another book, and an order form.

The following front matter can be placed in the back matter if you prefer: acknowledgments, lists of illustrations, tables, contributors, and permissions.

Postscript

A postscript is a place to add something you were unable to include in the book. If you came across additional research, for example, give a brief synopsis.

About the Author

An about the author section is optional. It is an opportunity to tell the reader who you are and why you wrote the book. It should include a brief biography and a photograph is customary. Often, a brief version is placed on the back cover, or a longer version on the dust jacket flap of a hardcover edition.

Appendices

Items in an appendix may explain, elaborate or clarify information that do not fit neatly into the narrative.

The following are examples:

- A complete list of names from a military unit
- A list of which people are buried in which cemetery

- A complete transcription of a document mentioned in the text
- Information, documents or photographs gathered too late to be included elsewhere
- Any difficult-to-find items mentioned in the book (reproduction pieces available by catalog or collector's website, for example)

Each appendix needs a title, a number or a letter. The first appendix should appear on a right-hand page. Each subsequent appendix could begin on the next available page, right or left, to avoid blank pages.

Addendum

An addendum is a section of new material that was unavailable when the book was written. Often, an addendum is added in a subsequent edition, updating information without a complete re-write.

Glossary

A glossary is optional, but appreciated if you use: foreign words; jargon or technical phrases (common if you are describing a process or a profession from a century or more ago); words used during an earlier era but not used today; or unfamiliar slang (e.g. military slang).

Alphabetize glossary terms followed by a brief explanation.

Endnotes

If you want to place endnotes in the back matter, they should begin on a right-hand page, be organized by chapter, and then by note number. Leave extra space before the start of each chapter's endnotes to create a visual break.

Bibliography

While a formal bibliography is optional in a memoir, readers may be interested in what books and articles you consulted in addition to any original source material you used.

You will find standard bibliographic style guides for published materials in *The Elements of Style* by William Strunk and E.B. White, or *A Manual for Writers of Term Papers, Theses, and Dissertations* by Kate L. Turabian.

Your bibliography could be organized by family, location, research facility or topic. If you organize in a way other than alphabetical by author's last name for the whole list, use a subhead to indicate the start of a new section, alphabetize within the section, and leave space before the subhead as a visual break.

Index

All non-fiction books that will be sold or used in libraries must have an index. If your plan is to give your book to friends and family members only, an index is not mandatory, but may be appreciated. Fortunately, most word processing and page layout software makes it possible to create index tags electronically within the body text, which are compiled into an index once the final layout is finished. It is important to compile the index last, to make certain text has not shifted from one page to the next during any final editing or touch ups to the layout.

Unfortunately, there is not one, single set of rules for creating an index. Most publishing houses have their own criteria, as do professional indexers. As the publisher, you have a great deal of latitude in what you will include.

Indexing takes time and adds pages to the book, but, first and foremost, it should be a useful tool. Be careful not to let the task of indexing determine the contents. It is not uncommon to find books where material in the beginning is over-indexed, and material at the end is under-indexed because the indexer tired of the process.

There are three types of index listings to consider: names, places and subjects.

Every person mentioned should be included in the index. A full-name index has become the standard.

Indexing places is helpful to other people researching the area described in your book.

Indexing subjects is a little trickier because it is hard to know what subjects are the most important to include. If you have spent time talking about battles, or the details of a profession, or have discussed the manufacturer of your grand-mother's bone china, those are the kinds of subjects worth including.

An index is not merely a list of names and places, it is a way for people to retrieve information quickly, so any subject you think would help the reader find what they are looking for will be appreciated.

Index the whole book—everything from the dedication to the appendices—with a couple of exceptions. There is no need to index the colophon or copyrights page, nor the bibliography because it is already alphabetical by author's name and therefore easy to search. Endnotes or footnotes may be a different matter, if you have included other explanatory material in the note. If there are relevant entries in the explanatory material, then index it.

Basic Index Formatting

The index should begin on a right-hand page and be typeset in the body font, one or two points smaller. Each page should have a running header and page numbers, the same as the rest of the book. Use hanging indents to keep the alphabetical first letter flush left, but the remainder of the listing along with the page numbers, indented about one-quarter of an inch. Use a slightly larger space between listings than the line leading for wrapped text to create a visual break or to add a bit of white space to the page.

When you begin a new letter in your alphabetical list, use a subhead in bold that is slightly larger than the index body text.

Some publishers use bold page numbers to indicate illustrations, and bold italicized page numbers to indicate boxed text or tables. If you have created a list of illustrations or tables in the front matter, there is no need for this type of formatting in your index.

Page numbers are formatted according to long-standing tradition. Information that occurs on sequential pages is formatted with an en dash in between the numbers, but only if the discussion of the subject is continuous across those pages. For example, a person may be mentioned on page 140 and again on page 141, but there is *not* a continuous discussion of this person, so the formatting would be 140, 141. If there had been a continuous discussion of that person, the formatting would be 140–141. This is a subtle difference and not crucial.

Most software-generated indexes will create a list of numbers separated by commas. You can save space in the index by combining a long list of consecutive page numbers (140, 141, 142, 143, 144), into a shorter run of 140–144. Whether you follow the long-standing convention of using the en dash only to indicate a continuous discussion of the subject, is up to you, although using the en dashes correctly is more accurate.

In a memoir, there may be chapters where the same individual is mentioned on every page. Another way to cut down on the number of pages where an individual is indexed, is to give the reader the first page plus a symbol (e.g. * or # or +) on which a major player is mentioned in a chapter, but no subsequent page numbers. If you shorten the number of listings this way, explain it at the beginning of the index—true of any deviation from convention—so that the reader knows what to expect.

There is no need to indicate how many times an individual, place or subject is listed on a single page. An index points the reader to the page, it does not absolve the user of reading what is there.

Formatting Subjects

Main subjects should be flush left, then broken down into minor subjects. The minor subjects should be indented one-quarter of an inch using a hanging indent so that any wrapping page numbers fall at half an inch. Main subjects are capitalized; minor subjects are not unless they begin with a proper noun. If you include a cross-reference, the word "see" should be in italics before the cross-reference subject. The following is an example:

Wagon
    Conestoga   33, 70, 104
    repair, *see* wainwright
    trains 21-24, 47

Formatting Place Names

Formatting place names can be tricky if the place is known by more than one name during different time periods. The New Netherlands is a good example. If your ancestors lived in the Manhattan area during Dutch rule, they would have lived in New Netherlands, not New York. If you are unsure whether your readers will be acquainted well enough with the location to know that New Netherlands became New York, you may want to include a cross-reference.

New Netherlands, *see also* New York.

Another way to deal with place names where the location is the same but the name is not, is to include an explanation, such as:

Denver, Denver County (then Arapahoe County), Colorado
Denver, Arapahoe County (now Denver County), Colorado

Index geographic names the way a reader would look for them, so:

The Dalles, Oregon.
    The Dalles, Oregon, not Dalles, The, Oregon because "The Dalles" is recognized as the place name.

Elms, The.
    However, if you have a property name such as The Elms, it would be indexed as Elms, The and not The Elms. (Indexing can be tricky.)

Florence, Italy.
    Florence not Firenze (for an English-speaking audience)

Pear Cottage.
    Pear Cottage, not Cottage, Pear

If you use abbreviations in your place names, do so consistently, such as:
    St. Louis or Saint Louis, but not a mixture of the two
    Ste. Genevieve County for Sainte Genevieve County
Or:
    Ste. Genevieve Co. (if you also consistently abbreviate county using Co.)

Formatting People's Names

Surnames are not universal, and they can be inconsistent over time. That makes them tricky to index if you have included people whose families are the same, but whose surnames are different. In general, whatever rule you followed for the text, repeat in the index, except where alphabetizing by your software becomes a problem. Not all software alphabetizes the same way. Microsoft Word, for example, will treat De la Rosa differently than de la Rosa, giving priority to the capitalized version. The index will show both versions, but the capitalized version will come first.

Most software will treat names with spaces in them differently than names without, so these words would be alphabetized as:

De la Rosa
Deify
Delarosa
Detrimental
Di Larosa

If the number of listings between the two versions of De la Rosa is substantial, use a cross-reference (e.g. *see* Di Larosa or *see* Du Larosa) so that the reader knows to look for another spelling. A different way to deal with this is to explain at the start of the index that you have made all versions of Vandergard (Vander Gard, Van Der Gard, van der Gard) the same for the purposes of indexing only.

If there are people with the same name, do something to distinguish them in the index, for example:

Josiah Smith (1830–1899)   33, 89, 90
Josiah Smith (1864–1919)   60, 71, 90
Josiah Smith (1880–1956)   78, 91, 106

Or:

Josiah Smith (the elder)   33, 89, 90
Josiah Smith (the baker)   60, 71, 90
Josiah Smith (the son)   78, 91, 106

If you have many people listed with the same surname, so you will list the surname once, flush left, then alphabetize the first names indented one-quarter of an inch (.25") with the hanging indent leaving any wrapping page numbers indented one-half inch (.5"). For example:

Foster
    Allen 71, 77
    Bruce 50
    Carter 44

If you have a long list of people under the same surname, when you reach the next column or page, repeat the surname followed by (cont.).

Foster (cont.)
Wesley
William, Jr.

Women's names can be problematic because in order to create the most useful index, you need to refer to women by both their maiden and married names, if appropriate, and on occasion, by multiple married names. The following are examples of how to handle this.

If a woman's name was Mary Jane Jones Rankin Scarborough, meaning she was born as Mary Jane Jones, married a Rankin and subsequently married a Scarborough, she should be listed as:

Jones, Mary Jane (*see* Rankin, Mary Jane, *see* Scarborough, Mary Jane)
Rankin, Mary Jane (Jones)
Scarborough, Mary Jane (Jones) (Rankin)

People with hyphenated surnames should be listed under both names as well. For example:

Gowan-Saroyan, Jane (*see* Saroyan, Jane Gowan)

If there are women who are referred to by *only* their married names, they should be listed as:

Brice, William (Mrs.)—not, Brice, Mrs. William.

If there were many women named Mrs. Brice, for example, they would all alphabetize under Brice, M (for Mrs.) and not under the letter of their husband's first name where they should.

Incorrect:
Brice, Keith
Brice, Mrs. Adam
Brice, Mrs. William
Brice, Nathan

Correct:
Brice, Adam (Mrs.)
Brice, Keith
Brice, Nathan
Brice, William (Mrs.)

The use of titles such as Miss and Dr. is a matter of preference in the index, unless Miss Shaw or Dr. Reynolds is the only name you have for those individuals. If you have only a last name and a title, then the titles belong in the index.

In a transcription, using a name as you find it is proper; in an index, not necessarily. For example, if you find the name Daniel, Dan'l and Dan in the body text, in the index, you may not wish to have three listings for the same person under each of these iterations. If it is clear that you are referring to the same person, use the best, most complete name—Daniel.

If there are people who are referred to by only one name, or by none at all, include whatever you need to, to reference that individual:

> Horace (the watchmaker)
> Negro girl (b. ca 1850)
> Susannah (the neighbor)

The same goes if you have a surname but no first name, for example:

> Halford (cotton buyer)
> Rosenkranz, Miss (housekeeper)
> Surry, Miss (teacher)
> Tarbox, Mr. (land agent)

If you have people who used a nickname that does not suggest their formal name, and then use a cross-reference, such as: Rogers, Buzz (*see* Rogers, Alden).

Formatting Institutional Names

Formal names should be indexed as they are presented:

> All Saints Cathedral
> Miss Porter's School
> Van Pelt Cemetery

These places could also be indexed under subject headings:

Cemeteries
> Van Pelt Cemetery

Churches
> All Saints Cathedral

Schools
> Miss Porter's School

Institutions with the same name should include a way to differentiate one place from the next:

> Old Burying Ground (Boston, MA)
> Old Burying Ground (Waverly, NH)

Institutions using people's names can be tricky, as well. For the most part they should be indexed as written, so either:

Harrison Trimble High School
Or:
Trimble, Harrison. *See also* Harrison Trimble High School
But not:
Trimble, Harrison (High School)

In the 19th century, it was common for people to name their businesses after themselves. The best way to list them is both as they appear *and* by the founder's last name, for example:

C. Madison & Co.
Madison, Charles. *See also* C. Madison and Co.
Madison (C. Madison & Co.)

Index legal cases the same way as business names above. First by the full name of the case, usually plaintiff versus defendant, and then by the surname of the defendant followed by the full case name, so:

Delaney vs. Richards
Richards (Delaney vs. Richards)

Index consistently using listings that help readers find information quickly and easily.

Errata

An errata section is used to alert the reader to any errors that were discovered during production that are uncorrected in the narrative. For publishers who run thousands of books in a single press run, these sections are necessary because the publisher will not issue a corrected edition until the print run is sold out. Fortunately, if you use one of the print-on-demand printers that does not charge to upload a new version, you can correct errors as you find them by uploading a new interior file. There would be no need for an errata section.

An errata section is organized in order of the errors with the chapter number and page number, followed by what is listed and the correction. For example:

Chapter 2, page 26: 21 May 1767 should read 21 May 1867
Chapter 2, page 33: Richard S. Burton should read Richard L. Burton

Remember: Each time you make changes that move words from one page to another, you must re-create the index.

Colophon

A colophon is the design and production credits for the book: who created the cover and interior, the fonts and paper used, and the name of the printer. This information can also go on the copyright page above the copyright notice and cataloging data.

Excerpt

If you have written other books, or are writing or planning to write additional books, include an excerpt from another book at the end of this one, especially in an electronic version. In an electronic version you can also include a live link to your website, a blog where you will update readers on the progress of a new book, or to a place where the other book(s) is sold. Include the full links in your print edition as well so interested readers can find you online.

Include something exciting or useful in the excerpt. Then, tell the reader why they may be interested in other books you have written. Ask readers to check out the link. This is referred to as a "call to action" in marketing. You could also include a line such as, "If you enjoyed this book and would like to purchase a copy for a family member ... "

Format the excerpt the same way as the body text. If you have many other books, list them at the end of the excerpt so that interested readers can browse your list of titles. Include links for each of those titles as well.

Order Form

Including an order form is one way to make sure an interested person who has found your book in a library has a way to contact you to buy their own copy. Not everyone uses the Internet to place orders, even today.

An order form should occur on the last page, and should include:

- Your name or your company name
- Your address (where they should send the order)
- Your website address
- A call to action ("If you enjoyed this book and would like to buy a copy for a family member ...")
- All titles available (cross-sell your other books)
- The price of each item
- Shipping and handling charges for each item
- A discount for ordering more than one book (free shipping perhaps)
- Any additional merchandise you have to offer (photographic reprints or family tree charts, for example)
- A place to total the order

- A place to fill out their name, address, email address (make this area big enough for the person ordering to write legibly)
- An explanation of the payment methods you will accept (check, money order, PayPal or credit card)

Creating order forms can be tricky. Find a good catalog order form and use it as your guide.

❧❧

In the back matter, you have an opportunity to include whatever did not fit easily into the body of the book, or to clarify terms used or mistakes discovered after the typesetting was finished.

The most important item in the back matter is the index. Every non-fiction book that will be sold in a store or used in a library must have one, including a memoir. Even if you forgo the place names and subject entries, an every-name index has become the standard. The index is also a good marketing tool. Most people who see their names in the index are delighted and want to read more.

As the publisher, everything else in the back matter is up to you.

❧❧

Working with an Indexer

Most memoirs do not need the services of a professional indexer. You know your material as well as any indexer could. Professional indexing is often necessary for complex non-fiction or scientific works, but you should be able to either create the index yourself as you typeset, or be able to work with your book packager to do so. If you choose to hire an indexer, consider the following:

Portfolio

A professional indexer should be able to give you the titles of books he or she has indexed, and an electronic copy of an index or two.

What to Include

Your index should include every name mentioned in the book, along with the names of groups or institutions. Include place names that are significant. The indexer may be able to suggest subject headings to you, since subjects are more commonly what professional indexers categorize, rather than names.

Fees

Professional indexers charge either by the page, or by the hour. If your indexer does not have much experience, pay by the page. Pay by the hour, only when hiring an accomplished indexer. Using a professional indexer can often run as much as book packaging or editing costs. If you have to choose, put the money into editing first, and then into the layout and design. Leave the indexing for last.

Final Layout

A professional indexer must work from your final layout—with all of the typesetting in place and pages established—in order to create an accurate index. Before you give the final layout to the indexer, make certain all revisions or corrections have been made. Then, print a final copy.

After the indexing is complete, if you make revisions to the text that alters on which page the indexed words appear, you will pay dearly to have the indexer make corrections.

Write a Formal Proposal or Contract

Use a formal proposal to indicate how the index is to be returned to you or your book packager—as a Word document, or an unformatted plain text document, for example. Make your expectations for the index and deadlines clear. If you have agreed to pay by the hour, include a do-not-exceed price to keep the indexer from running wild with your budget.

❧❧

It may seem as if there are a lot of rules to follow for typesetting, but it is the attention to detail in the typesetting that will make your book look as if it has been professionally published.

Chapter 21

Designing the Cover

It would be nice to think that readers do not judge books by their covers, but in reality, they do. Not only do they judge whether they want to buy the book, but often a book with a poor cover will go unread, simply because it looks uninviting. If your book is solely for the enjoyment of family you may not need much of a title. Your cover image and a simple title could speak for the contents of the book.

If your photo book will be sold (or given) to libraries or bookstores, it must have a title, and it should accurately describes the contents. If you have not given much thought to your book's title while you were writing, once you start designing the cover, you must. In fact, choosing the right title and making it look good on the cover may be the most difficult element of cover design. Fortunately, there is a fairly simple formula for the other elements expected on the front and back covers as well as on the spine.

Choosing a Good Title

The title will affect the perception readers have of the book and as such, the title should be the most prominent item on the cover. A non-fiction title is like a promise you are making to the reader for what they will experience reading the book. While it is tempting to use a title that is also a clever play on words (e.g. Deep Roots and Long Branches), if you want potential buyers to know what you are writing about, it is best to be specific in the title or subtitle.

You could use "The Life of ... " or "My Memoir ... " or "The Unusual Life of ... A Memoir" plus your, a time period or a region to distinguish you from others with the same name.

Most online bookstores will list both your title and subtitle in the short listings, so, if you prefer, you can use a shorter title followed by a more lengthy, explanatory subtitle.

The following are examples of good titles:

A Memoir: The Story of William A. Fellows and the 82nd Airborne

The Life of Abial Washburn: From Georgia to Tennessee and Back, 1930-1976

My Life on Wall Street: Hubert Miller and the Roller Coaster Ride of High Finance in the 21st Century

These titles are not as good:

My Life
The Third Child
I Was Born in Ohio

On the cover, typeset the title in a font large enough to be readable in a small thumbnail online. Online bookstores and eReaders will display your cover this way and often the small image is all a potential buyer has to evaluate the book.

Cover Layout Basics

How your cover is designed depends upon how it will be bound—hardbound, hardbound with a dustcover, or softbound (paperback).

A paperback cover is printed on a single sheet that wraps from the front around the spine to the back. It will be printed at a size larger than the book's pages, and then attached to the book with glue and trimmed so that the page and cover edges are smooth and even.

Hardbound covers can be made from either cloth or paper. They are glued to stiff boards to form a solid cover. A paper cover for a hardbound book will look like modern textbooks—full color with a glossy coating. Paper covers for hardbound books are designed even larger than those for softbound books because they must wrap around the edges of the boards and glued down to form part of the inside cover. An endsheet will be glued over the edges of the cover.

Cloth covers are made of anything from linen to leather, depending upon the printer's equipment and how much you are willing to pay. Cloth covers, typically, do not have much more than the title and the author's name. Many cloth-covered books also have a full-color, paper dust jacket that wraps around the cloth cover. The dust jacket uses flaps inside the front and back covers to keep it secure.

Whether you are designing a paper cover or a dust jacket, your printer should have a template for you to follow. Many printers have template generators that will give you an exact size based upon the number of pages in the book, which will determine spine width. You can assemble the elements at any time, however, and create the final cover once you have a page count.

Cover elements.

Cover templates will have three areas defined by the edge of the element: the bleed edge, the trim edge and the safe area.

The *safe area* is the innermost area that allows for any slippage when the printed cover is attached to the book's interior. Most templates will give you three safe areas, one each for the front cover, the back cover and the spine. The safe areas are away from the edges of the spine and the front and back covers. Keep all text, as well as the barcode, and any logo images within the safe areas.

The *trim edge* is where the book will be trimmed once the cover is applied to the interior pages so that the finished book will have clean, smooth edges.

The *bleed edge* is the area where photographs or solid background color should reach, so that when the book is trimmed, there is no danger of leaving a white line around an edge because nothing was printed in that area.

Cover Elements

Covers have three elements: the front, the spine, and the back. Most covers are designed in a single piece, and when laid flat, the front cover will be on the right-hand side, the spine in the middle and the back cover on the left.

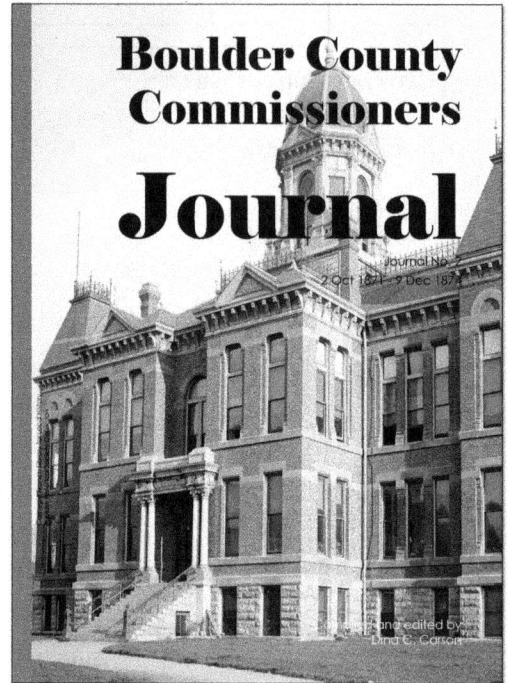

Cover photograph properly placed (left); Cover photograph making the title difficult to read (right).

If you use a print-on-demand printer that has an online cover generator—not a template but a design tool—you may be able to design the cover in three separate parts. Using one of these cover generators, however, will give you fewer options than designing the cover yourself.

If you design your own cover, create it as a single piece. You can use a word processor (although not ideal), an image editing program, a page layout program or a vector graphics editor such as Adobe Illustrator. One of the benefits of using a page layout program or a vector graphics editor is that they are built for creating cover files—to combine images with crisp, sharp type.

For ideas, take a look at Book Cover Archive (www.bookcoverarchive.com). This website offers a gallery of book covers created by professionals.

Front Cover

The front cover should get the reader's attention. The title should be the most prominent element on the cover, set in a font that is easy to read. The following are popular cover fonts: Baskerville, ChunkFive, Franchise, League Gothic, and Trajan.

For the background, use a photograph, a color, or a texture as long as the area where the title and subtitle are placed is plain (subtle) enough that the reader has no trouble reading the text at a glance. Avoid background elements that are too busy and those that do not create enough color contrast with the title text.

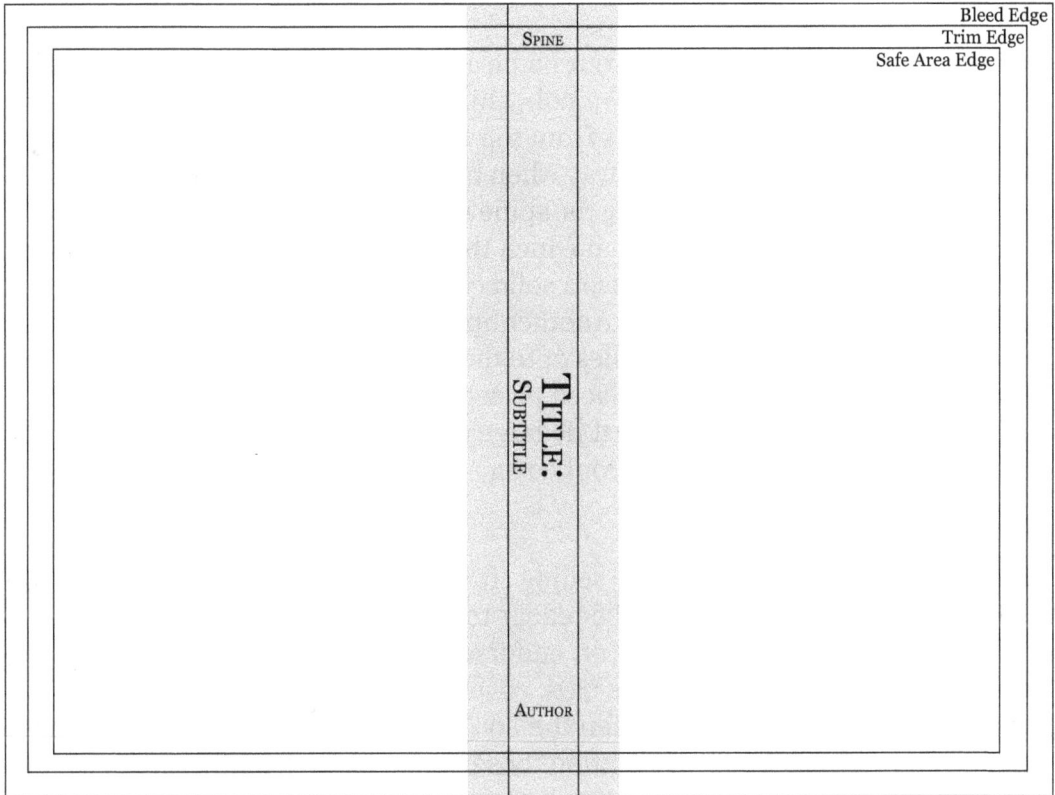

SPINE

TITLE:
SUBTITLE

AUTHOR

Bleed Edge
Trim Edge
Safe Area Edge

Spine wrap.

If you use an image, choose one that says something about the contents. The illustration shows two covers with the same title, but uses the background photograph in a different way. The key to making a book cover image look great is finding one that leaves a large, nearly solid area where you can place the title in a contrasting color. The cover on the left has enough plain sky to read the title and subtitle clearly. The closeup cover image does not.

If you do not have an appropriate photograph in your own collection, you may be able to find a historical photograph that you could license, or you could purchase an image from one of the online rights-managed image companies for a few dollars.

Size and resolution matter and your cover image is likely to be the largest image you use for this project. The resolution should be 300 ppi at a size big enough to cover the bleed area. A cover with a 2.5" spine, for example, would measure 19.5" x 17.5" which is 5850 pixels by 5250 pixels.

If you cannot find the perfect photograph for the cover, blocks of color or subtle patterns also work.

The Spine

The spine will contain your title, your name as the author (full name, initials plus last name, or last name only), and a publishing company logo, if you have one.

The lettering on the spine goes from top to bottom—never the other way—so that all of the titles read the same way when books are spine out on the bookshelf.

The tricky part about designing the spine is making the elements (background image) stop at precisely the point at which the cover bends, either to the front or back. One way to avoid this is to use a solid color, a texture, or a photograph that continues across the entire cover. Another option is to create a spine wrap, where a graphic element or color continues onto the front and back covers to disguise a little slippage if the cover is not placed perfectly during production.

The typeface on the spine must be large and legible, and typically, the same one you used for the title on the front cover.

Back Cover

The back cover does most of the selling. It should explain why the reader will want your book and gently asks the reader to buy a copy.

If you have solicited blurbs or endorsements, your best endorsement(s) should go on the back cover. The back cover should include a bit about you as the author, or why you have written the book. If there are other books you have written, there may be room to mention those books, or to show their covers, page count, ISBNs and price.

If you have a website where the book is sold, the URL should appear prominently on the back cover.

If you plan to sell your book commercially through a print-on-demand printer (such as Lulu or Amazon), you must place an ISBN barcode at the bottom right corner about one-quarter inch from the spine. The barcode can also include the price, although price is optional.

Some printers will include the barcode for you in their template. If you are using one of the ISBNs belonging to your print-on-demand printer, the barcode will be placed on the cover as you create it. If you are printing through an offset printer and must purchase an ISBN barcode, you can do so online. There are many companies offering barcodes for as little as $10. You will receive an EPS (.eps) image by email to use in your design. If you are purchasing your own ISBNs from the Bowker Company, they also offer barcodes for sale.

The other element you will need if you plan to sell your book to libraries or bookstores is a subject heading in the top left corner of the back cover. This is to give the librarians or bookstore employees an idea where to categorize the book.

Book Industry Standards Advisory Committee (BISAC) codes are the standard across the industry for subject headings. If you search online for BISAC codes, you will find a complete list. For most memoirs, the code will be Biography and Autobiography/Personal Memoirs. If you are using a print-on-demand printer, this question will come up as you are creating a listing for your book. Some printers make it easy to search for the BISAC code, others do not. Some printers allow you to list two or more categories, others do not. Search online for the complete list, then use the best subject heading on the back cover.

Advanced Cover Design

The following are additional tips for designing effective covers:

First, go to Amazon.com and take a look at Todd A. Stone's book, *Novelist's Boot Camp*. This is a simple cover, in two colors, black and olive, but it says something about what is in the book, and does so simply.

Now take a look at *Virginia Historical Genealogies* by John Bennett Boddie. This is a black-and-white cover that is about as simple as is possible, but it does not re-produce well as a thumbnail on screen. Arguably, this is a well-written book, but does the cover give you that impression? This book has been around for more than fifty years, so it is hard to be critical of a cover that was designed before major printing technology changes. However, the contents are deserving of a better cover.

Using Color

To make areas of solid black (such as your title text) look its best, use the formula for rich black, which is: 40% cyan, 40% magenta, 40% yellow, 100% black. You will notice that these are in CMYK colors. CMYK is the color palette most printers prefer. If you are designing your cover in your word processor or image editing program, you may not be able to choose the CMYK color palette, so the colors you are seeing on screen in the RGB palette may look slightly different when printed. Page layout and vector graphics programs are designed for working in CMYK.

Limit the cover's color palette to two or three colors and their various tints. That should be a sufficient variation unless you are using a photograph. If you are, choose colors from the photograph for other elements such as the subhead "About the Author" on the back cover. As with interior text, black text is still best for most elements on the cover.

If you need help choosing colors that look good together, use a good color picker. There are apps and online color wheels available, or buy one of Jim Krause's books, *Color Index*, or *Color Index 2*. If you want to go all out, buy one of the Pantone Color Guides (www.pantone.com).

Selecting great color combinations is not easy. If your spouse will not let you choose your own shirts, ask for help choosing colors for your book cover.

Other Cover Considerations

Once you have a cover design in mind, scale it down to a small thumbnail of one inch by one and a half inches (1" x 1.5"). This is how your cover will appear to people shopping at an online bookstore. A thumbnail image is how you will present the cover on your blog, website, Facebook, on a bookmark, or business card to give away to interested family members or other buyers. If the title is not easy to read at the thumbnail size, then revise the cover for those uses with bigger, bolder text.

Save your cover in different sizes. You may need an eBook version (600 pixels x 800 pixels), an online bookstore version (Amazon's requirement is 1880 pixels x 2500 pixels), one for your blog or social media (400 pixels x 600 pixels), and a small thumbnail 90 pixels x 108 pixels (the standard cover size in Amazon's email promotions).

If you have plans for writing more than one memoir, especially if the different books cover different periods of your life, consider using a branded look, that is, the same layout with different colors or photographs so that the books look like they belong together.

⁊⁊⁊

If you cannot design a cover yourself, the following are tips for working with a cover designer.

Working with a Cover Designer

Before you hire a cover designer, ask about the designer's experience. Cover design is a specialty, and most graphic designers have never designed a book cover. Most book packagers, however, either have cover designers on staff, or use freelancers who are familiar with book cover design.

Take a look at Book Cover Archive (www.bookcoverarchive.com). This website offers a gallery of book cover designs. Show the prospective designer four or five styles that you like, but be open to suggestions.

In addition to cover ideas, bring along a two or three paragraph synopsis, to help the designer understand the content of your book. The cover design should complement the content.

Portfolio

Ask to see the designer's book cover portfolio. Evaluate the full covers, front, spine and back, to make sure the designer is familiar with the elements needed for a commercially available book.

Estimate

Ask for an estimate. Most cover designers will offer two or three designs, plus two rounds of revisions before you start paying more than the initial estimate. You may even find that the cover designer has a few standard layouts that you can choose from to save money. Include a do-not-exceed price in the agreement, so the designer cannot go wild with changes before you have a chance to revise the estimate.

Deadlines

Make your expectations clear and set firm deadlines. Let the designer know when you will have a final page count, and when you expect the final cover finished once the page count is given. The designer should have the cover essentially ready, needing only a few minor adjustments once the page count is final.

File Type and Resolution

Let the designer know what type of file and resolution you need (usually a PDF) and any special instructions provided by your book printer. In addition, ask for web-ready book cover images in the different sizes you may need—an eBook version (600 pixels x 800 pixels), online bookstores (Amazon's requirement is a cover of 1880 pixels x 2500 pixels), and a small thumbnail 90 pixels x 108 pixels (the standard cover size in Amazon's email promotions). Make sure the final cover looks good and that the title is readable, even at the smallest thumbnail size.

Write a Formal Proposal or Contract

Use a formal proposal to indicate how and when the cover should be delivered to you—on a thumb drive, an external hard drive, an archival DVD, or through a file sharing service. Make sure deadlines for payment and a finished cover are clear. Include all prices and payment terms.

❧❧

Your cover is the ambassador for your book. Some family members will want a copy even if it comes as loose leaf sheets wrapped in newspaper. Most readers, however, will form an impression of the book's contents by looking at the cover. When designing your cover, you should be able to find many suitable possibilities from the hundreds of thousands of non-fiction books already published. Use one as your guide. Bottom line: all of your hard work writing the book deserves to be covered in something beautiful, and representative of the quality of the contents.

Chapter 22

Preparing the Final Files

Most memoirs are printed. However, some of your readers may prefer an electronic version, or, if you are not interested in selling the book, an online version may be a good choice to distribute it as widely as possible. You may choose to do all three or some combination of the three.

While this book focuses mainly on print publishing, there are ways that you can use what you have produced for print to also publish electronically or online. What follows are brief descriptions of the differences in setup between print and electronic or online versions. For complete instructions, please consult *Set Yourself Up to Self-Publish: A Genealogist's Guide*.

Final Files for Print

How you prepare your final files depends upon your printer. Most printers want PDF files because they are the least problematic. If you send a file in a word processing format such as Word, and you have used a font that the printer does not have, the text may re-format in a way you do not intend. By creating a PDF, there are rarely any font issues because the process of creating the PDF embeds the fonts into the document. Creating a PDF is, in some ways, like taking a snapshot of your manuscript. It will create a file that looks exactly like your manuscript file whether you created it in a word processing program or a page layout program. Most word processing and page layout software will save documents as PDFs.

Create Final PDFs

If you are using one of Adobe's software products to create your PDF (Acrobat or InDesign, for example), there are different PDF settings, including press quality or high quality print (what we want for a printed book), smallest file size (appropriate for emailing the book), and several other settings in between. The best settings for printed material are: Press Quality, High Quality Printing or PDF/X 1a:2001. Most page layout programs will give you a choice in PDF settings, your word processor may not. In most cases, the printed book will still look fine.

If you use a digital or offset printer, ask for their preferred PDF settings before saving your files. Most print-on-demand printers, on the other hand, will accept whatever file you upload, so the responsibility for creating a file that will look its best when printed is up to you.

After creating the PDF, print it out and check it over carefully by comparing the printed version to your original to make sure nothing shifted or was lost in the conversion. This is the process of typescript editing (mentioned in Chapter 15: Editing Your Manuscript). This is the time to catch widows and orphans, captions that do not match images, and other errors. Take a ruler and scan each line one at a time for errors. You may be surprised at what crept in as elements were typeset. The following are common post-typesetting errors:

- Widows and orphans
- Missed or incorrect formatting styles
- Hard returns mid-sentence
- Missing punctuation
- Incorrect quote marks (the symbol for inches)
- Spacing around images
- Spacing between different types of text blocks
- Images that fade into the page (missing outlines)
- Images that do not fit the grid
- Placeholder images not final images (at resolutions too low for print production)
- Pages that are mis-numbered

Uploading Files for Print

If you have created your final layout in chapters so that they are easier to work with, it is safer to send the printer a single file so there is no chance the files could be printed out of order. Programs such as InDesign will take your individual files and combine them into a single book-length PDF. The full version of Adobe Acrobat will also combine individual PDF files into a larger book-length file.

If you must upload your manuscript files individually, the best way to make sure they are printed in the correct order is to begin each file name with a number so that the computer arranges them in the correct order. If you followed the advice in Chapter 14: Writing a First Draft, you should be ready to go.

If you need to number your files now, the following is another way to make sure the computer arranges them in the correct order.

Unfortunately, if you number your files starting with a one (1), and you also have an eleven (11), the computer may order the files this way: 1, 11, 2.

The only way to avoid this is to count the total number of files, and use a sufficient number of zeros preceding the file number to force the computer to put the files in the correct order.

If there are fewer than ten files, there should be no issues, as the computer will number those files from one (1) to nine (9) in order. If there are ten or more files but fewer than one hundred, create two digit numbers from 01 to 09, so that subsequent numbers will be in the correct order. If there are more than one hundred files, file names require two zeros in front of the numbers from one (001) to nine (009), and a single zero before each and every number from ten (010) to ninety-nine (099). Numbers greater than one hundred will fall in order correctly.

Once you upload the files, the best way to see whether or not the files were placed in their proper order is to order a proof copy. Many print-on-demand printers offer a digital PDF proof for you to download. This should not cost you anything, but proofing on screen and proofing in print are different. You will catch different errors. It is worth the money to print a proof copy as well.

Examine the digital and print proofs carefully page by page. You may be surprised what you find. Missing punctuation and incorrectly applied styles are common errors. Watch for places where widows or orphans were created by text shift. It happens. Make sure your illustrations remain in place along with any captions or credits.

Other Information About Your Book

Once you start the process of uploading files to a print-on-demand printer, requesting ISBNs or creating marketing materials for your book, you will need the following information. Keep it gathered in a convenient place so that you can cut and paste whatever is required by vendors or websites.

If you have purchased your own ISBNs, much of this information will inform the book-buying community about your book. If you use a print-on-demand printer, they will ask for much of this information when you upload your files. Each printer has slightly different requirements. What follows is the information asked for most often.

Title

Title. Keep the title and subtitle separate.

Subtitle. Keep the title and subtitle separate.

Author and Publisher

Primary Author. List your name as the primary author. If you have co-authors or other contributors, you should have a chance to add their names.

Author Biography. Write a few paragraphs about yourself as the author and why you wrote the book.

Publisher. If you are acting as your own publisher, you have a choice whether to create a publishing company, or not. For tax and legal reasons you may wish to do so. One sign that you are a self-publisher, however, is naming the publishing company after yourself.

Language and Printing Location

Language. The primary language of the book.

Country. The country in which the book was published, not printed.

Important Dates

Copyright Year. The year in which the book was finished. Although your copyright existed from the time you put pen to paper, most publishers use the most current year as the copyright date, so that readers know that the information is current.

Publication Date. This is a fictional date used by the publishing industry to schedule book reviews ahead of the book's official launch. Use the date when your book is available for sale.

Audience

Target Audience. Unless you are writing a children's book, the audience will always be "Trade."

Metadata

Together, the title, license, description, category and keywords make up the metadata—cataloging information about your book that is key to book sales. Any mis-matches in the metadata will make it difficult for the big databases (online book catalogs) to place your book in front of the right potential buyers.

License. Indicate that you own the copyright to your work, that you are not re-packaging a work already in the public domain.

Description. This is your sales language, your chance to interest potential readers. Some sites use descriptions as short as 200 characters, others as long as 4000. Have several descriptions ready with the most important information wrapped up in the shortest description, and additional detail in the longer descriptions. If you want to sell your book, the description may be one of your most important marketing tools. Lulu describes "providing too little detail in the description" as the greatest mistake of new authors.

Category. Many printers will use the BISAC codes, others have a search option, still others make it as confusing as humanly possible. When in doubt, if Memoir is not a main category, look for Biography and Autobiography. A secondary category could be Personal Memoirs, or a category that describes your profession (e.g. Educators or Musicians).

Keywords. Most sites allow five or more keyword phrases separated by commas. Choose the five most important and put those first. For most memoirs, the keywords should be about your name and the location(s), your profession or where you have lived. For example, John Campbell memoir, John Campbell aeronautics engineer, or John Campbell Lincoln Nebraska. If you are able to add more keyword phrases, do. More keywords will help potential readers find the book. Think of the phrases another researcher would use to find the book. There are keyword search programs online that can help with this, such as Google Adwords Keyword Planner (adwords.google.com). This tool is free, but you must create an account to use it.

ISBN and Price

ISBN. If you have your own ISBN, use it. If you do not, leave this blank and the printer will assign one of theirs to you.

Price. Choose a price higher than the wholesale price if you want to make money. Another reason you may wish to choose a price higher than the wholesale price is to give the distributor (printer) the opportunity to price the book at a discount. Book buyers love bargains, but if you price the book at the wholesale cost, the distributor cannot sell the book for less than what it costs to manufacture it.

The following are a few items particular to Amazon (CreateSpace), Lulu and Bowker (the ISBN Agency).

Amazon (CreateSpace)

Distribution. Amazon offers the following outlets for distribution: Amazon. com, Amazon Europe, Create Space eStore, Bookstores and Online Retailers, and CreateSpace Direct. If you are using one of their ISBNs your book is also eligible for distribution to libraries and academic institutions—a plus for non-fiction books.

Prices. If you have chosen distribution outside of the United States, choose US Dollars, Euros, and British Pounds. Google's online currency calculator can help convert U.S. dollars to English pounds or euros. Round the prices up to the nearest .99 or .95, as prices ending that way have become customary.

Option to Publish on Kindle. If you use CreateSpace to publish your print book they will give you the option to create a Kindle version.

Publish a Memoir

Lulu

Private Access. One of my favorite features of Lulu is that you can publish a book and keep it completely private, meaning that only you can order copies. This is appropriate for books that you may wish to distribute to family members that have information about living people you would not want distributed outside the family.

Direct Access. Direct Access gives you a private URL to direct family members to buy the book for themselves. This option gives you less control over distribution than private access, but it is a good option if you have family spread out all over the country, and you want them to be able to buy their own copies and have the books delivered directly to them.

General Access. Any book you assign as general access will become available through Lulu's catalog as well as other online booksellers' catalogs.

Bowker Company (ISBN Agency)

ISBN 10. Older ISBNs had only 10 digits. If you have a newer ISBN it will have 13 digits. There is a calculator on the site to convert it to the older 10 digit version. This site asks for both, and checks one against the other for accuracy.

ISBN 13. The ISBN for your book.

LCCC. A Library of Congress Catalog Number.

Medium. Medium is the format of the book, usually print or eBook, unless you have chosen to distribute it as an audiobook, or on CD or DVD instead.

Format. In most cases the format will be paperback or hardbound.

Title Status. If you want the book industry to know that your book is available for sale, use Active. You can use the term Forthcoming, if you are months away from publishing. Be sure, however, to come back and change the status. The big databases that the book sellers use will show the book as unavailable until you change the status to Active.

Price Type. Choose Retail Price.

Keep a file with this information gathered in one place. When you are ready to let others know that you have a book available, having these details handy will save time.

SECTION 5

For most memoirs, marketing is not as much about making sales as it is about contacting the people who would be interested in reading your book or adding it to a library collection, and providing information about where they can obtain a copy. Marketing—spreading the word—is about using methods that get results at a cost you can afford, in both money and time.

Baby Steps

If your intent for writing your book is solely to provide a lasting legacy to family members, then once they have copies, you can stop marketing.

Next Steps

If, however, you would like your book to remain available well past the current generation, contribute it to the major genealogical collections around the country, and establish a sales channel that will last awhile. Creating a website for the book or selling the book through an online bookseller such as Amazon are two ways to keep the book out in the marketplace long after you have turned your attention to other projects.

Giant Leaps

If you have a compelling story that would be of interest to the general public, then by all means, market the book wherever you can. Your work may be the inspiration other memoirists need to write their own stories. It may help another researcher answer questions about your profession or the era you grew up in. It may interest a local historian who is researching the places where you lived. There may be many people who are interested in your book that you will remain unaware of unless you spread the word far and wide.

Note: In this section, the expression "pitch" means to make an appeal or to make your case about your book.

Chapter 23

Creating a Marketing Plan

Quite often, when I speak to groups about marketing, I get moans and groans about not wanting to "sell" something. Not all selling is the equivalent of selling used cars. Some of you will generously give your books away to family members. If you have the means to do so, hooray.

Many of you will sell your book, if for no other reason than it is more practical for your family members to order a copy online and have the printer ship the book to them directly, than for you to buy hundreds of copies, store them (and dust them), and have to run to the post office every time someone orders one.

In this section, marketing (and its side-kick, selling) is more about getting the word out that you have a book available, than becoming a tycoon selling books to unsuspecting cousins.

Marketing 101

Marketing has five elements: identifying the target market, determining a method to reach out to the target market effectively, giving interested people a reason to buy, showing them where they can buy, and asking them to do so.

Identify the Target Market

Most of you will have more than one target market. For this discussion, a target market is a group of people with similar interests. The reason you want to narrow down a wide group of potential buyers into narrow target markets is to be able to reach them effectively. People who have similar interests tend to gather in the same places, belong to the same (or similar) groups, read the same books or magazines, and use the same websites. Once you identify where you can reach the target market, you can let them know the book is available.

Reach Out to the Target Market

Let us use your immediate family as an example. Most people have multiple ways to reach parents, grandparents, siblings and children. You have phone numbers, email, and home addresses. That gives you many ways to reach this audience. You could call each person and discuss the book. You could create an email list and send a group email, or you could write a letter or create a sales sheet and send it to each family member's home. You could make an announcement on the social media your family follows. You could talk about the book at the next family gathering. Contacting your family should be easy. Unfortunately, you may not have as many easy options with other target markets.

Every target market has a way to contact the group and its members. You may have to decide, however, whether the effort or expense of reaching out to each target market is worth the cost.

Give the Target Market a Reason to Buy

In most cases, it is not enough to simply tell someone you have a book available. While your Mom will buy a copy without hesitation, other buyers will want to know what they will get out of reading your book. The most important part of your marketing plan is putting together a list of benefits.

Benefits are the reasons why a person will want to read your book. Distinguishing benefits from features can be confusing. The following are common book *features*:

- The book is 396 pages long.
- The book covers my education and career.
- The book begins in 1955.
- The book covers the space race with the Russians, the Mercury tragedy and each Apollo mission.

By contrast, this is an example of a benefit-rich statement: "With cinematic power and beauty, bestselling author David Laskin brings to life the upheavals of the twentieth century through the story of one family, three continents, two world wars, and the rise and fall of nations." That description, taken from the dust jacket flap of David Laskin's *The Family*, sounds much more like an enticement to read the book than a list of facts, does it not?

Remember back in Chapter 22: Preparing the Final Files in the discussion about your book's description and how vital the description can be to sales? It is worth your time to write a compelling enticement to read the book. In fact, it is worth writing, and re-writing, if necessary. Once you have a vivid, enticing description, you can use it in all of your marketing materials.

Show the Target Market Where They Can Buy

Let potential book buyers know where they can buy a copy, whether by contacting you directly, by buying from your website or at an online bookstore such as Amazon. If you have multiple options for sales, give the buyer a choice. Not everyone is comfortable purchasing items online. And, if you want to offer autographed copies, state where those copies are available, as well. For some people, autographed copies are an additional inducement to buy.

Include a Call to Action

One of the biggest mistakes in marketing is forgetting to ask for the sale. You do not have to include an obnoxious, flashing "Buy Now!!!" button. A simple, "purchase your copy today" will do. Or offer free shipping if the buyer purchases a book by a certain date. Enticements to act sooner rather than later often work.

Setting the Price

Before you can sell your book, you have to determine its price. If you do not plan to make any money on the book, you can set the price a few cents over your wholesale cost.

In the publishing industry, the standard price is set at eight times (8x) the wholesale cost to account for the cost of marketing and fulfillment. That cost is based upon long print runs, however, that keep the wholesale cost of each book very low.

Realistically, your wholesale costs will be a bit higher and depending upon which type of printer you have chosen, the cost may be substantially higher. You will have to decide which is more important to you, making the book widely available—meaning keeping the retail price low—maximizing the amount you make on the sale of each book, or something in between. The higher you set the price, however, the fewer you will sell.

If you plan to offer an eBook version, understand that eBook readers do not expect to pay the same price for their electronic version as they would for a printed book. Amazon has recognized this fact and has structured their royalty payments to reflect what readers want. Amazon pays a royalty of 70 percent to any eBook priced under $9.99, but only a 30 percent royalty for books priced at $10 or higher. Amazon has analyzed a lot of buyer data to discover that $9.99 price point. Consider pricing your electronic version under $9.99.

For most memoirs, making the book more widely available at a lower cost is the best way to get your hard work out there to the people who are interested in your stories.

The Offer

Use the following formula to build your marketing pieces: attention-catching headlines and sub-headlines, text that supports the headlines while giving readers details, and a call to action. I have added bullets and keywords to the formula to make your offer easy to scan, and easy for the search engines to find if you post the offer online.

Headline

The headline should get the reader's attention and interest them enough to read more. For most memoirs, this would include the main surnames or most important events covered in the book (e.g. New Book Follows the Career of Cary L. Finch, Aerospace Engineer, 1950-1990).

Sub-Headlines

Sub-headlines break up the rest of the text into small, easy-to-read sections. Subheads also make it easy to scan the piece from beginning to end. Subheads are an opportunity for you to catch and keep the reader's attention (e.g. A Front Row Seat to the Mercury Tragedy).

Supporting Text

After each headline and sub-head, give the readers details from the book. Tell a quick story, allude to the action, give something to pique the reader's interest.

Bullet Points

Give the reader a bulleted list of the book's main features:

- Subjects covered
- The most important places or events covered
- Number of pages
- Number of photographs or illustrations (you could name any that are especially enticing [e.g. The only known photograph of Hurricane Betsy taken from space])
- Price (include shipping and handling charges)
- ISBN (if you have one)

Keywords

If you will place your marketing piece online, include a few important keywords within the text to help the search engines find it. Using the example above, keywords could include: Cary Finch Space Program, Cary Finch Aerospace Engineer, 1965 Hurricane Betsy, and so on.

Call to Action

A call to action is a marketing term for asking the reader to buy (e.g. "Buy by November 1st and receive free shipping").

Pre-Publication Offers

One method publishers use to jump-start their sales is to send a pre-publication offer letting potential readers know that the book will be available soon, while offering a discount of some type as an enticement to buy before the book's release.

Before print-on-demand, the proceeds from a pre-publication offer was a way to pay for the first print run. It was also a way to fill the time between when the book went to the printer, and when the books were delivered. With print-on-demand, there is no longer much of a delay or the need to pay for an initial print run. Today, a pre-publication offer is more a thank-you to the people who purchase right away.

Ongoing Offers

Continue to market your book for as long as you want readers to buy it. Memoirs do not go out of style, so you could repeat your offer every now and again for years to come. Even after your family members have copies, there will be new members of the family who may enjoy reading the book as well. As the kids start having kids of their own, they may become more interested in their roots. In addition, there will always be a new generation of genealogical researchers who were unaware of their interest in your book when it was released.

Check Out the Competition

If you are ever at a loss for how to get the word out about your book, look for ways in which other authors are marketing their books. Check out book-related websites. Read the About the Author pages. Sign up for book-related emails. Check YouTube for book trailers. Spend some time on Amazon and other online booksellers' sites and read the description of other memoirs. Read the blurbs about the authors.

Learn from the best. Use the search engines to find all the marketing and publicity about a family-related book. David Laskin's, *The Family* would be a good model since it is a relatively new book, and it is a personal narrative. David Laskin, however, is a Harvard-educated writer with some major-league writing credentials, so you may not be able to replicate precisely the kind of attention for your book that he has garnered for his. You should, however, be able to get some ideas for increasing sales of your book.

Create a Marketing Plan

For many authors, once a book is complete and that huge project is off the desk, it may be difficult to jump right back in to create awareness for the book. If you will create a plan with just one marketing technique per week over the first six months after your book is finished, you will be surprised at how many people you will reach. Like many things, you are more likely to accomplish your marketing goals if you write them down and schedule them on the calendar.

※✦

The most important thing about marketing is being able to identify your target market, finding a way to contact these potential buyers, and describing your book in such a way that they simply cannot resist placing an order.

Chapter 24

Reaching Your Audience

One of the biggest mistakes novice marketers make is believing that "everyone" will want a copy of your book. With a memoir, that is not likely. With most books, it is better to identify the people who are the *most* likely to buy in order to save marketing money and time. The natural markets for your book are a starting point. There may be other, unanticipated buyers, however, who surface through your marketing efforts.

Family Members and Friends

The obvious target market for your memoir is members of your family. Your friends may also be interested in reading your book. The following are marketing techniques you can use with family members and friends.

Email Campaign

Send an email announcing the book. Add a signature to your regular email so that each time you correspond, a message will go out showing you as the author, the title, a link back to your website or a place where the book is sold and any social media you are participating in that concerns the book. If you include "http://" before any website address, the link will become click-able within the email.

Ask family members and friends to forward your book announcement email to anyone else who may be interested in the book. This is a good way to have family members help spread the word, especially if you do not have email addresses for cach of the distant cousins.

Family Gatherings

Bring a few books with you to each and every family gathering in case there are people who have been waiting to buy directly from you.

Autographed Copies

Autographed copies are a nice touch when you know the buyer personally. They also make some books more valuable. In order to offer autographed copies, you must purchase enough books to keep a few on hand to fulfill the orders, or ask family members to bring their copies with them to reunions, or other family gatherings for you to sign.

Make an Announcement

Make an announcement on any social media sites where your family and friends participate. Google+ has a new service called Google Hangouts (LIVE) that enables you to hold a town meeting of sorts with friends and family using the Internet. (More on the workings of Google Hangouts in Chapter 25: Generating Publicity.)

Send a Card

Some of your family members may not use email. There are services such as Send Out Cards (www.sendoutcards.com) that enable you to create a personalized card that the company will print and send through the postal service. Use your cover image and images from the book to create your personalized card. Have the description and buying information for the book ready to copy and paste into the card. Write a quick personal note, as well. Personal notes take only a few seconds to compose but mean a lot to the recipients.

Genealogical Researchers

Other genealogical researchers who are working on your family—whether as a direct line or a collateral line—may be interested in the book. The key to finding the people in a target market is to evaluate where they gather and make an announcement where they are likely to see it. In the announcement, do not try to sell directly. Let the group know that there is a new book out and where interested members can go for more information.

Family Trees with Links to You or Your Family

If you did not do so during your research, check the major genealogical research sites (Ancestry, FamilySearch, MyHeritage and FindMyPast) for member trees that link to you or your family and contact the owners of those trees.

Genealogical Forums

Many of the major genealogical research sites have forums by surname and location. You can leave a message for members in the forum. Use an informative headline (e.g. New Book Follows the Aerospace Career of Walter Richmond, 1944–1990). Within the post, use your description of the book. And, if you are posting in a locations forum, make ties to the location clear (e.g. New Book about the Aerospace Career of Walter Richmond, 1944–1900, in Houston, Texas).

Some of the older forums have stopped accepting new posts, but their older posts remain online and contain contact information. Although you can no longer post a message, you could contact anyone who is researching your family.

Blogs

Finding a surname-based blog will be relatively easy because so many people are blogging, but finding a surname-based blog that is also researching family history is not. My best suggestion is that you use both "family" and "genealogy" in your keywords when you search.

Surname Groups

Look at Cyndi's List (www.cyndislist.com) for surname groups and reunions. The categories list alone will keep you busy. Some links will take you to personal websites, and others to surname societies or newsletter websites.

Conferences

If you stayed in one area of the country for a substantial amount of time, ascertain whether there is a regional genealogical conference where you could post an announcement for attendees. Most conferences sell inexpensive advertising space in their giveaway bags or programs that you could use to make your book announcement.

Contact as many like-minded researchers as you can find. They may have a greater interest in your book than some of your distant family members.

Local Historians

How much you can interest local historians or history buffs in your memoir depends upon how much local history you included in the book. If you have good stories about a particular area or time period, contact local historians and make your pitch, mentioning the parts of your book that may appeal to them.

Historical Societies and Their Museums

Societies appreciate being able to offer special deals to their members, so offer to give society members a discounted price in exchange for mentioning the book in their member newsletter and on the society's website. Set up a special landing page on your website where society members can go to place a discounted order.

The most likely opportunity for in-store sales may be at a local historical museum bookshop. There you will find like-minded local history buffs who buy local history books. Approach a museum shop buyer by making the book's ties to the community obvious in your pitch.

Offer a small discount if the museum shop buys only one book, and a larger discounted price if they buy three or more books. Most museum shops will not stock an abundance of any one book until they see how well the book will sell.

Not every historical museum is connected to a historical society. The independent museums in the area may be willing to sell your book, as well.

Living History Societies and Re-Enactors Groups

Re-enactors are individuals who are so fascinated with how people lived during an era that they spend time and money re-enacting what life was like then. If your memoir includes detailed research about an era, a profession, war-time, or military groups, there may be a society of like-minded historians or re-enactors who may be interested.

One of the most interesting re-enactors I have found is a Victorian Photographer who demonstrates historically accurate wet-plate photography to interested photographers, and who takes photographs of re-enactors in Victorian dress. Check out Alex Burnham's website (historic-photographer.co.uk).

Collectors Groups

Although collectors will rarely refer to themselves as re-enactors, many of them have an interest in the historical era from which their collections came. As an example, consider the Winchester Arms Collectors Association (winchestercollector.org). They feature historical articles and host events for collectors. Collectors groups may be willing to feature an article about your book if there is a significant tie from the book to their members' interests.

Complete Strangers

"Complete strangers" is a difficult target market to define, but there are a few ways in which to reach interested individuals without knowing who they are.

Website

Host your own website with enough information about the book that someone who is researching your family, the time period or the place, could find the site using a search engine. Use appropriate keywords in the copy and the metatags to help the search engines correctly categorize the site. Look back at the cheat sheet of "Other Information About Your Book" you should have standing by and pump up the keywords to include the same type of information that other genealogical researchers, history buffs or collectors would use to find the website. (More about hosting your own website in Chapter 27: Selling Online.)

Email Signup

One way to make contact with complete strangers is to ask them for an email address when they visit your website. Many companies use this technique to send product or service offers. If you are not planning a regular newsletter, indicate that you will only be contacting them with news of the book, either when it is finished or when a new book is offered so that they will not be fearful of dozens of emails a day clogging their email box.

Book Trailer on YouTube

Create a quick book trailer on YouTube showing some of the photographs from the book and giving a little taste of the stories told in the book. You can create a book trailer quite easily using movie or slideshow software such as Windows Movie Maker or iMovie for the Mac. Watch a few episodes of Ken Burns's *Civil War* to see how the master uses still photographs and voice-overs to tell a compelling story. Search for book trailers on YouTube to see other examples.

Social Media Page or Group

Create a specialty page (fan page) or group for the book or a part of the contents that would appeal to other researchers, local historians or collectors. The expectation with a fan page or group, however, is that you will contribute to it regularly enough to keep members interested. If you do not have the time to commit to updating it at least once every couple of weeks, you may want to skip this step. I would give you the same advice about establishing a blog for the book. The expectation of people who read social media or blogs is that you will provide updated content often.

Make Yourself Available to Answer Questions

If you are able to help another writer who is working on a memoir, and are willing to answer questions about your process, say so on your website, a public blog, or a post to your social media account. The same goes for letting genealogical and historical societies know that you are willing to help their members, and give them a way to contact you. Being helpful can translate into book sales.

Libraries

Most libraries have limited budgets, and the books they want to buy are ones that patrons will check out over and over. In other words, libraries will buy the latest bestsellers but may not be interested in buying a memoir unless they have a genealogical, biographical or local history collection.

If you have a local connection, it would be a grand gesture to send the library a free copy, along with a note about how you are connected to the area. To go the extra mile, help the library's indexer by sending a list of the main characters with their birth and death years, along with the synopsis that explains how you are connected to the area.

If you are planning to sell to the library market, however, the following are a few things to consider:

Obvious local ties. Libraries are more likely to buy if there are strong ties to the area, or if you have done extensive research about the local area included in the book.

General appeal. If your story has broader, general appeal, make sure your description of the book includes that information.

Price. If you are able, offer the library a discount on the book or sell it to them at cost plus shipping. Librarians must look after their budgets.

Bookstores

In general, bookstores are lousy places to sell books. Bookstores play by a different set of rules than other retail outlets. Bookstores expect to put your books on their shelves, wait ninety days to see if the books sell, and if they do not, to return them to you for full credit. You pay the shipping to get the books to them; they return the books, and oftentimes, you get back books in no condition to re-sell.

Bookstores can be a good place to sell books if you can be there to give a talk about your book to an eager audience. Book signings are a long-standing tradition in publishing, but the only people who make money by signing books, are celebrities. If you are well known, you can sit and sign books for a couple of hours and make some money. If you are not well known, you must create a reason for people to come into the store, usually by offering a free, informative talk.

In either case, a bookstore hosting a book signing or a talk will expect to buy the books from you at a discount of about fifty percent. You will be expected to bring enough books to the store to satisfy the expected crowd, and the bookstore will sell the books at full price to the audience. Afterward, the bookstore will pay you the negotiated price for each book sold.

Non-Book Stores

The list of non-book stores is nearly endless. Any retail outlet that you can establish a tie with could sell your book for you. Books are sold at restaurants, tire stores, copy shops, outdoor stores, indoor stores, bait and tackle shops—nearly everywhere there is a cash register.

The best news regarding selling to non-book stores is that they do not expect to return the books. They will expect the same deep discount as bookstores and will likely take only a few copies to see how sales go. They also may expect a counter-top display. Fortunately, you can pick up an easy-to-assemble cardboard display form online or at most office supply stores.

Complimentary Copies

For the sake of posterity, other genealogical researchers, and the possibility that some major catastrophe will happen somewhere at some time, please send a complimentary copy of your book to the following major genealogical collections:

The Library of Congress
101 Independence Ave, SE, Washington, DC 20540

The Family History Library
35 North West Temple St, Salt Lake City, UT 84150

The DAR Library
1776 D Street, NW, Washington, DC 20006

The Denver Public Library
10 W 14th Ave Pkwy, Denver, CO 80204

The Allen County Public Library
900 Library Plaza, Fort Wayne, IN 46802

The Wisconsin State Historical Society
816 State St, Madison, WI 53706

The Midwest Genealogy Center
3440 S Lee's Summit, Independence, MO 64055

The New York Public Library
31-11 Thomson Ave, Long Island City, NY 11101

If you are able, add to your list the local libraries in the places where you have lived. I have often been surprised by the amazing collections of local history in even the tiniest of local libraries.

ಲ∿ಶ

Reach out to people who may want to buy a copy of your book, and to stores that could sell the book for you. Start with the natural target markets. If you are interested in expanding your reach, the next few chapters will show you how.

Chapter 25

Generating Publicity

There is an old saying in marketing: "When you advertise, you pay for the privilege of saying good things about yourself. Publicity allows other people to say good things about you free of charge." Publicity often sets the "word-of-mouth" train in motion, but it is not without work. If you want to gain publicity for your book, you will need to pitch it to the people who can help spread the word.

Gaining publicity for a memoir is going to be a stretch, except for those with stories that would be interesting to the public, or are of such an extraordinary nature that they will generate interest in the news.

Book Reviews

Book reviews are a long-standing publishing tradition. Unfortunately, the most widely read book reviews are out of reach for a memoir unless you write for a major magazine or newspaper.

Book Review Magazines

The book publishing industry fills the review pages for *Kirkus Reviews*, *Publishers Weekly*, *Library Journal*, *Booklist* (American Library Association), *Library Review*, and the book review columns in the major newspapers. The likelihood of being able to get a memoir reviewed in one of these outlets is slim.

Local Newspapers

You are much more likely to have success with your local newspaper if they feature local authors. There are two approaches you can use when pitching a local newspaper: one is to ask for a book review; the other is to offer a good story from the book that features a local connection. Most newspapers today, even small local papers, have online editions. To make the pitch to the right person, check the online edition for book reviews and local human interest stories. If the newspaper runs a local history column, even better.

Online Bookstores

Most of the major online bookstores such as Amazon and Barnes&Noble offer reader reviews. Whether or not your book appears in these catalogs is largely a function of which print-on-demand printer you use.

The best thing about online reviews is that friends and family can easily post them. Ask people who have read the book to write an online review. If you asked people to write blurbs for the book, ask them for a review, as well.

Your Associations

You may belong to associations, clubs or organizations that would feature a review of your book in their member newsletters. Consider school groups and alumni associations, sororities or fraternities, civic groups, philanthropic groups, religious organizations, sports teams—any group you have an affiliation with that would be willing to let their members know that you have written a book.

The Press

The key to working with the press is making it easy for them to help you while meeting their deadlines.

Help a Reporter Out

One way to get the attention of busy reporters is to join the website, Help a Reporter Out (www.helpareporter.com). Every day, reporters seek information from experts. To use the site effectively, do not overstate your expertise and respond to the digest of queries in a timely manner. The free account will send queries in your field of expertise three times a day. There is a paid option as well, if you want to become known to a wide range of journalists as an expert in a particular field. Help a Reporter Out is not the only press leads website available, but it offers a free option where many others do not.

Google Alerts

One of the easiest ways to keep track of events that are happening in the news is to set up Google Alerts (alerts.google.com) for the places and events that occur in your book. For example, if you have researched the Battle of the Bulge, and a re-enactors group is conducting a demonstration at a military museum, you could pitch the local newspapers, any societies associated with WWII, and the re-enactors group to include stories from your book, or a mention of your book in their coverage of the event.

Press Releases

The standard pitch tool for the media is a press release. The key to an effective press release—first and foremost—is sending it to the correct person or media outlet. The likelihood of getting any attention by sending a fax to the *Chicago Tribune* is a lot lower than sending an email to a local reporter who covers historical events for a small town.

Press releases follow a formula. The following is the standard formula for most press releases:

The Header. The header should include the line "For Immediate Release" unless you wish the news outlet to hold the release until a specified date.

Headline. The headline often includes a hook that helps the journalist provide something of value to the readership, usually in the form of entertainment, information, analysis or assistance. So, a curiosity piquing headline could go something like this: "Mrs. O'Leary's Cow Started the Great Chicago Fire ... Or Did She? New Book Offers Eye-Witness Testimony of Arson and Murder."

First Paragraph. The first paragraph after the headline backs up the headline with facts and should include the who, what, where when, and why of the story.

Subheads. Subheads help journalists skim through the press release quickly.

Body Paragraphs. The body paragraphs contain more about the book, perhaps a quote from you as the author, or a quote from an expert concerning the substance of the book, all of which support the main headline's promise of content.

Contact Information. If a journalist is on a deadline and wants a quick quote from you, he or she must be able to reach you quickly. Include your email address and cell phone number.

Distributing Your Press Release

Once you have a press release ready to go, make it available one or all of the following ways: by sending it directly to a journalist from a local news outlet, posting it on a free online press release site, paying a press distribution site to deliver it to targeted journalists, and including it in your own media kit (more on media kits shortly).

If you have done your homework and found the correct journalist from a local newspaper, email the press release to him or her directly. If you do not hear anything back, wait a few days, and then send an email asking whether he or she received the release. If nothing happens after that, there is no sense in pestering the journalist. Not every journalist has the time to respond to every press release sent to him or her.

Free Online Press Release Sites

At one time, there were dozens of free online press release sites. Many of those sites have become subscription sites. CyberAlert, a media monitoring service (www.cyberalert.com), posts its top free press release distribution services list every so often, and these are the top three from their latest list:

- PRUrgent (www.prurgent.com)
- PRLog (www.prlog.org)
- Newsvine (www.newsvine.com)

Paid Press Release Services

Book Publicity Services (bookpublicityservices.com) has a list of the best paid and free press release services. Unfortunately, paid distribution services are expensive and may not yield worthwhile results for a memoir. Regardless, the following are the top three paid sites from their list:

- PRWeb (www.prweb.com)
- eReleases (www.ereleases.com)
- PRNewswire (www.prnewswire.com)

Media Kit

The purpose of a media kit is to answer questions for the media quickly. At bare minimum, your media kit should include: a press release, an author biography and suggested interview questions in case the media person would like to conduct a quick interview about the book. You could also include: links to any social media you are using for the book, a link to your YouTube book trailer, story ideas, a fact sheet, current event tie-in ideas, quizzes, a resource list, FAQs, a review copy request form, any honors or awards the book has received, reviews and a list of interviews you have given.

Keep these items together as a PDF to attach when you reply to email queries that come from the media. Each piece of the media kit should have your full contact information in case only one page from the PDF is printed for reference.

Your online media kit (or media room) should go one step further. In addition to the media kit as a quick PDF to download, also provide each page of your media kit in plain HTML so that the text is available to the search engines. In the online version, also provide: low and high-resolution images of your book cover, an image of you as the author, and any interesting images from the book—low resolution for the Internet, high resolution for print; any media clips—audio, video or a link to the media outlet where you have given interviews; as well as your speaking schedule or author events you have planned.

Bloggers

For those of you who are unfamiliar with blogs, blogs are web-logs—a type of website. Blogging software makes blogs easy to update. The most recent post (information) remains at the top of the page until the next post comes along and moves the older information down or into an archive.

Blogs are popular because they are easy and inexpensive to set up. If you can use email, you can post (add information) to a blog. That said, for a blog to become popular, it must be fed and followed. In other words, you must add useful, helpful, interesting information to the blog regularly enough to satisfy the audience—the blog's followers. (You will find detailed instructions for creating a blog in *Set Yourself Up to Self-Publish: A Genealogist's Guide*.)

There are two primary ways to encourage bloggers to help get the word out about your book: to provide content for the blog, or to become a guest host providing interesting information to or answering questions by the blog's audience.

First, however, you must locate blogs that are appropriate to a conversation about your book. Any aspect of your book may be interesting to a blogger's audience. If, for example, you studied recipes that your 19th century ancestors would have used, then you may have information of interest to a historical cooking blog, or a blog that features unusual recipes.

Finding an Appropriate Blog

Use a search engine to locate a blog by searching for your subject (i.e. historical recipes) and the word "blog," or you can use a blog directory. A search engine is likely to return individual blog posts that contain your keywords, whereas a blog directory is more likely to return entire blogs dedicated to the subject. The Search Engine Journal (searchenginejournal.com) keeps a current list of the top blog directories. The following are a few of the most popular blog directories:

- Blog Nation (www.blognation.com)
- Best of the Web Blog Search (blogs.botw.org)
- Bloggeries (www.bloggeries.com)
- EatonWeb Blog Directory (portal.eatonweb.com)
- Blogged (blogged.com)
- Blog Search Engine (www.blogsearchengine.com)

Providing Content

If you want a blogger to include your information on his or blog, it has to be of value to their readers. It pays to spend some time looking through the archives of the blog to see what has interested readers in the past before you contact the blogger and suggest content.

Become a Guest Host

Guest hosting on numerous blogs is a way to create a virtual book tour. Instead of going from city to city signing books in bookstores, you become a guest on blogs. To become a guest host, ask the blogger to set up an author interview. The blogger will let his or her audience know in advance when the interview will take place, and the audience will submit questions for you through the blog. At a set date and time, you will become available on the blog (from your computer) to answer the audience's questions. The best thing about an author interview by blog, is that you can remain in your office to participate. No traveling is necessary.

Provide Something of Value

Another way to encourage a blogger to help you is to offer something of value to their readers. Offer a discount on your book, or free shipping, or a free sample (recipe, chapter, quiz) by email. Or offer a copy of the book as a prize for your guest appearance. Allow the host to choose the winner.

Social Media

There are two ways to use social media to spread the word: you can post (write short tidbits of information) on your social media pages, or you can comment on other people's pages.

Many people use social media as a private way to communicate with friends and family. If you are going to generate any publicity about your book, however, you must establish a public page. On some sites, that means creating a different account for you as an author, or creating a business or fan page about the book. Each social media site is different, so you will need to establish an account and test it out to see what will suit you and your book best.

Social Media Sites

The following are, currently, the most used social media sites. Trends on social media change over time, so do not be surprised if a year from now, something new has come along to grab the interest of the public. To use these sites, establish an account, give yourself a public profile and post.

- Facebook (www.facebook.com)
- Twitter (www.twitter.com)
- LinkedIn (www.linkedin.com)
- Pinterest (www.pinterest.com)
- Google+ (plus.google.com)
- Tumblr (www.tumblr.com)
- Instagram (www.instagram.com)
- Flickr (www.flickr.com)

There are specialized social media sites such as: regional sites (e.g. VK is a European site); subject-based sites (e.g. GenealogyWise is a genealogy social network); format-based sites (e.g. YouTube is a site for video); or activity-based sites (e.g. MeetUp is a site that puts people together for activities such as running).

Post to Your Own Page

The best social media posts are brief—two to three sentences, max. Share links if there are websites that have more information on the topic of your post. Use hashtags to enable people interested in the subject to find the post. A hashtag is the symbol "#" followed by a subject (e.g. #MichelleFullertonMemoir).

Use an image. Images get attention and posts with images are more likely to be read. If you want to spread the conversation, include the names of followers. On some social media sites such as Facebook, typing another person's screen name is enough to alert them that they have been tagged (written about) in a post. On others such as Twitter, using the symbol "@" plus their screen name is necessary.

Most social media sites give viewers a chance to:

- Like (indicate their interest)
- Share (re-issue the post on their own timelines)
- Comment (write something about the contents of the post)

The terms for each of these activities may vary in different social media sites, but the effect is the same. Ideally, you will write something that is interesting enough to your followers (the people reading your posts) that they will pass the information along to their followers. Or, you can encourage them to share by asking that they do so.

Brand Your Social Media Account

Most social media platforms allow you to upload a cover (banner) image. Use this opportunity to show your book cover. In most cases, your cover image may be too small for most people to easily read the title, so place the title in a larger font beside the cover image, along with your name as the author and your website address.

Link Back to Your Social Media Pages

Once you establish social media accounts, you will have a unique URL (website address) that you can link to, on your website, social media accounts, blog or email signature to direct viewers to other information you have posted online.

Comment on Other People's Posts

Commenting on other people's posts can be a great way to introduce yourself as an expert on a subject. Unfortunately, it can be a potential minefield. Be positive, choose your words carefully so that they cannot be misinterpreted, and offer something helpful to the discussion. Leave controversial topics alone. There are people who revel in the worst, base culture of the Internet. There is no sense in painting your book with that kind of brush. Take the high road.

Book Lovers

There are a host of websites devoted to book lovers and posting an announcement on these sites is a good way to spread the word about your book. There are three types of sites for book lovers—sites devoted to readers, books, and book promotion.

Reader Websites

Each of the following sites provides information for readers, and each has its own rules of participation. What you will be allowed to post about your book varies from site to site. Please read the rules before you post.

GoodReads. GoodReads (www.goodreads.com) is a social media site for book lovers that allows you to share what you are reading with your friends. GoodReads also has an author program similar to Author Central on Amazon where you can post information about your book (www.goodreads.com/author/program).

LibraryThing. LibraryThing (www.librarything.com) is a social media site for book lovers and a place to catalog your books.

BookTalk. BookTalk.com (www.booktalk.com) describes itself as "all the buzz about books." BookTalk.org (www.booktalk.org) a free book discussion group.

Shelfari. Shelfari (www.shelfari.com) is Amazon's "encyclopedia for avid book lovers."

ReadingGroup Choices. ReadingGroup Choices (www.readinggroupchoices) helps book clubs choose their next book. It may be hard to break into book clubs, but you will not know unless you try.

Discussion Groups

Many eReader platforms have their own discussion groups (forums) for book lovers. The following are three of the most popular:

Kindle Boards. Kindle Boards (www.kboards.com) is a discussion forum for all things Kindle.

NookBoards. NookBoards (www.nookboards.com/forum/) is a discussion forum for Nook users.

MobileRead. MobileRead (www.mobileread.com) is a cross-platform forum for people who use eReaders.

Book Sites

There are a growing list of book search engines, including:

Open Library. Open Library(openlibrary.org) is building an enormous encyclopedia of books by devoting "one web page for every book." You may as well have your book listed on this site.

BookHitch. BookHitch (www.bookhitch.com) is a search engine for books and authors.

Book Promotion Sites

Every place you can leave a mention of your book is a book promotion site, but the following are free sites where you can upload your cover, leave a sample of your writing, and other promotional materials.

Nothing Binding. Nothing Binding (www.nothingbinding.com) allows you to upload cover images, excerpts, reviews, an author image and other promotional items.

The Book Report. The Book Report (www.bookreportradio.com) is a digest of radio stations where author interviews are conducted. Listening to other authors give radio interviews can be helpful if you are planning to do any interviews of your own.

News Feeds

It is difficult to get a mention on a NewsFeeds site, but they are valuable if you want to follow social trends or breaking news to provide a hook for a pitch about your book to a local journalist.

Mashable. Mashable (mashable.com) follows the headlines, social media, tech and business, but also has a "watercooler" section of interesting headlines. One recent headline detailed how easy it is to get lost in the New York Public Library's Massive Map Collection.

Alltop. Alltop (alltop.com) has a good range of categories to follow that will digest the news across the Internet for you. While there is no genealogy subject heading, there is a history section.

Digg. Digg (digg.com) collects headlines across the Internet including headlines from social media sites and uploaded video.

StumbleUpon. StumbleUpon (www.stumbleupon.com) describes itself as "a giant collection of the best pages on the Internet." They will evaluate your interests and recommend pages for you to explore.

Google+

If there was ever a way to shout out to the world that you have a book available, Google+ may have figured it out.

Google+ has a feature entitled Hangouts on Air (www.google.com/+/learnmore/hangouts/onair.html) where you can "broadcast to the world for free." The live streaming feature allows you to create live video and have it broadcast on Google+, YouTube, and your website. It will be recorded and automatically saved to your YouTube channel.

You must establish a Google+ account, a YouTube channel (also a Google product) and have a webcam in order to record your broadcast. You can let others know about your broadcast, and they can view it on their computers, tablets or smartphones.

؏ؖ

Most publicity you can do for yourself, if you are willing to learn the ins and outs of what media outlets require. If your book would benefit from national publicity, you may want to hire a publicist, because they specialize in gaining the attention of hard-to-reach, national media outlets.

Working with a Publicist

The only time you should consider working with a publicist is if you have a family history that is of interest to the general public. Publicists are specialists in enticing media to cover you and the stories in your book. They perform a valuable service, and they charge accordingly.

Find the Right Publicist

Most publicists are specialists in one aspect of the media or another. Find a publicist who specializes in books and authors, and one who can conduct whatever type of media campaign you are interested in—online, newspaper, television, radio or all of the above. Publicists offer a multitude of services including: writing press releases, posting to blogs and social media, arranging for public appearances, scheduling interviews on television or radio, pitching feature stories, and locating media outlets appropriate to your media plan.

Research other book campaigns the publicist has worked on. The publicist should be able to tell you which books have gotten what kind of coverage.

Ask About Fees

Some publicists charge a retainer for a certain number of hours worked, others charge by the package. What the package includes can be a matter of negotiating. Many publicists offer a starter book package that includes: sending your book to a specific list of reviewers; sending press releases to a select group of media; scheduling you for interviews on radio, TV or blogs; and seeing that you get media training before any interviews take place. You may be able to find a publicist who will offer even smaller packages such as a single press release or a media kit.

Create a Media Plan

Before you approach a publicist, create a rough media plan so that you have a general idea of what you want the publicist to do for you. Where do you want your book mentioned? Local newspapers and journals? On local radio or television? Or do you think you can interest a national newspaper, radio show or television program in covering your book? If you are shooting for the moon, understand how hard it is to reach it. A local campaign may be a better way to start.

Be Realistic About Your Expectations

Before you add a media outlet to your plans, do your homework. If you think a *New York Times* book review is in order, then head to the library and read the reviews over the last month. Is there anything resembling your book in those reviews? If there is, great. Look at the way the book was covered and see how it could apply to your book. If there is nothing resembling your book in the reviews, there is a reason. The same goes for other media outlets—local or national. Asking a publicist to do the impossible will waste their time and your money.

Prepare the Publicist

Before a publicist can prepare a media campaign, they will need a copy of your book and any marketing materials you have generated.

Expect Criticism

Publicists are marketing experts. If you hire one, trust them to do what is right for you and your book. There may be a more effective way to get the word out than the marketing materials you prepared yourself. On occasion, using a good graphic designer to make your marketing materials look more professional is all it takes.

Ask How the Publicist Would Pitch Your Book

Publicists know how to sell ideas to the media and how to phrase a hook to pique interest. If a publicist struggles with how to describe your book to a journalist, there is little possibility that a journalist will be interested enough to interview you or write a story about your book.

PUBLISH A MEMOIR

Work With the Publicist's Schedule

Publicists work around the deadline schedule of the media. Your publicist should welcome input and questions, but ask for the best time to call or send your questions by email so that there is time for a thoughtful response.

Educate Yourself

The best way you can help your publicist help you is to learn how to market books by attend publishing association meetings and conferences, giving public talks to make yourself a better public speaker, and training to interview well on television and radio.

❧❦

Publicity is another way to describe word of mouth. For most books, word of mouth does not happen naturally. It must be generated and encouraged.

Chapter 26

Expanding Your Audience

Expanding your audience will help you reach potential buyers. The following are many of the same steps a business would use to reach out to new prospective customers, and a few techniques used primarily to market books.

Promote Yourself as an Author

For many authors, promoting one's self is uncomfortable, but your book sales will be the better for it if you do. The following are a few ways to promote your book while you promote yourself.

Promote Yourself Whenever You Can

Carry a few copies of your book wherever you go. You never know when you can strike up a conversion about your book or yourself as an author. Carry a few collaterals, such as bookmarks or business cards as well. (More about collateral materials shortly.)

Amazon's Listmania

Amazon allows users to create lists of books and other products within the Amazon catalog. When a user searches for a product that fits your list, the name of your list will pop up in the right-hand bar letting the user know that there are other similar products available in the list. This is one way to show what other books or products you found on Amazon that helped with your research, along with your book, of course, at the top of the list.

Amazon's Author Central

If your book is listed on Amazon, you can sign up for Author Central (authorcentral.amazon.com). Even if you do not use Amazon (CreateSpace) as your print-on-demand printer, your books could show up in the Amazon catalog a number of other ways—as a Kindle edition (through an eBook aggregator), Amazon's link to your POD printer's catalog (print books), or as a re-sale item. Many people re-sell their books on Amazon. In fact, you can sell your own books as a re-seller.

However your book made the list, you can use Author Central to promote yourself as an author. You can add book extras such as their "ridiculously simplified synopsis" or a longer excerpt. Your profile can include up to eight photos, eight videos, your speaking engagements calendar, a "from the author" note, reviews sent to you, additional details about the book, and your blog's RSS feed (more on RSS feeds in Chapter 27: Selling Online).

One of the best features of Author Central is that readers can see everything you have written in one place, which may generate additional book sales. One way to direct interested people to your Author Central page is to include a link to it on your author's website, in your profiles at social media sites, or anyplace online where you have your book listed.

You could get the URL (domain name) for yourself as an author (e.g. www.your-name-author.com) and redirect the URL to your Author Central page. You could also include a link in your email signature so that every time you send out an email, you encourage readers to check out your author's page.

Pixel of Ink Author's Corner

Pixel of Ink (www.pixelofink.com) also has an author's corner if you have a book for the Kindle and are willing to sell the book at bargain prices for a short time. Selling your book for $0.99 or giving it away free can spur other sales when the time for the deal has elapsed.

Create an Author's Website

Host a website that focuses on you, the author. There are a couple of ways to do this, and the next chapter will provide more details for creating websites, blogs and using URL re-directs to establish a presence online. For now, include the following in your author's website:

A Photograph (or Two). Invest in a decent head shot (portrait photograph). If you want to let your personality show a bit more, include a few candids.

A Biography. Write a quick biography about yourself, including the story of why you wrote the book. Provide a few details of your story, describe any discoveries or difficulties you encountered while writing, and explain why the book is a "must read."

The Media Kit for the Book

In the last chapter, I described what should go into a good media kit. The media kit for your author website should include the book's media kit, examples of any articles you have written, lectures you have given about your book, and interviews you have given to the media.

Content

Provide a few book excerpts. Give away a story or two. Enticing stories are a great hook into to the book. If you have written additional articles from your research, include them.

Lectures List

If you speak to groups frequently, include a lectures list. Interested professional, service, historical or genealogical societies may be interested in one of your talks and ask you to speak to their group.

Ask for Reader Feedback

Ask people who have read your book to comment on it, and then post their comments. This is similar to asking for a testimonial about a business.

Links for Purchase

Make sure that anyone who is interested has an easy way to purchase the book. Provide a link to websites where the book is sold, or provide an order form. If you book is sold in more than one format (print and electronic), or is sold through different outlets, use an icon for the format (i.e. Kindle or iBooks) as a link to the sales venue.

Email Subscription List

If you would like to contact readers about future books, or if you are planning to write additional articles about your book, ask readers to subscribe to your email list. An email list can be valuable in the event you write another book.

Contact Information

Make sure readers have a way to contact you, either through a form on the website, an email address, a mailing address or a telephone number.

If you are serious about promoting yourself as an author, there are companies such as @uthors on the Web (www.authorsontheweb.com) who produce author-centric websites for big-name authors such as David Baldacci and Debbie Macomber. If you want to take a look at a good author's website, look at David Baldacci's website (davidbaldacci.com). His site includes the following categories: Home, About David, Books, Author Events, FAQ, Photo Gallery, In The

News, Philanthropy (The Wish You Well Foundation), and Contact. He used to have a full-blown press room at this site, but has opted for a contact form for readers, and contact information for his speaker's bureau, publicist and the director of his foundation.

Author David Louis Edelman (science fiction novelist, http://www.david-louisedelman.com) has an interesting list of other places to find him online including: Amazon, DeepGenre, Facebook, FiledBy, GoodReads, Google Profile, LibraryThing, LinkedIn, LiveJournal, MySpace, Nextcat, Picasa, Red Room, SF-Novelists, Shelfari, Twitter and Wikipedia. David Edelman created his website using WordPress. His list of all the places he can be found online is a good example of promoting one's self as an author.

Start a Blog

Another way to expand your audience is to start a blog. Blogs are popular because they are so easy to set up and get going. One advantage to using a blog to spread the word about your book is that you do not have to seek out readers. If you publish a blog, readers can find you using a search engine based upon similar interests. The downside of establishing a blog for marketing, however, is that you have to provide content regularly in order to keep followers happy.

If you are interested in establishing your own blog, you will find detailed instructions in *Set Yourself Up to Self-Publish: A Genealogist's Guide*.

Join a Publishers Association

I believe that there is always something to learn from other people who have blazed a trail, and that is especially true when it comes to marketing books. Attending local publishers association meetings may inspire you to keep up your marketing efforts, and offer ideas for new avenues that have worked for other members of the association.

Many associations have negotiated special deals that can help with your marketing efforts, such as: annual conferences, cooperative mailings or catalogs, awards, advocacy in disputes or lawsuits, networking, freight discounts, rights negotiations, legal or financial services, distribution channels, reviews, networking and printing.

The following are publishers associations that you may find helpful:

- Small Publishers Association of North America (www.spannet.org)
- Independent Book Publishers Association (www.ibpa-online.org)
- Christian Small Publishers Association (www.christianpublishers.net)
- Association of Publishers for Special Sales (www.spanpro.org)

There are local and regional associations that may be helpful to you, as well.

Collaterals

Businesses rely upon collateral materials to get the word out to potential new clients. Everything a business would use can be useful to book marketing. The cost of full color printing has come down so much that I consider a box of 1,000 business cards a starting point, and I challenge myself to give them all away within a few weeks of a book launch.

Consider the following printed collaterals:

Business Cards

Use your book cover for one side of the business card and the other side to give a quick list of benefits, the ISBN, the price and a website where the book is sold.

Bookmarks

Think of a bookmark as an oversized business card. It should include the same information as a business card, along with quotes or images from the book.

Postcard

If you have a large list of people to contact by mail, create a postcard announcing the book to send to your list.

Rack Cards

Rack cards are the size of about one-third of a sheet of paper (4" x 9"). If you have more than one book to announce, use a rack card. Rack cards will fit inside a standard #10 business envelope. Use the extra real estate on a rack card to offer a discount, excerpts, tips, or images from the book.

The following are sites where you can order business cards and other collaterals at a reasonable cost. There are undoubtedly many others online.

- GotPrint (www.gotprint.com)
- VistaPrint (www.vistaprint.com)
- Moo (us.moo.com)

Leave Behinds

If you have a larger budget, the following are a few ideas for leave-behinds: flyers, postcards, mini cards, stickers, refrigerator magnets, note cards, sticky notes, table tents, or calendars. Use your book cover image or title on these products.

You can "leave behind" these items wherever people gather or wait—doctor's offices, community bulletin boards, chambers of commerce, public building lobbies—any place that will allow you to leave your materials behind.

Swag

If you have lotto winnings to throw at your book marketing, step up to items commonly found in swag bags at conferences, such as: key chains or other photo gifts, thumb drives, phone cases, tote bags, mugs, mousepads, tape measures, pens or calendars.

The following are promotional products companies where you can purchase leave-behinds and swag to give away:

- VistaPrint (www.vistaprint.com)
- 4Imprint (www.4imprint.com)
- Positive Promotions (www.positivepromotions.com)

Attention Getters

If you want to garner attention, consider the following products: banners, yard signs, window decals, window clings, car door magnets, posters, bumper stickers, t-shirts—even aprons. You can put a photograph on just about anything with a surface, and your book cover is a good image to place on items that will be seen by the general public. Car door magnets promote your book(s) while you are out and about, wherever you go.

The following companies provide customized products:

- CafePress (www.cafepress.com)
- Zazzle (www.zazzle.com)
- VistaPrint (www.vistaprint.com)

There are hundreds of companies around the country that supply printed and promotional products. You may find local providers as well.

Speaking Engagements

There are ample opportunities to speak to groups about your book. Groups often looking for speakers at their meetings include: historical or genealogical societies, clubs, church groups, PTAs, or service groups (Kiwanis, Elks, or Optimists).

Consider educational opportunities such as life-long learning programs or other adult education providers in your community. Teachers welcome speakers if you can talk about subject that would tie in with their lesson plans. Some businesses offer learn-at-lunch opportunities. Businesses such as cruise ships and ski lodges invite speakers to entertain their patrons.

If you are uncomfortable with public speaking, Toastmasters International (www.toastmasters.org) has groups in nearly every community where you can test out your talk on people who will offer constructive criticism. The more you practice, the more comfortable you will be in front of a group.

Community Events

Community events are good places to sell books with local ties. Consider book fairs, farmer's markets, local festivals, town or county fairs, and holiday events. Check with the local historical society as well as civic and service groups for their event schedules. Many times, you can rent a booth at one of these events for little money, giving you and your book exposure to hundreds, if not thousands, of potential book buyers.

Articles, Columns, and Blog Posts

One way to give your book exposure and re-use the research you have already done is to write articles for magazines, columns for newspapers, or posts for blogs. Every media outlet is looking for content, and they are under pressure to find good material before every deadline. Their need creates an opportunity for you to obtain a mention of your book.

Write a Query Letter or Email First

Before you write any article, it is worth your time to query the media outlet with your idea first. A good query is similar to a good press release in that it uses a hook to gain attention, and then gets to the idea quickly. Boil it down to three paragraphs: the who, what, where, when and why; the meat of the idea; and why you are the perfect person to write the article. End with a thank you for considering your idea and your contact information.

Find an Appropriate Media Outlet

Before you submit a query, do your homework. The article should be appropriate for the media's readers. A genealogical magazine, for example, may be interested in an article about research methodology, but a local newspaper would not. An article about the history of the county fair may interest a local newspaper, but may not be right for a Revolutionary War blog. Some media outlets have specific submission guidelines. Look for the guidelines and follow them closely. Submissions outside of the guidelines likely will be tossed.

Article Ideas

Become a curator of information or website links. Most people do not have time to search for everything they may like to know for themselves, so your article could comprise something along the lines of: "The Top Ten Websites for Local History" or "The County's Best Historical Museums and Why You Should Visit."

Write about your experience writing the book. There are fledgling writers in nearly every audience.

Write about your experiences. If you have an interesting story to tell about why you decided to write a book, tell it.

Write about your adventures with research. If you reconnected with your pals from the first grade, write about it and tell others how they can do the same.

Write in-depth stories of the neighborhood, city, area, region, time period or how tasks were accomplished.

Write a how-to article. If you learned enough about tatting to describe your great-grandmother's winter pastime, show others how they can learn too.

Proofread and Fact Check

Before you submit anything, proofread carefully and check your facts. It never hurts to give an article a thorough going over for spelling, punctuation, grammar and accuracy. The most common reason editors reject article submissions is sloppy copy editing.

Include a Signature with Your Article

At the end of each submission, include a signature (also called a resource box) with as much information as the magazine, newspaper or blog will allow.

Your signature could include:

- A photograph (of you or an image from the book)
- Your Name, Author of (the title of the book)
- Available at (local bookstore or online bookstore)
- Your website address (include the "http://" in any electronic communication to create a live link)

YouTube

YouTube can be useful to your marketing efforts beyond just a video book trailer. Consider filming each of your author events and posting those clips on YouTube. Look at the list of article ideas in the last section. Each and every idea for an article could also be an idea for a quick YouTube video.

YouTube is a Google company, and you can establish your own YouTube channel using your Google account. Google accounts are free and they give you access to Gmail (email), Google+ (social networking), Blogger (a free blog platform), Picasa (image editing), GooglePlay (apps), Google Books, Google Maps and more.

Brand your YouTube channel the way you did for other social media sites by uploading a cover (banner) image with your book cover, the title, your name as the author and your website address. Your YouTube channel will also have a unique URL (website address) that you can link on your website, social media accounts, blog or email signature to direct viewers to your videos.

Partner Up

One way to sell many books at a time is to partner up with a group that is willing to either let their members know your book is for sale, or to give your book to members as a membership perk.

If your book would interest the members of a local historical society, for example, ask the society to include a mention of your book along with a discounted price in their next email to members.

Asking the society to buy a book for each member is a little tougher sell, but with the right book, it is possible.

Stretch your imagination a bit to find partners. For example, if your book if you happen to be a famous local musician, you may be able to partner up with the local philharmonic to give members the book if they renew their season tickets. Expect to offer the book at a significant discount to interest a group in partnering with you in this way.

Cross Promotions

Cross promotions are similar to partnering. You will offer to promote a group, business or society in your social media pages and on your website if they agree to promote your book to their members. Consider cross promotions with reunions and family associations, genealogical and historical societies, or local groups or businesses with which you have ties.

Viral Marketing

Another way to expand your audience is to offer something that others will be willing to share with their friends, family, and colleagues. In marketing, these offers are called viral marketing tools. Usually, these tools come in the form of information—a helpful article that readers would pass along to someone who would also benefit from reading the article.

One way to offer viral marketing tools is to put them on your blog or website with a download link to a PDF document. Another way is to set up an autoresponder in your email program. Most email programs offer a way to send an automatic response based upon the email address or a subject line. Gmail, for example, calls autoresponders "canned responses" but it works the same way as an autoresponder.

To use autoresponders effectively, set up a new email box as an autoresponder, with an email greeting along with your PDF attachment. Anyone who sends an email, for example, to "5Tips@mycompany.com" will receive back a thank you for the inquiry along with the PDF containing the 5 Tips article. The other way to set up an autoresponder is to use your email box with a filter that catches the subject line and returns an automatic response. So, for example, you would tell interested readers to send an email with the subject line "5 Tips" to youremail@yourcompany.com and your email program would receive the email and automatically send a return email with your PDF attachment.

Make sure the PDF has your signature (resource box) or contact information on it, in case someone passes along the article to another person. You will want every person who receives the article to know how to contact you or where to go to order your book.

Ongoing Communication

One way to market your book(s) continuously is by maintaining some ongoing communication with your readers.

The most popular method of ongoing communication is an email list, often referred to as an email blast or an eZine (electronic magazine). Keeping in touch is particularly helpful if you plan to write another book. It is also a way for you to ask for stories and photographs while writing the next book.

You could ask interested readers to sign up for your email newsletter on your website, your blog, or in the signature in your email.

To make ongoing email communication easy, consider using an email service. One advantage to using a service is that they cue up the email from your list one at a time to avoid triggering the spam filters in most email programs that catch any email with more than eight to ten recipients. Group emails get sent to the spam filter most of the time. Using an email service means your email is more likely to be delivered, and most email services have tools that allow you to see which emails are being opened and which are not. Analyzing which emails are going unopened should help you write more attention-getting subject lines in the future.

The following are email services to consider. Some are free (or have free options); others charge a monthly fee based upon the number in your list.

- MailChimp (www.mailchimp.com)
- AWebber (www.awebber.com)
- Constant Contact (www.constantcontact.com)
- iContact (go.icontact.com)
- ActiveCampaign (www.activecampaign.com)
- Benchmark (www.benchmarkemail.com)

☙ঙ৯

There is almost no limit to the ways in which you can reach out to the general public to raise awareness for your book. A little bit of effort and creative thinking goes a long way.

Chapter 27

Selling Online

Selling your book online is a convenience for many readers, but also the most practical way to sell books. Bookstores are only interested in books that sell quickly, and convincing a bookstore to carry a memoir can be difficult unless you are well known or your story will have appeal to the general public. Not to mention, that once the book is in the store, you must inspire interested readers to go there to purchase the book.

Fortunately, there are a multitude of ways to offer your book for sale on the Internet.

Create a Website

If you want to sell your book online at your own website, you will need a domain name, a web host with server space to hold your website files, a way to build the website, a method of sending files to the server, and a way to allow customers to pay for the book.

Domain Name

A domain name (also called a URL—Uniform Resource Locator) is the address where web browsers will locate your website in order to display it. Google's domain name, for example, is www.google.com. If you know a website's domain name, you can type it directly into the search bar.

You can obtain a URL through one of the many registrars online, such as:

- Register.com (www.register.com)
- Domain.com (www.domain.com)

Registering a domain name will cost anywhere from a few dollars per year to about twenty-five dollars per year. If you stop paying the annual fee, you will lose the domain, and Internet users will no longer be able to find your website.

Web Hosting

The files that make up your website must sit on a server (computer) that is connected to the Internet all the time.

You can obtain free server space for a website. The most popular free website hosts are:

- Weebly (www.weebly.com)
- Wix (www.wix.com)

The following are sites where you can obtain free space for a blog. The sites marked with an asterisk also have paid options. You can use a blog to sell your book online instead of a website, if you prefer.

- Blogger (www.blogger.com)
- WordPress (www.wordpress.com)*
- Squarespace (www.squarespace.com)*
- Tumblr (www.tumblr.com)

There are hundreds of others. Free websites or blogs include a domain name, although, it may be a subdomain of the company, such as, www.yourname.webhostingcompany.com. If you have your own domain name, you could employ domain forwarding to point your domain name to the site. For example, your domain could be something simple such as www.RogerWilsonStory.com. That is the URL you would print on your business cards or use in your email signature because it will re-direct anyone who types that address into their web browser to the site which may be located at a more complicated address such as www.rogerwilsonstory.domainhostingcompany.com.

Note: Domain mapping is a bit more detailed than simply forwarding. Once you establish the domain map, all of the interior files that the site creates will use only the shorter, easier domain name, rather than the complete URL. For example: www.rogerwilsonstory.domainhostingcompany.com/10-Best-Pictures-from-Space.html will become *www.rogerwilsonstory.com*/10-Best-Pictures-from-Space.html using domain mapping.

Many free website hosts offer simple HTML editing tools to help you create a website. How much control you will have over the look and the organization depends upon the type of tools offered. Blogs work a little differently than HTML sites. Blogs are built primarily upon templates that hold the code for the blog posts so that the latest post goes to the top until it is replaced with something newer. Most blogging software also allows you to create static pages, and to add widgets (code) to a sidebar so that readers can click a button to go to your payment system or shopping cart.

Free sites often place advertising on your web pages. Some free sites limit the number of pages you can create. Others limit server space (often impacting the number of images you can use on the website) or traffic (the number of people visiting the site at a time and in a single month). Free is fantastic, as long as the hosting company stays in business.

Another option is to purchase hosting for your website from an Internet Service Provider (ISP). Three of the biggest ISPs are:

- HostGator (www.hostgator.com)
- NetworkSolutions (www.networksolutions.com)
- GoDaddy (www.godaddy.com)

There are thousands of local and regional ISPs offering different levels of services at all price ranges.

Some ISPs offer web-building tools, many of which are drag and drop which means you do not need to know much about creating websites in order to use them. Most ISPs charge for a certain amount of server space before you have to buy more. If you have many large files, such as videos, you may need more space. Some ISPs also charge for traffic, so if you have a popular website, you may pay more for the number of people visiting the site. Thankfully, most ISPs allow a generous amount of space and traffic in their basic (least expensive) packages.

HTML Editor

If you do not have the option of using your ISP's website building tools, or want to have more control over the look and contents of your website, you will need a way to build it. The most common way to build a site is in the computer coding language HTML, using an HTML editor. HTML editors come in all levels of sophistication and price from free downloads found on the Internet to Adobe Dreamweaver (www.adobe.com). For the most part, you do not need the most sophisticated program available to sell your book online.

Note: If you choose a blog-based site, you will not need an HTML editor. The blog software contains all of the editing tools you will need.

Uploading Files

If you build a website using an HTML editor, you must upload your files to the server space reserved for your site by your Internet Service Provider (ISP). Some ISPs have file transfer protocol (FTP) tools available from your account dashboard. Others will give you an FTP address and you must use an FTP program to upload your files from your computer to the ISP's server. The following are some of the most popular FTP programs. Those with an asterisk are free.

- WS_FTP Pro (www.ipswitchft.com)
- SmartFTP (www.smartftp.com)*
- CuteFTP Pro (www.cuteftp.com)
- WiseFTP (www.wise-ftp.com)
- FileZilla (www.filezilla-project.org)*

Uploading files to or downloading files from the Internet is simple. To send new files to the Internet, you choose files from the panel showing your computer, and hit the arrow key pointing to the side showing the server's files. If you want to download files from the server to your computer, you choose files from the server side, and hit the arrow key pointing to the files on your computer.

Payment Method

If you want to sell your books online, you must provide a way to receive payment. You can use a simple form that readers can print and send to you in the mail with a check, but most people who shop online expect to pay online. The simplest way to accomplish this is to set up a business PayPal account. These accounts are one step up from personal accounts in that they allow you to pay for items, but also receive payment. And, the site will create the code for a unique "buy now" button for each product you wish to sell, that you can copy and paste into your website or blog allowing readers to make a purchase online.

Organizing Your Website

Organizing the website well is key. At a glance, readers should be able to look at the home page and understand what to do next.

Banner Images. Most websites use a banner across the top to identify the website, display a logo, and tell viewers what the website is about. Use the banner to show your book cover and give the title, subtitle and your name as the author.

Navigation. Every page of the website should have essential navigation (links or buttons), so that readers can go from place to place within the website without losing track of where they are, and without having to use the back button on their web browser repeatedly to access other sections of the website.

Place the essential navigation in a vertical column down the left-hand side of the website or across the top beneath the banner. These are the two most common areas for navigation, and where the reader will expect to find links.

Website Real Estate. Most websites are wider than they are tall to keep viewers from having to scroll. If you can, keep whatever information you wish to impart on each page short enough to keep scrolling to a minimum.

What to Include in Your Website

Once you have the essentials—the domain name, hosting space, a way to build the site, and a payment method—there are other elements that will help potential readers find your site, and obtain enough information to purchase the book.

Home Page. Your home page should let readers know enough about the book to make them want one. Include a book cover image (even if you have one in the banner area), along with a "buy now" button, and the same type of information you used in your press releases—headline with a hook, follow up paragraphs with who, what when where and why, as well as a call to action (asking the reader to purchase the book).

Autographed Copies. If you plan to offer autographed copies, let readers know how to request one. This should be a different process than your "buy now" button so that you can tell which books must come from your stock and be autographed, and which ones you can ship directly from your book printer to the buyer. If you are using PayPal to create your "buy now" buttons, simply set up a different button to indicate a request for an autographed copy.

Author. Use this page to promote yourself as the author, or to explain why you wrote the book and how you went about the research. Show your event schedule or give a list of lectures you have prepared about the book, and give interested readers a way to contact you to book a lecture.

Excerpts. Include an excerpt or two so that readers get a feel for the contents.

Reviews. If you have good reviews, put a few on your website or blog.

Social Media Links. If you are using social media to promote the book, use an icon for each of the social media sites where you are active (Facebook, Twitter, YouTube or others) to link to your page on those sites. If you have a video book trailer, you can use the YouTube icon to link to your YouTube channel (where viewers can see all of your videos), but the site also produces the code to embed a small video window into your website or blog.

Ask for an Email Address. If you are planning any ongoing communication with readers, ask them to give you an email address. You could also capture email addresses by adding some viral marketing pieces to the site. Viral marketing was discussed in the last chapter.

Media Kit. If you are doing any publicity for the book, put your media kit online.

Contact Information. Give readers, people who may want to book you as a speaker, or members of the media a way to contact you.

Bookstore. Give readers information about other books you found helpful in writing your book. You can make a few dollars with your bookstore by becoming an affiliate of other online bookstores (see Affiliate Programs below).

Search Engine Optimization (SEO). In order for the search engines to correctly categorize your site so that users can find them you need the following:

Good Content. Search engines will look for matches between the content (the words on the page) and the keywords (metatags in the background). The closer the match, the more "relevant" the page is to the search term. In other words, if a person is searching for "Hubert Wilson Story" and you include that phrase in the content and the keywords, your site will show up higher in the search engine's list than a site using "Woodrow Wilson History" in the text.

Clean Design. Clean design means error-free code. If you use blogging software or your ISPs website building tools, you should not have to worry about the code. If you use an HTML editor, as long as you follow the software's basic design process, you should have clean code. If you edit the code on your own—all bets are off. If you edit the code yourself, be sure to check each page for missing images or bad links.

Keywords that Make Sense. Most website-building software allows you to add keywords (metatags) to the code of the website that will remain unseen by the user. Keywords are used by the search engines to help determine relevance. By choosing your keywords or phrases wisely, you will help boost your website's rankings in the search engines. Keywords are separated by commas, and can include more than one word (e.g. Hubert Wilson Mathemetician, Hubert Wilson and NASA, Hubert Wilson Remembers Springdale, etc.). Do not stuff the keywords with anything that is irrelevant to your book or the search engines will push your page rank down. Also, use the best eight to ten keywords or phrases. Any more than that, the search engines will ignore them.

Description Tags. Keywords are one metatag; the description is another. The description tag is what appears in search engine results underneath the headline link. It should give the viewer an idea of what the site is about in one sentence. Look at the first sentence of the description you wrote for your book. That sentence should hook the reader or pique his or her curiosity about the book, and is probably the best description for your website as well.

Title Tags. Each page in your website should contain a title tag. The title tag is what appears in the top left-hand portion of the web browser when visitors are on the site, but also is used as the click-able headline in the search engine results. A good title tag for the home page should be short and sweet (e.g. New book. Hubert Wilson's Career (1940–2001): WWII to Space and Back.).

Image Tags. Image tags are used by the search engines to determine relevance. Image tags can boost your ranking by adding more keywords to the page. Image tags are also used by the "Images" tab on the major search engines, so if you tag an image with the names of each person in the image, anyone searching for those names may find your image which will lead them back to your website.

Image Basics Online

The goal when preparing images to use on the Internet is to keep the file sizes small enough that web pages load quickly. One way to accomplish this is to use thumbnail images with links to full-sized images so that readers have the option of looking at a photograph or a document at full size or downloading the larger image for themselves. Full-sized images can be used to order prints, as well, which is a nice way to share photographs with your family without having to print them yourself and send them.

If you place a full-sized image online, however, expect that people will save the image for themselves. If you do not want your images saved or used in ways you cannot control, there are ways to disable right clicks and copy/paste, or use thumbnail-sized images only, and give interested people a way to contact you for a full-sized image.

If your thumbnails are linked to larger images, explain that somewhere on the home page. Not everyone will understand that the thumbnails are click-able links unless you explain. Also post a warning about large file sizes so that readers are prepared for how long a full-sized image may take to download. Oftentimes, large images will take a minute or two to appear in a web browser making the viewer believe that nothing is happening and close the window prematurely.

Book Cover Image

Use your book cover image in the banner or in the right-hand column of the page. To keep pages loading quickly, convert your book cover image as you would any other image for the website. If you use a small thumbnail which can make the title hard to read, you can link it to a larger image or add your title, subtitle and author's name in the banner area in a larger font.

File Formats

Save full-sized images as smaller thumbnails using the "for the web" setting in your image editor, or at 72 ppi because the monitor cannot display an image at any higher resolution anyway. While web browsers will recognize and display TIFF, BMP, JPG, GIF, and PNG files, you will achieve the best quality with the fewest compatibility issues if you stick to JPG or PNG. Use PNG if you want to maintain a transparent background if the image is an icon or a logo, for example, with sharp lines and distinct areas of color. Use JPG for photographs, maps or illustrations. Play with the image format for your documents to see what gives you the best results. Typically, documents that are fairly clean, with easy-to-read handwriting will look fine as a JPG.

Animation

While you can include animated graphics, such as animated GIFs or flash animations on your website, please do so sparingly. Flashing or rotating graphics have fallen out of fashion and tend to annoy viewers.

If you have many images to share, create an animated slide show. The most common website building software have simple plugins that create slideshows, or you can use stand-alone software such as Adobe Flash (www.adobe.com) to create a file that plays like a video. Microsoft Movie Maker comes pre-installed on most Windows machines or is free to download. Macs have iMovie that is similar. Both iMovie and Movie Maker create web-ready video slideshows.

Another option is to find (or purchase) a flash gallery where the slideshow is already built, you just add the images. Search for "free photo gallery download" on the Internet and you will find hundreds of sites with flash galleries to download. One you have a flash gallery filled with images, upload it to the server and create a link to it in the navigation of the website.

Video

If you have video, you may want to use a thumbnail or link to take readers to a full-screen version of the video. If you create a "channel" on YouTube, you can store your video files there (saving server space that you may have to pay for), and YouTube will give you the code to bring a small video window into your website. You will copy and paste the code into the page on your website. Viewers will then click on the video window to play the video from your website.

Audio

Audio files also can be large. While audio alone can generate memories, you could use your audio as the soundtrack behind a slideshow, and load it on YouTube.

Websites can be a dynamic way to showcase what is in the book, add extras, share photographs and documents, and provide an easy way to sell books online.

Online Ads

Typically, I do not recommend that you purchase ads to sell your book because there are an infinite number of ways that you can plug your book without having to purchase advertising. However, there are a few ways that you can do so without busting your budget.

Adwords

Adwords is a Google company that sells advertising which appears in the Google search engine results (usually the top three listings on the page, plus the top ten items in the right-hand sidebar), and on selected websites that have allowed an advertisement window to be placed on the site. To purchase an ad, you will set up an account, choose the keywords you would like to bid on and set a budget for how much you are willing to pay per day to let the ad run. The best thing about Adwords is that you only pay if a viewer clicks on the ad and goes to your website. Because the best keywords for a memoir are not often searched, you may not pay a great deal to get interested people to your website to buy the book.

Note: Adsense is also Google company that pays for advertising if you allow an advertisement window to be placed within your website. It is a way to make a few dollars, but unless you have an often-visited website, do not expect much more than dinner or movie money.

Facebook Ads

Facebook advertisements show up in the news feeds on individual's facebook pages based upon what they have "liked" on other pages. In other words, if you choose "genealogy" in the likes and interests field, your ad will be shown to other people interested in genealogy. A recent search showed that choosing "genealogy" as an interest returned more than two million interested people. A search for "genealogy family history" returned only eighteen thousand, and "genealogy research" only sixteen thousand. Unfortunately, there is no way to know more specifically if any of these people are interested in your story. Select the option to only pay for clicks to your website, which will narrow the number of people down considerably. The fewer clicks through, the lower the cost of the ad.

Trade an Ad

Make an offer to a local historical or genealogical society to trade ads. You host an ad for the society on your website, while they host an ad for your book on theirs. Agree to a length of time you will keep each other's ads up.

Book-Related Sites that Sell Ads

There are several book-related sites that sell advertising. The following are two of the most popular:

Ereader News Today. Ereader News Today (ereadernewstoday.com). This site sends emails to its subscribers daily that offer readers free and bargain books for their Kindles. This site also spreads the word through their Facebook page. If you want to price your book at $2.99 or less in order to reach their enormous audience, buying an ad on this site will help you do so. They also offer a Bargain

Books ad that takes 25 percent of whatever you sell through the ad, measured by their affiliate code through Amazon.

BookBub. BookBub (www.bookbub.com). This site offers bargain eBooks to their subscribers across many eReader platforms. You coordinate the sales price with each of your retail outlets (Amazon, Barnes&Noble, BooksaMillion, etc.) or through your eBook aggregator, if you used one. You purchase an ad based upon the genre and the sales price. Their primary focus is on fiction and, unfortunately; there is not a category listed for family histories. There are categories for Biographies and Memoirs as well as Advice and How-To, which may fit your book.

Online Bookstores

There are many bookstores besides Amazon that sell books online. If you are using one of the big print-on-demand printers, chances are good that your book will be included in the catalogs of:

- Amazon (www.amazon.com)
- Barnes&Noble (www.bn.com)
- Books-a-Million (www.booksamillion.com)
- Powell's Books (www.powells.com)
- Alibris (www.alibris.com)
- Abe Books (www.abebooks.com)
- Biblio (www.biblio.com)
- The Tattered Cover (www.tatteredcover.com)

If your book is not included in these catalogs automatically, look for the "publisher" information on their websites to see what you must do to have your book added. Amazon, however, remains the largest online book seller. As long as your book is listed there, you may not want to go to a lot of trouble to have your book listed in other online stores.

Wherever your book is listed online, use every tool available to enhance your listing. Make sure each site has a cover image. Enable all features that allow readers to get a feel for what the book entails. Add a description, an author biography or an excerpt. Everything you can do to help buyers find your book will increase book sales.

Amazon

The three most important sales tools on Amazon are the "Look Inside the Book" function, reviews that come from readers, and Author Central, where you can showcase yourself along with the book. These features have been discussed, but here is one more. On your book's listing, below the cover is a link to "share your own customer images." If you have other photographs related to the book that would entice readers to buy, by all means, add the photographs.

Affiliate Programs

One way to earn a little bit more for selling your own book is to join an affiliate program. Affiliate programs give you credit (and a percentage of the sale) every time someone goes to your website or opens your email, clicks through to the online bookstore, and makes a purchase. Amazon has one of the most comprehensive affiliate programs online.

One way to be helpful to your readers is to suggest other books (or products, if appropriate) to enhance the reader's experience. For example, if you have a travel guide, you could recommend travel gear or a translation guide that would be helpful while visiting the area your travel guide describes. For a family history, you could recommend other books about the area or era. Amazon does this expertly with their "customers who bought this item also bought" feature.

Amazon also has a "recommended for you" feature based upon your prior purchases. You could set up a "recommended reading" list with links to any books (or movies) you used in your research.

If you think viewers would appreciate buying from their favorite online bookstore, or in different eReader versions (Kindle, Android, etc.), set up multiple affiliate links giving readers a choice.

Each affiliate program will give you a coded link to the products on their website so that when viewers on your website make a purchase using the affiliate link, you get credit for the sale.

Online Non-Book Stores

Bookstores are not the only places books are sold online. There are online sales outlets such as eBay (www.ebay.com) where you can set up an account and sell items directly to eBay's buyers. There are also museum shops and historical or genealogical organizations that sell books.

Conduct a quick search of the area(s) where you have lived and see whether there is a Chamber of Commerce, independent bookstores, a college or university, a local library, and what tourist attractions exist. You may be able to sell books through a local hotel or bed & breakfast.

You can negotiate with any place that has a website where products are already being sold to list your book on their website. They will collect the full retail price, send you payment for the wholesale price through PayPal or a wholesale page on your website, and you will ship the book to the reader.

❧✦❧

Selling online is one way to expand your audience because potential readers can find your book using a search engine. You will make the most per book if you sell directly to the reader, but there is something to be said for gaining access to the customer base of an existing group or online store. You may make more money by selling books at a discount through an association, for example, because of the larger volume of sales, than selling one book at a time through your website.

Conclusion

Whether you took only the baby steps or jumped headlong into the giant leaps, I am sure you have stories that deserve to be told and published for interested family and others to read and appreciate.

I am confident that if you can follow the steps outlined in this guide, you can publish. Although most memoirs are published in print, if you choose to publish electronically, let me encourage you, once again, to publish at least a few copies in print to contribute to the major genealogical or historical collections around the country. Your story and your hard work deserve to be preserved and available for generations to come.

If you are just beginning, I trust you are inspired enough to pick a project to publish. In fact, I hope to have inspired half a dozen projects you cannot wait to begin, and caused many more ideas to tumble around in your imagination.

If the book is underway but the writing is not yet complete, I anticipate that you will reach out to family members and others who can be of assistance to gather photographs, information, and details you may have forgotten.

If you are starting with a box of documents or photographs, my aim was to motivate you to begin scanning and organizing, sharing with family, and preparing the images for when you are ready to lay out your manuscript.

If your story is sitting in your computer yearning to bust out of the bytes and into the hands of family members and other interested readers, I trust this guide has made you believe that you *can* publish and reach out to others who may be interested in the stories you have written.

About the Author

Dina C. Carson has been involved in publishing and genealogy for more than two decades. She brings her experience with all phases of book publishing to help first-time self-publishers create quality family or local histories that are both believable and achievable.

She is the coordinator of the Boulder Pioneers Project, a comprehensive look at the original source documents for Boulder County during the territorial period (1858–1876) and is the author of more than a dozen annotated indexes of Boulder County source materials.

She lectures frequently to genealogical, historical and philanthropic societies, gives workshops on publishing, pioneers and other topics, and is working with the Colorado State Archives on state-wide records indexing projects.

Although her formal education is in international law and economics, she owns Iron Gate Publishing, a publishing company that focuses on genealogy, local history and reunion planning. She is also a partner in Imagination Technology, a graphic design and marketing firm working with local businesses.

When she's not at a computer working on a publishing project, you can find her photographing the pioneer cemeteries of Colorado.

Bibliographyx

RESEARCH

Blumenson, John J-G. *Identifying American Architecture: A Pictoral Guide to Styles and Terms, 1600-1945*. New York, NY: W W Norton, 1981.

Butchart, Ronald E. *Local Schools: Exploring Their History*. Nashville, TN: American Association for State and Local History, 1986.

Carpenter, Will. *The Life and Times Of ...: Researching and Writing American Local History*. Cookeville, TN: HistoryWorks, 2009.

Carson, Dina. *Directory of Genealogical and Historical Societies, Libraries and Museums in the U.S. and Canada, 2014*. Niwot, CO: Iron Gate Publishing, 2014.

Danzer, Gerald A. *Public Places: Exploring Their History*. Nashville, TN: American Association for State and Local History, 1995.

Davidson, James West and Mark Hamilton Lyle. *After the Fact: The Art of Historical Detection*. Boston: McGraw Hill, 2000.

DeBlasio, Donna M. *Catching Stories: A Practical Guide to Oral History*. Athens, OH: Swallow Press, 2009.

Dudley, Roger L. *In Their Time: A Timeline Journal for Placing Family Events into Historical Context, 1000-2076*. Denver, CO: Warfield Press, 2013.

Evans, Tonya Marie and Susan Borden Evans. *Literary Law Guide for Authors: Copyright, Trademark and Contracts in Plain Language*. Philadelphia: Literary Entrepreneur Series, 2003.

Field, Marion. *The Writer's Guide to Research: An Invaluable Guide to Gathering Material for Features, Novels and Non-Fiction Books*. Oxford, England: How to Books, 2000.

Filby, William. *A Bibliography of American County Histories*. Baltimore, MD: Genealogical Publishing Company, 2000.

Foster, Gerald. *American Houses: A Field Guide to the Architecture of the Home*. Boston, MA: Houghton Mifflin, 2004.

Hart, Cynthia and Lisa Samson. *The Oral History Workshop: Collect and Celebrate the Life Stories of Your Family and Friends*. New York: Workman Publishing Company, 2009.

Henderson, Nancy. *The Genealogist's U.S. History Pocket Reference: Quick Facts & Timelines of American History to Help Understand Your Ancestors*. San Diego, CA: Family Tree Books, 2013.

Howe, J. and Delores A. Fleming, Emory L. Kemp, Ruth Ann Overbeck. *Houses and Homes: Exploring Their History*. Walnut Creek, CA: Alta Mira Press, 1997.

Hunt, R. Douglas. *American Farms: Exploring Their History*. Malabar, FL: Krieger Publishing Co., 1996.

Jacobson, Judy. *History for Genealogists: Using Chronological Time Lines to Find and Understand Your Ancestors*. Baltimore, MD: Clearfield Publishing Co., 2009.

Jones, Thomas W. *Mastering Genealogical Proof*. Arlington, VA: National Genealogical Society, 2013.

Kammen, Carol. *On Doing Local History: Reflections on What Local Historians Do, Why and What it Means*. Nashville, TN: The American Association for State and Local History, 1986.

Kammen, Carol. *The Pursuit of Local History: Readings in Theory and Practice*. Walnut Creek, CA: Alta Mira Press, 1996.

Kerr, K. Austin and Amos J Loveday, Mansel G Blackford. *Local Businesses: Exploring Their History*. Nashville, TN: American Association for State and Local History, 1990.

Kyvig, David E. and Myron A. Marty. *Nearby History: Exploring the Past Around You, 2nd Edition*. NY: Alta Myra Press, 2000.

Lynch, Daniel. *Google Your Family Tree*. Baltimore, MD: FamilyLink, 2008.

McAlester, Virginia and A. Lee McAlester. *A Field Guide to American Houses*. New York, NY: Knopf. 1984.

Mills, Elizabeth Shown. *Evidence Explained: Citing History Sources from Artifacts to Cyberspace*. Baltimore, MD: Genealogical Publishing Co, 2007.

Ritchie, Donald A. *Doing Oral History*. New York: Oxford University Press, 2003.

Szucs, Loretto Dennis and Sandra Hargreaves Luebking. *The Source: A Guidebook to American Genealogy, 3rd Edition*. Provo, UT: Generations Network, 2006.

Urend, James P. *Places of Worship: Exploring Their History*. Nashville, TN: American Association for State and Local History, 1990.

Yow, Valerie Raleigh. *Recording Oral History: A Guide for the Humanities and Social Sciences, 2nd Edition*. Walnut Creek, CA: AltaMira Press, 2005.

WRITING

Ackerman, Angela and Becca Puglisi. *The Emotion Thesaurus: A Writer's Guide to Character Expression*. Jupiter, FL: JADD Publishing, 2012.

Ackerman, Angela and Becca Puglisi. *The Negative Trait Thesaurus: A Writer's Guide to Character Flaws*. Jupiter, FL: JADD Publishing, 2013.

Ackerman, Angela and Becca Puglisi. *The Positive Trait Thesaurus: A Writer's Guide to Character Attributes*. Jupiter, FL: JADD Publishing, 2013.

Amato, Joseph A. *Rethinking Home: A Case for Writing Local History*. Berkeley, CA: University of California Press, 2002.

Barany, Beth. *The Writer's Adventure Guide: 12 Stages to Writing Your Book (for Novelists and Creative Nonfiction Writers)*. Oakland, CA: Barany Pub, 2009.

Beckett, John. *Writing Local History*. Manchester, England: Manchester University Press, 2007.

Bickham, Jack M. *The 38 Most Common Fiction Writing Mistakes (And How to Avoid Them)*. Cincinnati, OH: Writer's Digest Books, 1997.

Blake, Gary and Robert W. Bly. *The Elements of Technical Writing: The Essential Guide to Writing Clear, Concise Proposals, Reports, Manuals, Letters, Memos, and Other Documents in Every Technical Field*. NY: Simon & Schuster Macmillan Company, 1993.

Block, Lawrence. *Spider, Spin Me a Web: A Handbook for Fiction Writers*. NY: William Morrow Paperbacks, 1996.

Block, Lawrence. *Telling Lies for Fun and Profit: A Manual for Fiction Writers*. NY: William Morrow Paperbacks, 1994.

Block, Lawrence. *Writing the Novel from Plot to Print*. Cincinnati, OH: Writers Digest Books, 1985.

Borg, Mary. *Writing Your Life: An Easy-to-Follow Guide to Writing an Autobiography*. Fort Collins, CO: Cottonwood Press, 1990.

Bowerman, Peter. *The Well-Fed Self-Publisher: How to Turn One Book into a Full Time Living*. Atlanta, GA: Fanove Publ, 2007.

Boyer, Carl III. *How to Publish and Market Your Family History, 4th Edition*. Santa Clarita, CA: Carl Boyer, 1993.

Brohaugh, William. *Write Tight: How to Keep Your Prose Sharp, Focused and Concise*. Cincinnati, OH: Writer's Digest Books, 1993.

Browne, Renni. *Self-Editing for Fiction Writers: How to Edit Yourself Into Print*. New York, NY: Harper Paperbacks, 2004.

Carpenter, Will. *The Life and Times Of ...: Researching and Writing American Local History*. Cookeville, TN: HistoryWorks, 2009.

Casagrande, June. *It was the Best of Sentences, It was the Worst of Sentences: A Writer's Guide to Crafting Killer Sentences*. New York: Ten Speed Press, 2010.

Cheney, Theodore A. Rees. *Writing Creative Nonfiction: How to Use Fiction Techniques to Make Your Nonfiction More Interesting, Dramatic and Vivid*. Berkeley, CA: Ten Speed Press, 1991.

Chicago Manual of Style, 16th Edition. Chicago: University of Chicago Press, 2010.

Clark, Roy Peter. *Writing Tools: 50 Essential Strategies for Every Writer*. New York, NY: Little, Brown and Company, 2008.

Clausen, John. *Too Lazy to Work, Too Nervous to Steal: How to Have a Great Life as a Freelance Writer*. Cincinnati, OH: Writer's Digest Books, 2001.

Cleaver, Jerry. *Immediate Fiction: A Complete Writing Course*. NY: St Martin's Griffin, 2005.

Collier, Oscar and Frances Spatz Leighton. *How to Write & Sell Your First Nonfiction Book*. NY: St. Martin's Press, 1994.

Collins, Brandilyn. *Getting Into Character: Seven Secrets a Novelist Can Learn from Actors*. NY: John Wiley & Sons, 2002.

Dalton, Judy. *The 29 Most Common Writing Mistakes and How to Avoid Them.* Cincinnati, OH: Writer's Digest Books, 1985.

Dibell, Ansen. *Plot: How to Build Short Stories and Novels that Don't Sag, Fizzle, or Trail Off in Scraps of Frustrated Revision—and How to Rescue Stories That Do.* Cincinnati, OH: Writer's Digest Books, 1988.

Dickson, Paul. *War Slang: American Fighting Words and Phrases since the Civil War.* Washington, D.C.: Brassey's, 2004.

Edgerton, Les. *Hooked: Write Fiction That Grabs Readers at Page One and Never Lets Them Go.* Cincinnati, OH: Writer's Digest Books, 2007.

Einsohn, Amy. *The Copyeditor's Handbook, 3rd Edition: A Guide for Book Publishing and Corporate Communication.* (Berkeley, CA: University of California Press, 2011).

Ellis, Sherry. *Now Write! Nonfiction: Memoir, Journalism and Creative Nonfiction Exercises from Today's Best Writers.* New York, NY: Tarcher, 2009.

Embree, Mary. *The Author's Toolkit: A Step-by-Step Guide to Writing and Publishing Your Book (Revised Edition).* New York: Allworth Press, 2003.

Finley, Carmen J. *Creating a Winning Family History.* Arlington, VA: National Genealogical Society, 2010.

Franklin, Jon. *Writing for Story: Craft Secrets of Dramatic Nonfiction.* New York, NY: Plume, 1994.

Friedlander, Joel. *A Self-Publisher's Companion: Expert Advice for Authors Who Want to Publish.* San Rafael, CA: Martin Bookworks, 2011.

Fruehling, Rosemary T. and N. B. Oldham. *Write to the Point! Letters, Memos, & Reports that Get Results.* New York, NY: McGraw-Hill Book Co, 1988.

Garrison, Webb. *The Encyclopedia of Civil War Usage: Everyday Language of Soldiers and Civilians.* Nashville, TN: Cumberland House, 2001.

Gaughran, David. *Let's Get Digital: How to Self-Publish, and Why You Should.* US: Arriba Arriba Books, 2011.

Genealogy Publishing Service. *How to Write & Publish Your Family Book.* Franklin, NC: Genealogy Publishing Service, 1992.

Gerard, Philip. *Creative Nonfiction: Researching and Crafting Stories of Real Life.* Cincinnati, OH: Waveland Pr Inc, 2004.

Goldfarb, Ronald L. and Gail E. Ross. *The Writer's Lawyer: Essential Legal Advice for Writers and Editors in All Media.* NY: Times Books, 1989.

Gouldrup, Lawrence P. *Writing the Family Narrative.* Salt Lake City: Ancestry Publishing, 1987.

Gutkind, Lee. *In Fact: The Best of Creative Nonfiction.* New York, NY: W. W. Norton & Company, 2004.

Gutkind, Lee. *Keep it Real: Everything You Need to Know About Researching and Writing Creative Nonfiction.* New York, NY: W. W. Norton & Company, 2009.

Gutkind, Lee. *The Art of Creative Nonfiction.* New York, NY: Wiley, 1997.

Hale, Constance. *Sin and Syntax: How to Craft Wickedly Effective Prose*. New York, NY: Broadway, 2001.

Hart, Jack. *Storycraft: The Complete Guide to Writing Narrative Nonfiction*. Chicago: University of Chicago Press, 2011.

Hatcher, Patricia Law. *Producing a Quality Family History*. Salt Lake City: Ancestry, Inc., 1996.

Howard, V. A. and J. H. Barton. *Thinking on Paper: Refine, Express, and Actually Generate Ideas by Understanding the Processes of the Mind*. New York, W Morrow, 1986.

Kawasaki, Guy and Shawn Welch. *APE: Author, Publisher, Entrepreneur—How to Publish a Book*. US: Nononina Press, 2013

Kempthorne, Charley. *For All Time: A Complete Guide to Writing Your Family History*. Heinemann, NH: Boynton/Cook Publishers, 1996.

Kidder, Tracy and Richard Todd. *Good Prose: The Art of Nonfiction*. New York: Random House, 2013.

Kitchel, Dwain L. *Writing and Marketing a Family History in the 1990s*. Knoxville, TN: Tennessee Valley Publicatiions, 1990.

Kramer, Mark. *Telling True Stories: A Nonfiction Writer's Guide from the Nieman Foundation at Harvard University*. New York, NY: Plume, 2007.

Krull, Kathleen. *12 Keys to Writing Books that Sell*. Cincinnati, OH: F&W Publications, Inc. 1989.

Lashier, Kathleen. *Grandma [Grandpa], Tell Me Your Stories*. Waverly, IA: Cq Products, 1992.

Lashier, Kathleen. *Mom [Dad], Share Your Life With Me*. Waverly, IA: Cq Products, 1992.

Lashier, Kathleen. *To the Best of My Recollection*. Waverly, IA: G&R Publishing, 1996.

Leland, Christopher T. *The Creative Writer's Style Guide*. Cincinnati, OH: Writer's Digest Books, 2002.

Levin, Donna. *Get that Novel Started and Keep it Going until You Finish*. Cincinnati, OH: Writer's Digest Books, 1992.

Lopate, Phillip. *To Show and to Tell: The Craft of Literary Nonfiction*. New York: Free Press, 2013.

Lukeman, Noah. *The First Five Pages: A Writer's Guide to Staying Out of the Rejection Pile*. New York, NY: Fireside, 2005.

Lukeman, Noah. *The Plot Thickens: 8 Ways to Bring Fiction to Life*. New York: St. Martin's Griffin, 2003.

Marshall, Carl and David Marshall. *The Book of Myself: A Do-it-Yourself Autobiography in 201 Questions*. New York, NY: Hyperion, 2007.

Marshall, Evan. *The Marshall Plan for Novel Writing: A 16-Step Program Guaranteed to Take You from Idea to Completed Manuscript*. Cincinnati, OH: Writer's Digest Books, 1998.

McCutcheon, Marc. *Building Believable Characters*. Cincinnati, OH: Writer's Digest Books, 1996.

Merriam-Webster's English Usage Dictionary. New York: Merriam-Webster, 2010.

Morris, William. *Morris Dictionary of Word and Phrase Origins, 2nd Edition*. New York, Collins Reference, 1988.

Noble, William. *The 28 Biggest Writing Blunders (And How to Avoid Them)*. Cincinnati, OH: Writer's Digest Books, 1992.

Noble, William. *Noble's Book of Writing Blunders (And How to Avoid Them)*. Cincinnati, OH: Writers Digest Books, 2006.

Noble, William. *Writing Dramatic Non-Fiction*. Forest Dale, VT: Paul S Eriksson, 2000.

Nuwer, Hank. *How to Write Like an Expert About Anything: Bring Factual Accuracy and the Voice of Authority to Your Writing*. Cincinnati, OH: Writer's Digest Books, 1995.

Obstfeld, Raymond. *Fiction First Aid: Instant Remedies for Novels, Stories and Scripts*. Cincinnati, OH: Writer's Digest Books, 2002.

Orion, Dean. *Live To Write Another Day, A Survival Guide for Screenwriters and Creative Storytellers*. US: Sky Father Media, 2013.

Perl, Sondra. *Writing True: The Art and Craft of Creative Nonfiction*. Boston, MA: Wadsworth Publishing, 2006.

Plotnik, Arthur. *Spunk & Bite: A Writer's Guide to Bold, Contemporary Style*. New York, NY: Random House Reference, 2007.

Polking, Kirk. *Writing Family Histories and Memoirs*. Cincinnati, OH: Betterway Books, 1995.

Poynter, Dan. *Writing Nonfiction: Turning Thoughts into Books*. Santa Barbara, CA: Para Publishing, 2007.

Pyne, Stephen J. *Voice & Vision: A Guide to Writing History and Other Serious Nonfiction*. Cambridge, MA: Harvard University Press, 2011.

Q&A a Day: 5-Year Journal. New York, NY: Potter Style, 2010.

Rampolla, Mary Lynn. *A Pocket Guide to Writing History*. Boston, MA: Bedford-St Martin's, 2007.

Raymond, Stuart A. *Genealogical Jargon for Family Historians*. Bury: Federation for Family History Societies, 2005.

Reminiscing: 21st Century Master Edition. Itasca, IL: TDC Games, n.d.

Rodale, J.I. *Synonym Finder, Completely Revised*. New York: Grand Central Publishing, 1988.

Roerden, Chris. *Don't Murder Your Mystery: 24 Fiction-Writing Techniques to Save Your Manuscript from Turning up D. O. A.* Rock Hill, SC: Bella Rosa Books, 2006.

Rubie, Peter. *The Elements of Storytelling: How to Write Compelling Fiction*. NY: John Wiley & Sons, 1995.

Rubie, Peter and Gary Provost. *How to Tell a Story: The Secrets of Writing Captivating Tales*. Cincinnati, OH: Writer's Digest Books, 1998.

Schmidt, Victoria Lynn. *Story Structure Architect: A Writer's Guide to Building Dramatic Situations and Compelling Characters*. Cincinnati, OH: F&W Publications, 2005.

Sellers, Heather. *Page After Page: Discover the Confidence and Passion You Need to Start Writing and Keep Writing (No Matter What!)*. Cincinnati, OH: Writer's Digest Books, 2005.

Silverman, Sue William. *Fearless Confessions: A Writer's Guide to Memoir*. Athens, GA: University of Georgia Press, 2009.

Smith, Michael C. and Suzanne Greenberg. *Everyday Creative Writing: Panning for Gold in the Kitchen Sink, 2nd Edition*. Lincolnwood, IL: NTC Publishing Group, 2000.

Stewart, James B. *Follow the Story: How to Write Successful Nonfiction*. NY: Touchstone, 1998.

Strong, William S. *The Copyright Book: A Practical Guide, 4th Edition*. Cambridge, MA: MIT Press, 1993.

St. Maur, Suzan. *How to Write Winning Non-Fiction: The Complete Writing and Publishing Handbook for Non-Fiction Authors*. London, England: Publishing Academy, 2010.

Stone, Todd A. *Novelists' Boot Camp: 101 Ways to Take Your Book from Boring to Bestseller*. Cincinnati, OH: Writer's Digest Books, 2006.

Strunk, William and William Strunk, Jr. *The Elements of Style (Updated 2011 Edition)*. New York: The Style Manual Press, 2011.

Szucs, Loretto Dennis. *Family History Made Easy*. Salt Lake City: Ancestry Publishing, 1998.

Truss, Lynne. *Eats, Shoots & Leaves: A Zero Tolerance Approach to Punctuation*. New York, New York: Gotham, 2004.

Tuchman, Barbara W. *Practicing History: Selected Essays*. New York: Ballantine Books, 1935.

Turabian, Kate L. *A Manual for Writers of Research Papers, Theses, and Dissertations, 8th Edition*. Chicago, IL: University of Chicago Press, 2013.

Walsh, Bill. *Lapsing into a Comma: A Curmudgeon's Guide to the Many Things that Can Go Wrong in Print—And How to Avoid Them*. New York: McGraw-Hill, 2000.

Walsh, Bill. *The Elephants of Style: A Trunkload of Tips on the Big Issues and Gray Areas of Contemporary American English*. New York: McGraw-Hill, 2004.

Walsh, Bill. *Yes, I Could Care Less: How to Be a Language Snob Without Being a Jerk*. New York: St Martin's Griffin, 2013.

Wilson, Lee. *Make it Legal*. NY: Allworth Press, 1990.

Zinsser, William. *Inventing the Truth: The Art and Craft of Memoir*. NY: Mariner Books, 1998.

Zinsser, William. *On Writing Well*. New York, NY: Harper Paperbacks, 2006.

Zinsser, William. *Writing About Your Life: A Journey into the Past*. New York, NY: Da Capo Press, 2005.

Zuckerman, Albert. *Writing the Block Buster Novel*. Cincinnati, OH: Writer's Digest Books, 1994.

EXAMPLES

Alcott, Louisa May. *Little Women*. New York: Grosset & Dunlap, 1947.

Bruce, David. *Mark Twain Anecdotes and Quotes*. Smashwords, 2014.

Colletta, John Philip. *Only a Few Bones: A True Account of the Rolling Fork Tragedy and its Aftermath*. Direct Descent, 2000.

Doyle, Sir Arthur Conan. *The Hound of the Baskervilles*. London, McClure Publishing, 1902.

Edgerton, Les. *Hooked: Write Fiction That Grabs Readers at Page One and Never Lets Them Go*. Cincinnati, OH: Writer's Digest Books, 2007.

Frazier, Ian. *Family*. New York: Picador, 2002.

Jackson, Buzzy. *Shaking the Family Tree: Blue Bloods, Black Sheep, and Other Obsessions of an Accidental Genealogist*. New York: Touchstone, 2010.

Laskin, David. *The Family: Three Journeys into the Heart of the 20th Century*. New York: Viking Adult, 2013.

Mantel, Hilary. *Wolf Hall*. New York: Henry Holt and Co., 2010.

McInerney, Jay. *Bright Lights, Big City*. New York: Vintage, 1984.

Mendelsohn, Daniel. *The Lost*. New York: HarperCollins, 2007.

White, Bailey. *Mama Makes Up Her Mind: And Other Dangers of Southern Living*. New York: Trafalgar Square, 1995.

Wouk, Herman. *The Winds of War*. New York: Little, Brown and Company, 1971.

PRODUCTION

Ashford, Janet and John Odam. *Start with a Scan: A Guide to Transforming Scanned Photos and Objects into High-Quality Art, 2nd Edition*. Berkeley, CA: Peachpit Press, 2000.

Blatner, David and Glenn Fleishman, Steve Roth. *Real World Scanning and Halftones: The Definitive Guide to Scanning and Halftones from the Desktop*. Berkeley, CA: Peachpit Press, 1998.

Bonura, Larry S. *The Art of Indexing*. New York, NY: John Wiley & Sons, 1994.

Bringhurst, Robert. *The Elements of Typographic Style*. Point Roberts, WA: Hartley & Marks, 2008.

Carter, David, ed. *Big Book of Design Ideas*. New York, NY: Harper Collins, 2000.

Cohen, Sandee and Robin Williams. *The Non-Designer's Scan and Print Book: All You Need to Know About Production and Prepress to Get Great-Looking Pages*. Berkeley, CA: Peachpit Press, 1999.

330

Ctein. *Digital Restoration from Start to Finish*. London: Elsevier, 2010.

de Bartolo, Carolina. *Explorations in Typography: Mastering the Art of Fine Typesetting*. 101 Editions, 2011.

Evans, Poppy. *Designer's Survival Manual: The Insider's Guide to Working with Illustrators, Photographers, Printers, Web Engineers, and More ...* . Cincinnati, OH: How Design Books, 2001.

Felici, James and Frank Romano. *The Complete Manual of Typography: A Guide to Setting Perfect Type*. San Francisco: Peachpit Press, 2002.

Hendel, Richard. *On Book Design*. New Haven: Yale University Press, 1998.

Hoff, Henry B. *Genealogical Writing in the 21st Century: A Guide to Register Style and More*. Boston: New England Historical and Genealogical Society, 2002.

Krause, Jim. *Color Index—Revised Edition*. Cincinnati, OH: HOW Books, 2010.

Krause, Jim. *Color Index 2*. Cincinnati, OH, HOW Books, 2007.

Lee, Marshall. *Bookmaking, 3rd Edition: Editing, Design, Production*. New York: Norton & Co., 2004.

Lupton, Ellen. *Thinking with Type: A Critical Guide for Designers, Writers, Editors and Students, 2nd Revised and Expanded Edition*. NY: Princeton Architectural Press, 2010.

Masterson, Pete. *Book Design & Production: A Guide for Authors and Publishers*. El Sobrante, CA: AEonix Publishing Group, 2007.

McClure, Rhonda R. *Digitizing Your Family History: Easy Methods for Preserving Your Heirloom Documents, Photos, Home Movies and More in a Digital Format*. Cincinnati, OH: Family Tree Books, 2004.

Pantone Graphics. *Formula Guide: Solid Coated & Solid Uncoated*. Carlstadt, NJ: Pantone Graphics, 2014.

Smith, Brian R. *Dollarhide Numbering for Genealogists—An Authorized Guide for the Serious User*. Orting, WA: Family Roots Publishing, 2011.

Spaltro, Kathleen. *Genealogy and Indexing*. Wheat Ridge, CO: American Society of Indexers, 2003.

Sperry, Kip. *Abbreviations & Acronyms: A Guide for Family Historians*. Orem, UT: Ancestry, 2000.

Steinhoff, Sascha. *Scanning Negatives and Slides: Digitizing Your Photographic Archive*. Santa Barbara, CA: Rocky Nook, 2009.

Tally, Taz. *Avoiding the Scanning Blues: A Desktop Scanning Primer*. Upper Saddle River, NJ: Prentice Hall, 2001.

Wellisch, Hans H. *Indexing from A to Z*. Bronx, NY: The H. W. Wilson Company, 1991.

Wheildon, Colin. *Type & Layout: How Typography and Design can Get Your Message Across—Or Get in the Way*. NY: Strathmoor Press, 1995.

White, Jan V. *Great Pages: A Common-Sense Approach to Effective Desktop Design*. London: Serif Publishing, 1990.

Williams, Robin. *The Mac is not a Typewriter, 2nd Edition*. San Francisco, CA: Peachpit Press, 2003.

Williams, Robin. *The Non-Designer's Design Book, 3rd Edition*. San Francisco, CA: Peachpit Press, 2008.

Williams, Robin. *The Non-Designer's Type Book*. San Francisco, CA: Peachpit Press, 1998.

MARKETING

Amir, Nina. *Authorpreneur: How to Build a Business around Your Book*. Los Gatos, CA: Pure Spirit Creations, 2014.

Daffron, Susan C. *Publishize: How to Quickly and Affordably Self-Publish a Book That Promotes Your Expertise*. Logical Expressions, 2011.

Eager, Rob. *Sell Your Books like Wildfire: The Writer's Guide to Marketing and Publicity*. Cincinnati, OH: Writer's Digest Books, 2012.

Gaughran, David. *Let's Get Visible: How To Get Noticed And Sell More Books*. US: Arriba Arriba Books, 2013.

Kremer, John. *1001 Ways to Market Your Books: For Authors and Publishers*. Taos, NM: Open Horizons, 2006.

Levinson, Jay Conrad. *Guerrilla Marketing, 4th edition: Easy and Inexpensive Strategies for Making Big Profits from Your Small Business*. Wilmington, MA: Mariner Books, 2007.

Miller, J Steve. *Sell More Books! Book Marketing and Publishing for Low Profile and Debut Authors: Rethinking Book Publicity after the Digital Revolutions*. Acworth, GA: Wisdom Creek Press, 2011.

Schriever, Norm. *The Book Marketing Bible: 99 Essential Marketing Strategies for Self-Published and First-Time Authors, or any Writer Looking to Skyrocket Sales*. Seattle: Amazon Digital Services, n.d.

Scott, David Meerman. *The New Rules of Marketing & PR: How to Use Social Media, Online Video, Mobile Applications, Blogs, News Releases, and Viral Marketing to Reach Buyers Directly*. Seattle: Amazon Digital Services, 2013.

Scott, Steve. *61 Ways to Sell More Nonfiction Kindle Books*. US: Amazon Digital Services, n.d.

Weber, Steve. *Plug Your Book*. Falls Church, VA: Weber Books, 2007.

Index

Order Form

If you borrowed this copy from a library or would like to order a copy for a friend or family member, please send a check or money order to: Iron Gate Publishing, P.O. Box 999, Niwot, CO 80544. Our books are available online to institutions through Lightning Source, to individuals at Amazon.com and on our website:

www.irongate.com

Set Yourself Up to Self-Publish: A Genealogist's Guide
     ISBN 978-1-879579-99-6 $19.95 + $5.00 S&H

Publish Your Genealogy: A Step-by-Step Guide for Preserving Your Research for the Next Generation
     ISBN 978-1-879579-62-0 $24.95 + $5.00 S&H

Publish Your Family History: A Step-by-Step Guide to Writing the Stories of Your Ancestors
     ISBN 978-1-879579-63-7 $24.95 + $5.00 S&H

Publish a Local History: A Step-by-Step Guide from Finding the Right Project to Finished Book
     ISBN 978-1-879579-64-4 $24.95 + $5.00 S&H

Publish a Memoir: A Step-by-Step Guide to Saving Your Memories for Future Generations
     ISBN 978-1-879579-65-1 $24.95 + $5.00 S&H

Publish a Biography: A Step-by-Step Guide to Capturing the Life and Times of an Ancestor or a Generation
     ISBN 978-1-879579-66-8 $24.95 + $5.00 S&H

Publish a Photo Book: A Step-by-Step Guide for Transforming Your Genealogical Research into a Stunning Family Heirloom
     ISBN 978-1-879579-67-5 $24.95 + $5.00 S&H

Publish a Source Index: A Step-by-Step Guide to Creating a Genealogically Useful Index, Abstract or Transcription
     ISBN 978-1-879579-68-2 $24.95 + $5.00 S&H

Publish Your Specialty: A Step-by-Step Guide for Imparting Your Research Expertise to Others
     ISBN 978-1-879579-76-7 $24.95 + $5.00 S&H

Order Form

If you borrowed this copy from a library or would like to order a copy for a friend or family member, please send a check or money order to: Iron Gate Publishing, P.O. Box 999, Niwot, CO 80544. Our books are available online to institutions through Lightning Source, to individuals at Amazon.com and on our website:
www.irongate.com

Set Yourself Up to Self-Publish: A Genealogist's Guide
  ISBN 978-1-879579-99-6 $19.95 + $5.00 S&H

Publish Your Genealogy: A Step-by-Step Guide for Preserving Your Research for the Next Generation
  ISBN 978-1-879579-62-0 $24.95 + $5.00 S&H

Publish Your Family History: A Step-by-Step Guide to Writing the Stories of Your Ancestors
  ISBN 978-1-879579-63-7 $24.95 + $5.00 S&H

Publish a Local History: A Step-by-Step Guide from Finding the Right Project to Finished Book
  ISBN 978-1-879579-64-4 $24.95 + $5.00 S&H

Publish a Memoir: A Step-by-Step Guide to Saving Your Memories for Future Generations
  ISBN 978-1-879579-65-1 $24.95 + $5.00 S&H

Publish a Biography: A Step-by-Step Guide to Capturing the Life and Times of an Ancestor or a Generation
  ISBN 978-1-879579-66-8 $24.95 + $5.00 S&H

Publish a Photo Book: A Step-by-Step Guide for Transforming Your Genealogical Research into a Stunning Family Heirloom
  ISBN 978-1-879579-67-5 $24.95 + $5.00 S&H

Publish a Source Index: A Step-by-Step Guide to Creating a Genealogically Useful Index, Abstract or Transcription
  ISBN 978-1-879579-68-2 $24.95 + $5.00 S&H

Publish Your Specialty: A Step-by-Step Guide for Imparting Your Research Expertise to Others
  ISBN 978-1-879579-76-7 $24.95 + $5.00 S&H

www.ingramcontent.com/pod-product-compliance
Lightning Source LLC
Chambersburg PA
CBHW080324270326
41927CB00014B/3096